POSTGRADUATE STUDY
IN SOUTH AFRICA

Surviving and Succeeding

EDITORS

LIEZEL FRICK
PULENG MOTSHOANE
CHRISTOPHER McMASTER
CATERINA MURPHY

Postgraduate Study in South Africa – Surviving and Succeeding

Published by SUN MeDIA Stellenbosch under the imprint SUN PRESS.

Copyright © 2016 SUN MeDIA Stellenbosch and the Authors

All rights reserved.

No part of this book may be reproduced or transmitted in any form or by any electronic, photographic or mechanical means, including photocopying and recording on record, tape or laser disk, on microfilm, via the Internet, by e-mail, or by any other information storage and retrieval system, without prior written permission by the publisher.

Views expressed in this publication are those of the authors and do not necessarily reflect the views of the publisher.

First edition 2016

978-1-928357-23-0
978-1-928357-24-7 (e-book)

DOI: 10.18820/9781928357247

Set in Futura Lt BT 10.25/14.5 pt

Cover design and typesetting by SUN MeDIA Stellenbosch

SUN PRESS is an imprint of AFRICAN SUN MeDIA. Academic, professional and reference works are published under this imprint in print and electronic format. This publication may be ordered directly from www.sun-e-shop.co.za.

Produced by SUN MeDIA Stellenbosch.

www.africansunmedia.co.za
africansunmedia.snapplify.com (e-books)
www.sun-e-shop.co.za

ACKNOWLEDGEMENTS

We hereby extend our sincere thanks to the following persons and institutions:

Prof Sioux McKenna (Rhodes University), whose scholarly insights into and passion for postgraduate education shine through in the foreword to this book.

Prof Eugene Cloete (Vice-rector: Research and Innovation, Stellenbosch University) for providing the necessary funding to make the publication of this book possible. As Stellenbosch University continues to be one of the leading research universities in South Africa, it is not only important for the institution to partake in national debates on postgraduate education but also to pave the way for development in this area as a field of scholarship.

SUN MeDIA, in particular Wikus van Zyl, Johannes Richter and Emily Vosloo, who expertly handled the publication of this book.

The peer reviewers, who provided expert advice on the initial manuscript, without which the final product would not have been possible.

Our partners who have supported us through the long hours of book development.

CONTENTS

List of Figures xv

Foreword – Sioux McKenna 1

Preface – the Editors 7

PART ONE

Chapter 1 • Addressing some of the elephants in South African research education: Race and reflexivity in postgraduate study
Daniela Gachago

Introduction: On starting difficult conversations 13
On troubled knowledge and mutual vulnerability 15
On the importance of dialogue 16
On comfort zones, vulnerabilities and critical emotional reflexivity 17
On openness and reciprocity 19
On gentleness 21

Chapter 2 • Student-supervisor relationships in a complex society: A dual narrative of scholarly becoming
Zondiwe L. Mkhabela & B. Liezel Frick

Introduction 23
A perilous but decisive start 24
Liezel's narrative 25
Zondi's narrative 25
Getting to know each other's contexts 27
Making headway 30
The oral examination and graduation 32
Understanding each other's contexts 33
Building mutual kindness and trust 33
No compromises on quality: the role of compassionate rigour in doctoral education 34
Utilising experts 34

Chapter 3 • **Research ethics and ethical dilemmas in the South African context**
Simangele Mayisela

Introduction	39
"Who am I?" The researcher identity dilemma	39
Have you obtained ethical clearance? Institutional ethical regulations	41
"I am not your subject": Ethical considerations for research participants	43
"I have a say too": Ethical principles in working with children as research participants	44
"Promise you will not tell": The ethical principle of confidentiality	45
"I can't take it": Potential harm to participants	46
Walking on a tight rope: Legal quandaries and harm to institutions	47

PART TWO

Chapter 4 • **Getting started: Surviving and succeeding during the pre-doctoral stage**
Shakira Choonara

Introduction	53
Full-time versus part-time study	54
The application process	55
Selecting a university	55
Application processes	56
Brief proposal	56
Identifying a supervisor	57
Funding constraints	58
Further considerations for international students	58
Support structures	59

Chapter 5 • **Close encounters: Becoming resilient through compassion and imagination**
Bella Vilakazi

Introduction	61
Compassion in the context of doctoral supervision	61
Cultivating imagination in the context of doctoral supervision	62
An encounter with a prospective supervisor: My story	63
Democratic justice in postgraduate student supervision	65

PART THREE

Chapter 6 • Surviving and succeeding: The first-generation challenge
Soraya Abdulatief

Learning in the Third Space	70
Creating a mental Third Space	71
From solitary learner to emerging academic	72
Asking and answering questions	73
Publishing and presenting research	74
Setting up a virtual study group	75

Chapter 7 • Caught between work and study: Exploring boundary zones as an employed postgraduate student
Andre van der Bijl

Introduction	77
Frameworks for navigating different roles	78
Power and knowledge	83
Application, transfer and use of knowledge	85

Chapter 8 • The inclusion of visually impaired students in post-graduate programmes: A personal and political perspective
Heidi Lourens

Introduction	89
Entitlement to support: Thoughts on imposters and structure	91
Access to the written word: Poverty in the currency of research	93
Getting there: Notes on supervision and research interviews	95
Travelling abroad: Notes on academic conferences	96
A last note on the research supervisor	96

Chapter 9 • Being a postgraduate woman: Relationships, responsibilities and resiliency
Guin Lourens

Introduction	101
Gender and education	101
Developing resilience	104
The role of family and friends	105
The influence of emotional pressures on female postgraduate students	106
Work arrangements	107

Building a social support system 108
Institutional services and support 109
Time management 111

Chapter 10 • Being my own coach: Achieving balance in the four domains of life
Delia Layton

Introduction 115
The Four Human Domains 117
The "Inner I" 118
The "Outer I" 119
The "We" 120
The "It" 122

PART FOUR

Chapter 11 • Seeing yourself in a new light: Crossing thresholds in becoming a researcher
Sherran Clarence

Introduction 127
Three thresholds to cross 128
Designing your "Theoryology": A house can only stand on firm foundations 129
Moving into the field: Out of the theory clouds into the data swamp 131
The first draft: "It's a thesis!" (but there's work to be done) 133
Reflections: Seeing yourself in a new light 134

Chapter 12 • Agency and Ubuntu: Exploring the possibility of complementarity in postgraduate study
Langutani M. Masehela

Introduction 137
Agency as a driver of the postgraduate project 138
The notion of Ubuntu 140
Finding the middle ground: Agency and Ubuntu as complementary
    perspectives in postgraduate supervision 142

Chapter 13 • Whose voice is right when I write? Identity in academic writing
Catherine Robertson

Introduction	145
Three identities of the writerly self	146
The "autobiographical self"	147
The "discoursal self"	148
The "authorial self"	151

Chapter 14 • The PhD process: Doctor or doctored?
Kasturi Behari-Leak

Introduction	157
Doctoral traditions and conventions	158
Doctoral or doctored?	160
The head, heart, hand of doctoral study	160
Knowing the Doctoral Scholar	161
Being the doctoral scholar	162
Doing: stepping into the space as doctoral scholar	163
Locating the doctoral scholar in an emerging paradigm	164

PART FIVE

Chapter 15 • So what do you think? The role of dialogue in doctoral learning
Jacqueline Lück

Introduction	171
Dialogic spaces and Communities of Practice (CoP)	172
Community Dialogue	174
Dialogue with supervisors	174
Dialogues with colleagues and critical friends	176
Dialogue at proposal presentation	176
Dialogue at conferences	177
Dialogue with experts	178
Dialogue with other doctoral scholars	178
Online spaces	179

Chapter 16 • The benefits of being part of a project team: A postgraduate student perspective
Puleng Motshoane

Introduction	183
Starting the doctoral journey as a team member	184
Working in a cohort project team	184
Different forms of support	186
Networking beyond the formal study cohort: the value of closed networks	187
The benefits of networking beyond your established networks	188

Chapter 17 • Sharing the quest of doctoral success: Creating a circle of critical friends
Liz Wolvaardt, Hannelie Untiedt, Mariana Pietersen & Karien Mostert Wentzel

Introduction	191
Setting up a circle of critical friends	192
What to address during meetings	194
Benefits and challenges of participating in a circle of critical friends	195
Survival strategies	197

PART SIX

Chapter 18 • Daring to be different: A postgraduate student perspective on originality
Emmanuel Sibomana

Introduction	205
Research needs to be original, but what does that mean?	205
Original but based on other people's work	209

Chapter 19 • The viva voce: The living voice of a doctoral thesis
Ndileleni P. Mudzielwana

Introduction	213
Phase 1: Before the defence	216
Phase 2: During the defence	217
Phase 3: After the defence	219

Chapter 20 • Publish or perish? Communicating research with the public
Collium Banda

Introduction 223
A quest for relevance 224
Communicating science as partnership and hospitality 225
Sharing research during postgraduate studies 226
Risks in communicating science to the public 228
Developing the skills of sharing your research findings 229

Index 233
Information about the Authors 237

LIST OF FIGURES

FIGURE 7.1 Engeström's (1987) Activity Theory model as presented by Engeström, Miettinen and Punamaki (1999, p. 31) 80

FIGURE 7.2 Articulated multiple activity systems (adapted from Bolton & Keevy, 2011, p. 7) 81

FIGURE 11.1 Pushing thresholds 130

FOREWORD

FROM THROUGHPUT TO THRIVING: CHANGING POSTGRADUATE STUDY IN SOUTH AFRICA

The push for postgraduate education has intensified internationally. Universities are under enormous pressure to ensure that they graduate more and more PhD and Master's scholars. South African universities have been given the target to graduate 5 000 doctorates per year by 2030 (National Planning Commission 2011). This is a significant increase from the 2 258 doctoral graduates in 2014 (HEMIS[1] 2015). To ensure we have enough supervisors to achieve this goal, there is the additional target that 75% of academics should have PhDs by 2030, rather than the current 34%.

However, as academics we need to view this drive with a healthy degree of skepticism. We need to look carefully at the reasons for increasing numbers so that we don't undermine the very basis of the system simply for the sake of output. We need to ask what it is that postgraduate scholars are expected to do with the high levels of skill they acquire. And we need to revisit what the doctorate is really for.

Most national policies and reports around the world stress that postgraduate education needs to be responsive to the labour market and attend to the developmental needs of the economy (DHET 2013; EUA 2013). In the knowledge economy, the ability to solve industry problems and thereby producing more goods for the market is worth more than physical expertise of almost any kind. Postgraduate scholars are the individuals we look to for enhanced efficiencies and improved outputs.

I would argue that we need to be very cautious of such discourses, as pervasive as they may be. If postgraduate education results only in private goods – better salaries for the graduate and higher production levels for the employer – why should the taxpayer subsidise it? If universities are structured as private corporations, why should public funds be spent on them? In a country as unequal as ours, the narrow conception of the postgraduate qualification as a private good has major implications for student access because the logical consequence of seeing education as a private good is that the burden of cost should rest with the person receiving such goods.

---

1 Many of the statistics used in this piece have been sourced from HEMIS, the national Higher Education Management Information System, as this allows for more recent statistics than from published documents. They were accessed in November 2015.

Such a dystopian view of postgraduate education as merely a set of highly advanced industry skills is of course flawed in every possible way. The PhD and Master's degrees may well offer private goods, but their primary function should be to serve the public good. As such, these qualifications should benefit far more than the university offering the degree, the industry employing the graduate and the graduate herself. The postgraduate qualification should be the space in which we strive for a better understanding of our planet and society, and where a critical citizenry is fostered to the benefit of all. It is the intellectual place in which we contribute to the "frontiers of a field" (HEQSF 2013). Postgraduate education is the place where new knowledge is created that can be harnessed for the good of the public and thereby assist all of us to live in more creative and compassionate ways.

Postgraduate education, perhaps more than any other form of higher education, offers a significant space for resisting the human capital model of education. The dominant focus on economic matters and in particular the ways in which postgraduates serve to grow our economies is far too narrow. It is imperative that we scrutinise the intrinsic value of the postgraduate education offered to our scholars. When we move beyond the sterile language of employability in postgraduate education discussions, we open conversations about how this highest level of education contributes to social justice and the sustainability of the planet. And these conversations crucially need to include the scholars themselves.

This book offers a range of scholars' voices and thereby looks at what postgraduate education means here and now for those engaged in it. The book is being published during a time in which higher education in South Africa is undergoing substantial self-reflection. Student protests have raised questions about our institutional cultures, troubled our curriculum assumptions and challenged dominant pedagogical approaches. Postgraduate education should not consider itself immune from such deliberations. We need to ask ourselves tough questions about the extent to which our postgraduate education has been inclusive and socially just. We need to scrutinise who gets admitted, who graduates, who supervises and who examines.

Issues of social inclusion and epistemological access, which have been central to debates about undergraduate education in South Africa, are rarely raised in discussions about postgraduate pedagogy. There is generally a view that at postgraduate level people already need to be working at the most advanced levels and so collective engagement and collegial support is somehow inappropriate. But the "always already" scholar (Manathunga & Goozee 2007:309) is as rare as the "always already" supervisor. If we want all higher education in South Africa to be socially just, we need to foreground this issue at postgraduate level too.

FOREWORD

In 2014, 54% of postgraduates[2] enrolled in higher education South Africa were black African[3], which indicates great strides made in the last two decades, but shows there is still much work to be done at the point of access. Sadly, the percentages at enrolment do not echo those at graduation and in 2014, only 47% of postgraduate graduates were black. The racially differentiated success rates found in all other qualification levels (CHE 2013) are thus sadly continued into the postgraduate sector. In terms of gender, 50% of Master's enrolments in 2014 were female, but this drops to 44% at doctoral level.

The issue of who participates is crucial as it has implications for who contributes to knowledge production in every sphere of society and is part of the explanation for the lack of racial transformation of staffing in South African universities. We need to ask serious questions about both equity of access and equity of success in postgraduate education.

Students are also raising questions about whose knowledge is being cited and extended, and which theories are privileged. The canon on which we rely is neither neutral nor inherently excellent simply because it is dominant. Drawing on a wider range of theories is often a challenge for the supervisor whose expertise generally arises because of her years of induction in knowledge from the "Global North". We therefore need to look carefully at ways of doing supervision differently, so that multiple perspectives and contextually relevant knowledge come to the fore. To do this, we will also need to reconsider our approaches to supervision.

In South Africa, we have retained the traditional apprenticeship model of supervision as the main approach, particularly in the Humanities and Social Sciences. Research demonstrates that this model often results in the PhD being experienced as a lonely journey by the isolated scholar (Harrison 2012). There have been challenges to the traditional apprenticeship model as we look for creative supervision pedagogies that make space for other ways of knowing and generating the powerful knowledge we need and expect at this level of study. In 2010, the ASSAf report on PhD study in South Africa found that the two major risk factors for non-completion were poor student-supervisor relationships and inadequate socialisation experiences. While there are multiple causes for these problems, many of which are explored in this

---

2 "Postgraduate" here *only* includes Master's and doctorates, the focus of this book, and thus excludes Honours and other postgraduate students.

3 HEMIS uses Department of Labour terminology for racial categories. According to the 2011 census data, black Africans made up 79% of the South African population. It should be borne in mind that the 54% black African enrolment referred to above also includes black African students from outside of South Africa.

book, the ASSAf findings provide a significant challenge to our current models of supervision. Alternative models are available and may be more suited to our context of needing to increase postgraduate numbers and widen our theoretical base. In some instances, universities are beginning to adopt alternative models of postgraduate education such as project teams, supervision panels and doctoral schools (Lotz-Sisitka *et al* 2010; McKenna 2014; Samuel & Vithal 2011).

To this end, a great many books have been written about postgraduate education that provide insights into the different models of supervision that are available and what is expected of a supervisor. These books generally foreground the experiences of the supervisor and offer useful insights for both supervisor and postgraduate scholar. But few texts give us access to the voices of the scholars themselves. We really need to hear reflections from those engaged in the doctoral process if we are to understand what we need to do to ensure that the doctorate is a stimulating and worthwhile endeavor that genuinely serves a public good. This book is thus a crucial contribution to this process as we come to make sense of the context of low retention and high drop-out, and move beyond surviving to genuinely succeeding (Cloete, Mouton & Sheppard 2015; ASSAf 2010). To do this, we have to change our focus from what will increase throughput to what will ensure thriving.

SIOUX MCKENNA

REFERENCES

Academy of Science of South Africa. (2010). *The PhD study: Consensus Report*. Pretoria, South Africa: ASSAf.

Byrne, J. Jørgensen, T., & Loukkola, T. (2013). *Quality Assurance in Doctoral Education – results of the ARDE project*. Brussels, Belgium: European Universities' Association.

Cloete, N., Mouton, J., & Sheppard, C. (2015). Doctoral education in South Africa. Pretoria, South Africa: African Minds.

Council on Higher Education. (2013). *A proposal for undergraduate curriculum reform in South Africa: The case for a flexible curriculum structure*. Pretoria, South Africa: CHE.

Department of Higher Education and Training. (2013). *White paper for post-school education and training: Building an expanded, effective and integrated post-school system*. DHET, Pretoria: South Africa.

Harrison, E. (2012). *Paperheads: Living doctoral study, developing doctoral identity*. Oxford, UK: Peter Lang Publishers. http://dx.doi.org/10.3726/978-3-0353-0276-9

Higher Education Qualifications Sub-Framework. (2013). As published in Notice No 549, Government Gazette No. 36721, 2 August 2013. Pretoria, South Africa: Government Printers.

Lotz-Sisitka, H., Ellery, K., Olvitt L., Schudel, I., & O'Donoghue, R. (2010). Cultivating a scholarly community of practice. *Acta Academica,* 1:130-150.

McKenna, S. (2014). Higher education studies as a field of research. *The Independent Journal of Teaching and Learning*, 9:6-44.

Manathunga, C., & Goozee, J. (2007). Challenging the dual assumption of the 'always/already' autonomous student and effective supervisor. *Teaching in Higher Education,* 12(3):309-322. http://dx.doi.org/10.1080/13562510701278658

National Planning Committee. (2011). *National development plan*: Vision 2030, Pretoria, South Africa: Department of the Presidency.

Samuel, M., & Vithal, R. (2011). Emergent frameworks of research teaching and learning in a cohort-based doctoral programme. Perspectives in Education*: The changing face of doctoral education in South Africa: Special* Issue, 3(29):76-87.

PREFACE

Postgraduate Study in South Africa: Surviving and Succeeding is timely given the currently evolving national narrative of emerging student voices that are making themselves heard from within the realms of higher education institutions across the country. Many of these students are voicing their concerns about the lack of higher education transformation around issues of equity, curriculum reform, language and race. Many of these debates have centred on undergraduate education, though some of the issues of course cut across under- and postgraduate levels. This book provides a glimpse of the postgraduate experience amidst these debates. As such, it aims to constructively contribute to a growing national discourse on how students navigate these complexities in order to survive and succeed during their postgraduate studies.

A variety of contextual factors may influence the initiation, development and progress, and eventual outcome of a postgraduate study – whether the student ultimately survives and succeeds. Institutional policies and regulations provide some direction. A myriad of published research literature, self-help guides, online resources as well as institutional support programmes may provide guidance, while supervisors may provide mentoring and subject-related expertise. Family and friends may share the initial euphoria of the (sometimes first-generation) candidate pursuing a postgraduate degree. The value of such contextual influences in supporting the study and in particular the student should not be underestimated, to which many of the authors in this book attest. However, the contributors to this book also show that surviving and succeeding demand more than a contextually rich support system. Students' own self-reflective abilities, creativity and pragmatic approaches to surviving and succeeding show that postgraduate student success is as much internally as externally determined.

The book explores these elements from various thematic perspectives. Part 1 sets the South African scene of postgraduate study in a complex society. The contributors to this section provide us with unique perspectives on postgraduate study in a relatively young democracy. The students' reflexive experiences of sensitive issues such as race, developing constructive student-supervisor relationships within a context characterised by cultural and linguistic diversity, and dealing with ethical dilemmas that may arise as a result of working amidst such complexities are addressed. Part 2 provides a student perspective on starting the postgraduate journey in the context described in the previous section. The contributors to this section explore the pre-doctoral stage and the role of imagination and compassion in becoming resilient. Part

3 challenges the notion of the "always already" prepared student in the South African context (a notion borrowed from the work of Manathunga & Goozée 2007). Aspects that define many a postgraduate experience in South Africa – including being a first-generation postgraduate student, a working academic caught within institutional transformation, a disabled student, a woman in a predominantly patriarchal society – are outlined in this theme. The section concludes with how postgraduate students might achieve a work-life balance as they navigate these multiple responsibilities and identities. Part 4 explores postgraduate study as identity work within the South African context. The contributors to this section focus on crossing transformative thresholds in becoming a researcher, the possibilities of merging both individualistic (agentic) and collective (Ubuntu) notions of being, developing a writerly identity, and a student voice. Part 5 positions postgraduate study as a social practice in South Africa. The role of dialogue in doctoral learning, the benefits of being part of a project team and circles of critical friends are social practices that receive attention. Part 6 helps us to make sense of postgraduate outcomes in the South African context. A student perspective on the notion of originality, the *viva voce* and science communication beyond academic circles provide student insights on how postgraduate outcomes can be valued and valuable.

In conceptualising this project, an open invitation was sent out through all our respective networks to potential contributors. Those interested were asked to send us proposals for possible chapters, thus opening the space for a truly student-driven perspective. The contributing authors in this book hail from 11 different South African universities and a variety of disciplinary backgrounds (including Health Sciences, Education, Language Studies, Sociology, Psychology and Theology), which enrich the diversity of perspectives offered here[1]. The book builds on the success of similar initiatives focussed on postgraduate students' experiences in Aotearoa New Zealand (McMaster & Murphy 2014), Australia (McMaster, Murphy, Whitburn & Mewburn, in production), the United States of America (McMaster & Murphy 2016), the United Kingdom (McMaster, Murphy, Cronshaw & Codiroli-McMaster, in press) and Scandinavia (McMaster, Murphy & Rosenkrantz de Lasson). Though each of these books has its own character and unique national flavour, it highlights the importance of hearing the student voice above and beyond its potential epistemic and discipline-based contribution. Therefore, each chapter included in this book speaks from a uniquely South African perspective and we have tried to remain true

---

1 The self-selection process followed through the open invitation process yielded a diversity of contributions; however, the sciences were relatively under-represented. Twenty of the 33 proposed chapters we received were accepted and developed further into full chapters included here.

to the voice of each contributor, while at the same time providing a coherent body of scholarly work. The contributors were tasked to move beyond a personal narrative (even though this might have provided the impetus for their ideas), and asked to also consider current scholarship in their area of interest, yet provide useful insights to those who follow in their footsteps, as well as to those who will supervise their successors. The chapters in this book are not limited to a specific discipline, but are as universal to postgraduate study as possible.

As editors, we not only share the experience of having been postgraduate students ourselves, but we also share a keen interest in encouraging postgraduate students' voices, as well as contributing to the broader field of postgraduate literature. As such, we believe that this book may provide the catalyst for a continued scholarly debate on surviving and succeeding the postgraduate student experience.

THE EDITORS
STELLENBOSCH
SEPTEMBER 2016

REFERENCES

Lin, L., & Cranton, P. (2005). From scholarship student to responsible scholar: A transformative process. *Teaching in Higher Education*, 10(4):447-459. http://dx.doi.org/10.1080/13562510500239026

Manathunga, C. (2005). The development of research supervision: "Turning the light on a private space". *International Journal for Academic Development*, 10(1):17-30. http://dx.doi.org/10.1080/13601440500099977

Manathunga, C., & Goozée, J. (2007). Challenging the dual assumption of the 'always/already'autonomous student and effective supervisor. *Teaching in Higher Education*, 12(3):309-322. http://dx.doi.org/10.1080/13562510701278658

McMaster, C., & Murphy, C. (Eds.) (2014). *Postgraduate study in Aotearoa New Zealand: Surviving and succeeding*. Wellington, New Zealand: NZCER Press.

McMaster, C., & Murphy, C. (Eds.) (2016). *Graduate study in the USA: Surviving and succeeding*. New York, NY: Peter Lang Publishing.

McMaster, C., Murphy, C., Mewburn, I. & Whitburn, B. (Eds.) (in production). *Postgraduate study in Australia: Surviving and succeeding*. New York, NY: Peter Lang Publishing

McMaster, C., Murphy, C., Cronshaw, S., & Codiroli-McMaster, N. (Eds.) (in press). *Postgraduate study in the United Kingdom: Surviving and succeeding*. London, UK: Libri Publishing.

McMaster, C., Murphy, C., & Rosenkrantz de Lasson (in press). *Postgraduate study in Scandinavia: Surviving and succeeding*. New York, NY: Peter Lang Publishing.

PART ONE

SETTING THE SOUTH AFRICAN SCENE: POSTGRADUATE STUDY IN A COMPLEX SOCIETY

PART ONE

ADDRESSING SOME OF THE ELEPHANTS IN SOUTH AFRICAN RESEARCH EDUCATION: RACE AND REFLEXIVITY IN POSTGRADUATE STUDY

Daniela Gachago

INTRODUCTION: ON STARTING DIFFICULT CONVERSATIONS

Conducting research in South Africa is not easy. It is a country reeling from the legacies of apartheid, characterised by continued structural inequalities. I live in Cape Town, a place where neighbourhoods are spatially segregated by race and income distribution. The inequalities are blatant: on one side of the railway line, you find "white" spaces, which are characterised by natural beauty, affluence and western standards, while on the other side, you find conditions of extreme poverty: no formal housing, little or no access to water and sanitation – the reality for the majority of the inhabitants of the city. In Cape Town, every event, be it a natural disaster such as fires on Table Mountain or a cultural event such as a literary festival in Franschhoek, is seen and discussed through a racial lens. On the surface, it seems as if the rainbow nation lives peacefully forever after, reconciled and transformed through the miracle that Nelson Mandela performed. However, once you scratch the surface, things change quickly: race bubbles to the top and shows its ugly head, as diversity consultant Freeth (2013) observes.

Whatever topic you choose for your research, in South Africa you will have to engage with issues of race and, closely interrelated, class and gender: you might find it in the composition of your lab team, the use of language in meetings, the way your colleagues engage with you and each other, or in snide comments that are made. You may find it in the opportunities you have or do not have access to, information that is or is not passed on to you, networks that you are or are not allowed into. Trying to engage your colleagues, supervisors, friends and research participants in these issues is like walking in a minefield. You may be met with discomfort and silence, or with an explosion of emotions leaving you frustrated, confused and helpless, as well as feeling hopelessly inadequate at dealing with this complex situation. In my research I was hit by the depth of trauma and pain in personal stories shared by black and coloured students, and the daily violence they were exposed to, as well as the complete lack of knowledge about these stories within the white student body. I was similarly fascinated by the reaction of black students, after listening to some of the white students' stories of pain and struggle, when they realised that white people had problems too. I was mesmerised at the extent of misconceptions students had about the "Other"[1]. I kept wondering, do these students never engage with each other? Do they never listen to each other's stories?

I am an outsider to this country, which added an additional layer of complexity to my research. My family and I arrived in Cape Town in 2010, after living in Scotland and in Botswana. My husband is from Kenya and we have two mixed-race children. Until we moved to South Africa, we had only encountered openness, support and curiosity towards our colourful family. After our arrival in South Africa, this open acceptance changed. I soon realised that race and, in my case, whiteness, mattered in a way that I had never experienced before. This made me uncomfortable yet also curious to better understand the issue of race in the South African context. I started to ask a lot of questions.

While you might think that being an outsider makes it harder to engage in difficult conversations, it actually made it easier in some ways: it allows you to ask questions and notice things that others do not. Social practices that seem "normal" for people who have grown up here to the extent that they do not even notice them, will hit those new to South Africa right in the face. What struck me most when I first started teaching in South Africa were, for example, students' seating arrangements. While the class consisted of a diverse range of students, each group of students sat with peers of their own skin colour. Not only was I met with discomfort and silence when pointing this out to my colleagues and students, nobody seemed to care.

I decided to make this part of my research: where does this lack of engagement across difference come from? And how could you disrupt this? How could you start a dialogue across difference, one that would not just reinforce beliefs and assumptions but actually open up spaces for understanding and learning? In this chapter, I will

---

1 I use "Other" (in capital letters and inverted commas) to foreground the socially and discursively constructed nature of the other: a "distant other" who in this case not only does not look like me but to whom I am always in some ways differently positioned in relation to power and privilege. This "Other" is always positioned as either more or less privileged than I am, and our relationship is always based on an unequal power distribution (see for example Zembylas 2011).

reflect on some strategies that I adopted to initiate and engage in conversations on race and privilege in South Africa with my students, research participants, peers, colleagues and friends. As a postgraduate student engaged in research in South Africa, I strongly believe that reflecting on one own's raced, gendered, classed positionality and how it may affect your research is a necessary part of conducting your studies empathetically, critically and ethically.

ON TROUBLED KNOWLEDGE AND MUTUAL VULNERABILITY

As you engage with difficult and complex conversations around race, oppression and privilege, it is important to find a theoretical home, a home with which you feel comfortable. As I read up on South Africa's history, on the legacy of apartheid on the South Africa of today and, in particular, on its impact on education and on how students engage (or not) with each other, I found resonance with South African educator Jansen's term *troubled knowledge* (2009). Troubled knowledge is the indirect knowledge which is passed on from generation to generation; knowledge that is not conscious, but that defines how we see and engage with others. Jansen also calls it "knowledge in the blood" (p. 171), and defines it as "knowledge embedded in the emotional, psychic, spiritual, social, economic, political, and psychological lives of a community" (*ibid*). Jansen argues that it is this knowledge that keeps our communities apart; keeps us in our comfort zones. This knowledge has a darker side, as it draws out the "worst racial stereotypes, prejudices and aggressions" (Jansen 2004:121). He contends that for a social justice educator the most important thing is to disrupt this knowledge, as our classrooms are full of "bodies ... who carry knowledge within themselves that must be engaged, interrupted and transformed" (Jansen 2009:258).

I realised that my personal storytelling project disrupted some of the knowledges my students brought with them to class. It made students more aware of their assumptions and beliefs; it allowed them to see beyond the surface, beyond the masks that students across the rainbow nation were carrying in class, and made them care for each other. In their feedback on the project, they told me that they started to see each other as *humans* connected in a shared pain. In my readings I had also encountered the term *mutual vulnerability* (Keet, Zinn, & Porteus 2009), a key humanising concept in post-conflict societies that assumes we are all wounded in different ways and to different extents by the inhuman structure, in this case, apartheid. Could what my students were referring to be a growing recognition of this mutual vulnerability?

While in general this project was positively received by students, some of the feedback started to make me feel uneasy. In particular, feelings of pity by students associating with white privilege – comments such as, "Ah shame! If I only had known about the struggles this student went through to come to university, I could have helped." I noticed white students' defensiveness, their denial of any sort of responsibility in the continued structural inequalities characterising today's South Africa, and their difficulty recognising their own privilege. There was also a mounting anger expressed by some of the black students at this display of pity.

I found myself sitting with these explosive emotions in the classroom, unprepared and overwhelmed at how to deal with them, feeling more and more uncomfortable with what I was doing here. Did the telling of stories actually change anything? Or did I just re-affirm existing power relationships in the class? Who was I to challenge these knowledges? How could I prepare myself to challenge and question some of the emotions that were displayed in these conversations? What had I gotten myself into?

ON THE IMPORTANCE OF DIALOGUE

There was a distinct moment in my study where I felt that I needed help and advice at how to practically engage with the challenges encountered in this space. You might find that in your usual academic environment it is hard to find somebody who is willing to engage with you on difficult topics such as privilege or race. Whenever I tried to engage my colleagues at my university, my supervisors, even my friends in conversations around issues of difference and the emotions that I found in my teaching and research, I was met with the same discomfort and silence. At times I questioned myself as to whether my obsession with race was outdated or no longer that important in the rainbow nation as portrayed in media and policy. It felt to me as if this rainbow fairy tale was used to keep difficult questions at bay, to hide some of the uncomfortable truths from our conversations – an excuse to not engage in these difficult conversations. It felt as if people were too afraid to tackle these sensitive issues, too afraid to open this can of worms, or too afraid of not being able to contain the worms once unleashed.

Lacking a sounding board for my questions and doubts, I eventually decided to create a space for dialogue myself, outside of the academic reality. I was looking for a space where I could engage with issues around race and privilege in a different way: less theoretical, less academic, based on the lived experience of the people in South Africa. Together with a few other women I participated in a dialogue group. This group was founded in the spirit of hooks' (2000:8) feminist *consciousness-raising groups*, where, in our case, women of all colours and walks of life met on a monthly basis to engage in conversation and ask uncomfortable questions about what it meant to be human in today's South Africa.

If you can't find a space to discuss your thoughts and challenge your own understandings at your research site or university, consider creating such a space yourself. Connect with other postgraduate students to share, discuss and question your thoughts and even your findings. Find people in the community who share your passion and help you grow in your understanding and your postgraduate journey. Using social media to connect with others who are interested in discussing these issues could be another avenue to explore. I found various Facebook groups which helped me to understand current debates and discourses on race as well as gender in South Africa.

ON COMFORT ZONES, VULNERABILITIES AND CRITICAL EMOTIONAL REFLEXIVITY

While a theoretical framework to address the "elephant" may fit well with your lived experience, this might not always be shared by others. In my case, the notion of *mutual vulnerability and pain* (Keet et al 2009), became a bone of contention in our dialogue group. While black members of our dialogue group recognised white pain, they in some ways also invalidated this pain in relation to their own, and threw the term *white fragility* into our faces, warning us that listening to white pain could potentially re-traumatise black group members. White fragility is a term coined by DiAngelo (2011), an American anti-racist educator, and has been increasingly used in recent years to refer to white defensiveness in conversations around race. How did I, so keen on creating bridges for an understanding across difference, suddenly become the defensive "Other" – the white oppressor, the one who does not want to understand, transform or open up?

These debates coincided with the #RhodesMustfall movement, calling for the removal of the Cecil Rhodes statue at the University of Cape Town. Many of our black dialogue members actively joined this movement, which was clearly defined as a black movement, with a call for white allies to show – silent – support, emphasising the centrality of black voices and black pain (The Rhodes Must Fall Movement 2015). Mutual vulnerability was the last thing on their mind. My theoretical framework and lived experience clashed painfully; suddenly theory *antagonised* my lived experience (Britzman 2002). It was a painful and confusing moment and left me reeling, questioning all that I had believed in, read on, and used as central tenets for my PhD study. I thought I had it all figured out. But clearly not. As Nigerian writer Adichie (2015) recently stated in her commencement address to Wellesley College,

"Your standardised ideologies will not always fit your life. Because life is messy". What was my role in this struggle as a white European woman? If I did not believe in reconciliation, in the possibility of white and black students to find a shared space, a shared vulnerability to allow them to imagine and fight for a better future, what did I believe in? Where did this leave me, my study participants and my study?

This time, Boler and Zembylas's (2003) pedagogy of discomfort came to my rescue and helped me make sense of my messy emotions. The pedagogy of discomfort is based on the belief that only by moving out of our comfort zones will we be able to shake some of our own assumptions and beliefs about the "Other"; only by making ourselves vulnerable, and reflecting on our vulnerability and on the emotions that come with this vulnerability will we understand how our emotions are part of our socialisation. Zembylas calls this a *critical emotional reflexivity* (2011:1), which, as he explains, allows us to understand the historical nature and constructedness of the emotions we encounter.

The way I understand this is that we have to use our own emotions to recognise how our racial, classed, gendered identities have been constructed by our family, schooling, friends and communities. Our racial identities, for example, come with distinct emotional reactions in difficult dialogues. Through this lens my own defensiveness started to make sense. It was not just my own defensiveness, it was more; it was *white* defensiveness, born from *white* guilt and shame. Seeing emotions as politically and socially constructed helped me to distance myself from my own personal pain, to see the emotions I experienced in the bigger context of South Africa's painful history. I realised that our black group members did not necessarily react to me as an individual, but to what I was representing as a white woman in today's South Africa. In similar fashion black anger could be seen as politically, socially and historically constructed. Ahmed (2004) explains these emotions as symptoms of affective investments in social norms, accumulated over a lifetime, that make it so hard to shift our world views.

When I started to make sense of my emotional reactions in these difficult conversations, I found myself retreating more and more into an observer position, feeling like I had neither a voice nor an opinion. This is a difficult moment in postgraduate study, where you are seemingly supposed to have an opinion – a *standpoint* – at all times. But if you allow yourself to be vulnerable and to be open with your doubts, you might also find that over time you slowly learn to understand what *critical emotional reflexivity* could mean in practical terms; the slow and painful process of coming to terms with your own positionality and the emotions attached to it. I realised that I had to open myself up to challenge my own assumptions and beliefs, making myself part of the research process.

How do you become more reflective of your own affective investments? Personal storytelling, blogging and autobiographic writing might help. Write down your own story and see how your own understanding of self and other, of privilege and oppression might have changed over the course of your research. These do not have to be long stories – the digital storytelling format I adopted usually makes use of 300-500 words. They can be short vignettes that capture a moment, a feeling, or a doubt. Having to structure your thoughts into the form of a narrative can help you own and make sense of what and why you are feeling what you are feeling. Reflect on how your story supports or challenges the theories you chose for your study. Allow others to see your writing, comment on it and give feedback. This can be hard, especially if your thoughts are not fully formed or if you are struggling to find your argument. However, it is only in this exchange with others that you will be able to learn how to engage in difficult conversations in today's South Africa.

ON OPENNESS AND RECIPROCITY

Reflecting on your own emotions, taking yourself out of your comfort zones, and allowing yourself to be critiqued, challenged and questioned will allow you to understand your own and others' emotional responses better. It can also give you pointers of how to respond to them. When I engage in difficult conversations now, I try to be more aware of how I respond emotionally to certain topics but also of others' emotional responses. Instead of seeing emotions as getting in the way of conversations, I now see them as an entry point to start a conversation about the emotions we have learned and how to *unlearn* these emotions.

Being more reflective about your own emotional positionality will also help you become more aware of the underlying reasons you are conducting research. As researchers we have to be very careful and open about – what I would call – our *political* agenda when doing research. I do not believe that research can ever be neutral, as much as education can be neutral. We all have our own political agendas and our own beliefs of why we are teaching what we are teaching or researching what we are researching.

Opening up conversations about race and privilege can be highly emotional and stressful for both you and your research participants. Does your own political agenda match with the one of your study participants? What do empowerment, change and transformation mean to them? A risk in doing this kind of research as an outsider is that you could be seen and critiqued, as I would call it, a *data vulture*, coming from the north to feed on data of the south.

But even if you are South African, within this context of deep inequalities, conducting research ethically is a challenge[2]. Martha Nussbaum (2010:10) warns that, "[i]n a situation of entrenched inequality, being a neighbor can be an epistemological problem". Your interpretation of your data, in my case reading my own and my participants' stories, and your interactions with participants and colleagues will always be impacted by your cultural vantage point. Chaudry's (2009) reflections on her ethnographic work in Pakistan as a Muslim Pakistani woman educated in the United States of America is a useful account of how important it is to continuously critique your own biases and your own frames of thought. This self-critique, or reflexivity, might be the most important thing you do in this type of research, in particular within a social justice agenda.

Mutual vulnerability involves mutual reciprocity. How can you make your research participatory and reciprocal, so that not only you will gain from it? You can collect beautiful, heartfelt, honest stories. I found so much openness to share, so much support and gratefulness from my participants to have found somebody to listen to their stories and to take them back home. But what will your study participants have gained? Telling your own story, making yourself vulnerable to your research participants is the first step. But what more you can leave with them and what more of yourself can you give them? Think carefully about the professional and ethically implications of collecting and sharing your participants' data – about how you will present your participants to your audience, in particular if this is a foreign audience back home.

I watched an American student conduct research in one of the projects I was involved in and I loved her way of giving back. As an academic literacy lecturer she saw the need for academic writing support in her study participants and she gave this support generously during the time she was here. The way she conducted her study, her ethical and thoughtful engagement with her students, her lack of fear of critiquing our practice and her courage to challenge us deeply impressed me[3].

---

2 See Chapter 3 where Simangele Mayisela addresses this topic in more depth.

3 See Chapter 20 where Collium Banda argues that researchers have a responsibility to communicate their findings to the public, and in particular to their respondent constituencies.

ON GENTLENESS

In the struggle to understand yourself, do not forget to be gentle with yourself and your colleagues, fellow students and participants. Critiquing and questioning your own worldviews, from whichever part of the rainbow you may come from, can encourage a more understanding and empathetic approach towards the issues of race in postgraduate study in South Africa. In doing so, you might also be able to address your participants' questions (which may include uncomfortable questions about the motivation for your research) in ways that can facilitate a more open conversation with room for change and transformation.

I believe it is important to allow emotions into our lives as educators and researchers, to use emotions to reflect on why we react to certain situations in a certain way. It allows us to see our own lives as part of a larger social-economic and historically-shaped reality, to see our own emotional narratives as political. This also enables us the use our own narratives as a lens to understand how power and privilege is acted out in the micro cosmos that our classrooms or research sites represent – mirroring the larger society. By doing this, we may find ways to resist this normative nature of emotions governing how we act in and outside our classrooms or research sites to become critical yet ethical agents of social change.

Exploring the role of race in postgraduate research can be a process that takes you out of your comfort zone, leading you to engage with "Others", as well as yourself on deep levels. Do not be afraid to be challenged, critiqued and ultimately transformed in your relationship with others. Enter into a dialogue with the literature, your students, your research participants, your colleagues, your friends, and yourself. Be open and allow yourself to challenge and be challenged and transformed by this process.

REFERENCES

Ahmed, S. (2004). *The cultural politics of emotion.* Edinburgh, UK: Edinburgh University Press.

Boler, M., & Zembylas, M. (2003). Discomforting truths: The emotional terrain of understanding difference. In P. Trifonas (Ed.), *Pedagogies of difference: Rethinking education for social change* (pp. 110-136). New York, NY: RoutledgeFalmer.

Britzman, D. P. (2002). The question of belief. In E. Pierre & W. Pillow (Eds.), *Working the ruins: Feminist poststructural theory and methods in education* (pp. 27-40). New York, NY: Routledge.

Chaudry, L. N. (2009). Forays into the mist. In A. Y. Jackson & L. A. Mazzei (Eds.), *Voice in qualitative research* (pp. 137-164). Milton Park, UK & New York, NY: Routledge.

DiAngelo, R. (2011). White fragility. *International Journal of Critical Pedagogy,* 3(3):54-70.

Freeth, R. (2013). Just facilitation: Talking about race, privilege and sustainability. In *Proceedings of the 19th International Sustainable Development Conference* (pp. 149-162). Stellenbosch: Sustainability Institute. Available online at http://www.sustainabilityinstitute.net/newsdocs/document-downloads/doc_download/640-rebecca-freeth-just-facilitation-talking-about-race-privilege-and-sustainability

hooks, B. (2000). *Where we stand: Class matters*. New York, NY: Routledge.

Jansen, J. (2009). *Knowledge in the blood: Confronting race and apartheid past*. Stanford, CA: Stanford University Press.

Keet, A., Zinn, D., & Porteus, K. (2009). Mutual vulnerability : A key principle in a humanising pedagogy in post-conflict societies. *Perspectives*, 27(June):5-6.

Adichie, C. N. (2015). 2015 Wellesley College commencement address. Available online at https://www.youtube.com/watch?v=RcehZ3CjedU

Nussbaum, M. C. (2010). *Not for profit – why democracy needs the humanities*. Princeton, New Jersey, NJ: Princeton University Press.

The Rhodes Must Fall Movement. (2015, March 25). UCT Rhodes Must Fall Mission Statement. *RhodesMustFall Facebook Page*. Cape Town, South Africa. Available online at https://www.facebook.com/RhodesMustFall/posts/1559394444336048

Zembylas, M. (2011). *The politics of trauma in education*. New York, NY: Palgrave Macmillan.

STUDENT-SUPERVISOR RELATIONSHIPS IN A COMPLEX SOCIETY: A DUAL NARRATIVE OF SCHOLARLY BECOMING

Zondiwe L. Mkhabela & B. Liezel Frick

INTRODUCTION

Doctoral pedagogy is complex, partly due to the intricacies of the student-supervisor relationship. Manathunga (2005) refers to this relationship as taking place in a private space, which is especially true in the case of the apprenticeship approach to supervision where doctoral students often work in relative isolation with one or two supervisors.

In the South African context, this (relatively private) relationship can be even more complicated as a result of the complex historical past that still influences current learning spaces (as Daniela Gachago's first chapter in this book highlights). The racial inequalities enforced under the apartheid regime and which date even further back to colonial rule have left an indelible mark on South African education, including doctoral education. Waghid's (2015) recent reflection on his own experiences of doctoral supervision and the collection of papers edited by Aslam Fataar (2012) shed some light on this complex and complicated private space. Thus our narrative of an evolving student-supervisor relationship is not a unique one in the local South African context or even internationally (see, for example, Grant 2010a; Grant & McKinley 2011; McKinley et al 2011; Manathunga 2013; Winchester-Seeto, Homewood, Thogersen, Jacenyik-Trawoger, Manathunga, Reid, & Holbrook 2014). But we do not present our dual narrative as representative of these or others' stories, as each student-supervisor relationship is marked by its own particulars and peculiarities. What our story adds to the evolving South African national narrative on doctoral education is a unique perspective where *both* the student *and* the supervisor reflect on their *shared* so-called private learning space against the backdrop of a growing body of knowledge that sheds light on such spaces from either supervisors' or students' perspectives. As such, we put the spotlight on what is often the unspeakable truths marking our society and practices.

A narrative is a way in which meaning can be made from lived experience (Johnson 2006) and is by its nature socially situated (Pavlenko 2002) and contextual (Ollerenshaw & Creswell 2002). Thus documenting these experiences is essentially autobiographical in nature. The idea of narrative space consisting of three interconnected dimensions that provide a context for any particular story (Clandinin & Connelly 2000) was useful in making sense of our dual narrative. The three dimensions include (a) the participants, in this case our own experiences in interacting during the doctoral journey; (b) the timing of the story, how it relates to both the past and the future; and (c) the setting or locality of the story. Any story can be positioned within the space created by these three interrelated dimensions. The space creates the context within which the story is understood – by both the narrator of the story and the narrative researcher. In this case we took on both these roles as we autobiographically explored our narrated stories. Our choice of voice (Miles & Huberman 1994) is justified in Tierney's (2002:392) notion of narrative reflexivity. Johnson and Golombek (2002:4) also note the value of reflexivity in the narrative, in that "inquiry into experience ... can be educative if it enables us to reflect on our actions and then act with foresight". Our narrative highlights the individualised and contextualised nature of doctoral education and therefore does not aim to generalise, but rather explore the complexity of the student-supervisor relationship. Our shared space was characterised by many features that created scope for an uneasy relationship, as we explain further on. However, we also explore the means by which we were able to build and sustain a productive student-supervisor relationship leading to the successful completion of the study. As such, a dual narrative such as the one presented here becomes a useful vehicle by which other students and supervisors alike may chart their own complex postgraduate journeys.

A PERILOUS BUT DECISIVE START

Grant (2010b:351) presents doctoral supervision as a "pedagogy in which our raced, classed and gendered bodies are present", and when such supervision happens across ethnic cultures (as in this case), it "becomes a pedagogical site of rich possibility as well as, at times, a place of puzzling and confronting complexity". Our joint narrative speaks to both the possibilities and complexities of such a relationship.

Liezel's narrative

Our journey began in 2007, when a referral by a then recently retired colleague led to our paths crossing, and then ran in parallel until Zondi's graduation in March 2015. At the time, I (Liezel) had only recently completed my own PhD and was starting an academic career. I was young and inexperienced. At this stage, I had co-supervised one PhD student, but Zondi was the first student I took on as main supervisor. In addition, I am white and female. Zondi, on the other hand, had years of professional experience in the context where he wanted to conduct his study (even though he did not come into his study with a lot of research experience). He is black and male, and much older than me. Why are these personal characteristics of any importance? We came from very different places and spaces in a society where your social background, age, patriarchal traditions and ethnicity often still mark interactions between people. We were different in just about all possible respects, save our shared South African nationality and (most importantly) our mutual academic curiosity.

Zondi's narrative

In addition to the personal characteristics mentioned above, I (Zondi) brought into our student-supervisor relationship what I would now call stereotypes. Before I discuss this, I want to briefly explain why I pursued doctoral studies, my choice of university and how our student-supervisor relationship began. My doctoral studies were initially more a show of loyalty to my ancestors than a personal ambition for the highest academic accolades. I was raised by my grandmother after my mother passed on when I was nine years old. My grandmother believed in formal education as a vehicle to fight nothingness, and to build families and communities. Her wish was for my siblings and I to get a good education despite our indigent background – a wish I took seriously. My choice of university was influenced by the South African history of politics and education. Waghid (2015) argues that most non-white South African students have a bias towards achieving a qualification at a historically advantaged white university. I also developed a desire to intrude into universities that were intended for the other races and the elite of our complex South African society. My choice of university so far away from home was an attempt to break the barriers created by apartheid education, of which some are still intact today. I submitted a research proposal for consideration to the university where Liezel was employed and she was allocated to supervise my study given her expertise on adult education. I had never met Liezel before and did not know what to expect. As I was driving to our first meeting, a number of questions were running through my mind. Would she be accessible? Would she understand the narration of the problem I intended to investigate? Would the distance between our settings (approximately 1 800 km) be an obstacle or an enabler? Would she have an interest in a study that is located in a rural setting?

When I finally met her, even before we exchanged greetings, more worries crept in. I am a black South African while she is a white South African. Race was an issue to me because of the legacy of white supremacy and privilege that characterised the day-to-day life of South Africans. Waghid's (2015) argument that many black students still have feelings of mistrust and insecurity when supervised by whites held true for me at that stage. I was not sure if in this relationship there would exist what Lusted (1986) describes as a journey of production and exchange, or if my contributions would be subjected to merit or my blackness. I acknowledge that this naïve thinking was confirmation of racial stereotypes that are still embedded in the psyche of most communities in South Africa due to the experiences of the past apartheid regime and colonialism as Liezel mentioned earlier.

Liezel was also much younger than me. The age difference did not worry me, but age counts in my culture (Shangaan), especially between a man and a woman in any relationship, where the man is expected to be the leader and guardian. I understood that historically most white South Africans did not have to interrupt their schooling years to fend for their families and siblings. Most of them started and finished school before they would look for employment. Age and academic progress are therefore also linked to the history of South Africa. Liezel is female and I am male. Given the history of gender inequality and stereotypes across races in South Africa, I expected that she would want to prove that women can do better than men as this was the case with my earlier interactions with women in different professional contexts. These are some of the assumptions I brought to this new student-supervisor relationship. As we talked over a cup of tea, we began to agree on communication logistics and how we would go about the work going forward. So, this first meeting got us off on a perilous but decisive start with preparations for a journey and a student-supervisor relationship that lasted six years.

Liezel: This decisive cup of tea Zondi describes was marked by a tentative search for common ground from both sides of the relationship. Looking back, I think my young and inexperienced approach as a supervisor can be described by the saying, fools rush in where angels fear to tread. I was not immune to the stereotypes Zondi described. I also wondered whether he, as an older black man, would accept my guidance and critique as his supervisor. Would he judge my potential scholarly contribution to his work based on my appearance and background? Did I know enough about his study topic and context in order to give sound advice? I remember making a conscious decision at that time: to directly address the obvious things that could become issues in our student-supervisor relationship, and to be unequivocal about the basis from which I worked. If he did not like it, he could still decide to study somewhere else. So I asked Zondi directly whether he had a problem with me being a young, white female person supervising his study. I also told him that though I understood that each study and student made their own demands on a supervisor, I did not discriminate when it came to quality of work – I expected the same standard of academic engagement from each of my students, no matter who they were. I had no idea what effect this forthright approach might have had on him at the time.

Zondi: Liezel's forthright style unsettled me, especially her bold stance on quality of work and the hard work she expected from her students. I felt intimidated and I began to wonder if I would be able to meet her expectations. I was, however, reassured when she said that she was looking forward to learn from me as well, especially my culture and language. I felt at ease and began my first steps in building the relationship. Lusted (1986) claims that the supervisor, the student and the knowledge produced are bound together in a pedagogical relationship and that all three these agencies change as a result of this relationship. But at the same time, there is an unequal power relation at play in this relationship (Foucault 1986), based on class position, educational biography, familiarity and competence with disciplines and ideas, differences in cultural expectations, social experience, linguistic structures, as well as confidence, commitment and energy (Lusted 1986:5), as is evident from our dual narrative presented here. Thus knowledge production requires "deep processes that get under and into the skin, assembling psycho-social dynamics of struggle, submission and subjectification" (Green 2005:151). It was therefore essential for both of us to get to know each other and our respective contexts if we were to make sense of our joint doctoral venture.

GETTING TO KNOW EACH OTHER'S CONTEXTS

Liezel's commitment that she was prepared to learn from me as well was put to test when I sent her an email after I received her comments on my proposal. It was written in my language (Shangaan) with English interpretations. The email read as follows:

> *Eka Liezel (Dear Liezel). Inkomu nhlamulo ndzi yi kumile (Thanks for your response I received). Inkomu, salakahle (Thanks, regards).*

Her response was:

> *Eka Zondi. Inkomu for your revised proposal and thanks for the improvements. Inkomu, Liezel.*

Her use of "inkomu for your revised proposal" in the email was an indication to me that she was prepared to learn my language. I must confess that I did not do enough to teach her because after six years she could only greet and perhaps say goodbye in my language. My preoccupation with the study and the geographical distance between us are probably the reasons why I never taught her more. But she appreciated my effort, and her keen interest motivated me as I knew that her comments would ensure my progress.

Barbara Grant (2010b:351) eloquently points out that the complexity of both supervision and culture often go unrecognised in institutional conceptualisations of doctoral supervision:

> Supervision is cast as a mainly cognitive undertaking between rational, disembodied minds, in which the dominance of western knowledge systems is rarely acknowledged or challenged ...

My (Liezel's) background in adult education sensitised me to the importance of recognising students' prior knowledge and experience, as well as honouring who they are as people. Looking back, I can now see that we came from completely different epistemic and ontological positions. I had been schooled in a predominantly western epistemic tradition, putting me in a vastly different ontological position than Zondi. Mbembe (2015) claims that such western traditions often rest on a divide between mind and world, or reason and nature, where knowledge becomes divorced from context. Given our situation, there was much room for a kind of colonised scholarship where the powerful knower renders the non-western knowledge invisible. I needed Zondi to trust my scholarly judgement, but at the same time I had to own up that I did not know everything, least of all his epistemic and ontological background and current context. Making a small effort to cross the language barrier was an attempt at crossing a much larger cultural and epistemic divide.

The next year, I (Zondi) received confirmation that the university accepted my proposal. I was allowed to register as a PhD student, and a senior professor was appointed as co-supervisor with Liezel as my main supervisor. Next, I had to complete the first chapter of my thesis. This was challenging, as I had to lay the foundation that would guide the entire study. I visited the university where I met with my supervisors. It was my first experience in an environment where academics sat with me around a table as if I were their equal. I felt somewhat intimidated, and as I presented my ideas, it became clear that the journey would not be an easy one. Every single statement I made had to be accounted for. At some point the co-supervisor asked me if I were a politician. I was unsettled by this question. Did he think my proposal was a political presentation that would not meet academic standards? But Liezel kept probing into my presentation, which forced me to be more natural in the way I presented my ideas.

Fataar (2012:14) refers to what Zondi must have experienced as "the shifting identity of these students as they navigate the complex personal identity terrain involved in the process of developing a credible doctoral proposal". Zondi had to learn a whole new discourse that had not previously been part of his narrative, despite having successfully completed a Master's degree. Fataar (2012) refers to this notion as a pedagogy of supervision that requires a capital alignment between the student's life world and that of the university (where the supervisor often becomes the face of the university). The supervisory relationship created the space where Zondi could test his ideas, take risks, make mistakes, invent and reinvent knowledge, but I (Liezel) needed to earn his trust so he would have the confidence and courage to do so. My colleague and I also had to model what it meant being (responsible) scholars, which was not always easy in my case as I had only started on my own academic career. Green (2005) furthermore warns that doctoral pedagogy is as much about identity production as it is about knowledge production. I realised quite early on in the process that I would be doing Zondi a disservice if I tried cloning my own research identity in him – he needed to develop his own voice. The Socratic method – which Zondi refers to as probing (see Frick, Albertyn & Rutgers 2010) – helped me to get clarity on Zondi's ideas, so that I could guide him to own his intellectual project without me providing all the answers. I (Liezel) agree with Lin and Cranton (2005) that the transformative process that happens during a student's identity shift from being a scholarship student to becoming a responsible scholar is not easy or fast, and that it requires a gradual epistemic induction (Hugo 2009). In this case, it required a dual epistemic induction – Zondi needed to become eloquent in the dominant discourses on this chosen topic and research approach, whereas I needed to find ways to help him incorporate the co-present non-western knowledge systems that both Zondi and the nature of his study brought to our joint intellectual project.

When I next met with Liezel, I (Zondi) had lunch with her and her husband, who happened to know the area I come from. He was also in the process of completing his PhD. He gave me a few pointers, including how I could secure funding for my studies, as I had no financial support for my tuition. He linked me up with his friend, a businessman from my area, who provided me with funding for two academic years. Given the contextual complexity that marks our dual narrative, as described in the previous section, our student-supervisor relationship was evolving into the kind of scholarly friendship Waghid (2006) describes.

In the same year, I experienced a major setback. I was suspended from work, which affected the prospects of continuing with my studies as my work environment also formed my study site. I broke the news to Liezel. Although she was shocked, she surprisingly did not panic. She suggested that we take the study elsewhere. Her forward-looking attitude and the suggestion to take the study elsewhere inspired me to continue. We focussed on a local municipality that was also rural and shared the same social features as my initial study site. While we were initially granted permission to continue after Liezel and I met with the municipality officials and conducted a site visit within the affected rural area, the permission was subsequently withdrawn. It felt as if the study was doomed. I had to inform Liezel of these unpleasant developments hoping that we would help me find a way out of this mess. Effectively, I had lost a full year of my studies.

Later that year, a "not guilty" verdict was passed reinstating me retrospectively and I was granted permission to continue with my study at the original study site. I communicated these developments to Liezel, who had not lost hope that the study would continue. At this stage it was clear to both of us that we needed to work speedily given that we had already lost almost two years of study time. At least now I was allowed to do my study activities at work during working hours. The local authorities were keen to help me make up for the lost study time. I was also allowed unlimited internet access which facilitated my everyday contact with Liezel. This is evident in the numerous emails Liezel and I exchanged over the six years. Over the course of my study, Liezel visited me three times and I visited her four times at the university. These face-to-face-meetings were indispensable in making headway.

MAKING HEADWAY

In the midst of my studies, I (Zondi) remember discussions about my literature chapter. Reading created opportunities for constant communication between us, as everything had to be scrutinised, verified and approved. This process of managing progress was rigorous. It meant a lot of back and forth communication and required that we agreed before moving to the next step. At first I was not comfortable with the slow progress until I developed a habit of always going back to what I wrote before sending it to Liezel. This habit assisted me because when I was busy with one chapter, Liezel already looked at the chapter in relation to all the chapters that would follow. By the time I got to the next chapter, I already knew what was expected. We agreed that before going to the next chapter, we had to determine whether our work met the expectations of a doctorate. Liezel was very strict on standards. In my mind, this is what defined our student-supervisor relationship.

At a specific point during the study, an international expert related to the field of my study visited the university. Liezel invited me to a symposium featuring this expert. I had the privilege of meeting with him and we had discussions around my topic. Although his area of specialisation was slightly different, he gave me a better understanding of my topic in different contexts. Our discussions shaped the conceptualisation of my own study. He also donated his book to me, which gave me even more insights and was influential in conceptualising the theoretical framework for my study.

During our first meeting after I got reinstated, Liezel and I outlined a progress plan that I had to follow and it became evident that we were under enormous pressure to conclude the study. Liezel proposed timelines, but by mid-year it was evident that I needed more time to collect data. Liezel and I communicated on every little bit of progress made, and thus could jointly revisit our initial targets. As I drew closer to concluding the study, the municipality where I conducted my study was placed under administration (which meant it was declared bankrupt and placed under curatorship). This development had implications for my study. I informed Liezel about these developments. We agreed that we needed to integrate these developments into my study. This meant that I had to run additional interviews and rework the sample and analysis. It also meant that we had to allow more time for the study, but we were resolute that quality would not be compromised. We agreed to take more time and have a product both of us could be proud of. I had developed the habit of working on the dissertation like it was a lifetime journey. Sometimes I would forget that I needed to graduate. I remember that even after I had integrated the administration period, Liezel continued to refer me to yet more reading sources to update the literature I used.

As we drew closer to submitting the dissertation, the email exchanges increased. Liezel advised me to get a professional editor for the dissertation. Upon receiving her message, it dawned on me that we were nearing the end of our joint journey. I sent the edited dissertation to Liezel, to which she replied, "I shall work through it and see if any final changes are necessary". Quite clearly, Liezel was prepared to work through the dissertation until the last minute. This was confirmation of her commitment to quality when it came to academic work. When she finally said, "Maybe it's time we allow the chick to try out her own wings" (which meant it is time to release our work for external examination), I had mixed feelings and many questions. Is the work good enough for examination? Did I clarify the context of the study enough for the examiners to understand? Is the study of the quality expected for a doctorate? The time we spent with the document and the amount of work we put in, reassured me. Maybe the human factor was responsible for my feelings of discomfort. Although I developed a lot of trust in our work over the years, I was not comfortable having our work reviewed by individuals who were not part of our journey.

It took more than nine weeks for the results to come. Finally, I received an email from Liezel that read:

> It is good to be a carrier of good news on a Monday morning! We have received all your reports, and based on their feedback the oral examination will go ahead ... In general the three reports are quite positive (congratulations).

My response to the message was:

> I'm over the moon and ready for the oral exam.

Contrary to the message, I was anxious and confused, not knowing what questions the examiners were going to ask.

THE ORAL EXAMINATION AND GRADUATION

I was invited to the university for the oral examination. Liezel advised me to arrive a day before to allow time to prepare. On the day of the oral examination Liezel, the co-supervisor and I had a preparatory session. Liezel and the co-supervisor took me through the expected process and tried to reassure me, as I was very tense. They advised me not to give too much detail, to avoid volunteering information, and not to argue with examiners. This advice scared me even more, because I got the impression that examiners can be irritable and authoritative. After the session with my supervisors, we took a break. When we came back for the examination three hours later, the three of us were equally anxious. The oral examination took more than two hours. My supervisors were only allowed to observe. This arrangement put a lot pressure on me because I was worried that I would not represent my mentors well. When the examination was concluded, it was evident from the examiners' comments that it was an outright pass. This brought to conclusion a long journey, well travelled, and it was time to prepare for graduation.

The same evening Liezel introduced me to her Master's students. For the first time I learned how much she valued me, and I was extremely humbled. The day was concluded festively when Liezel and her husband took me out for supper the same way they did when I first became her student in 2008.

The graduation was an experience of a lifetime. It dawned on me (Zondi) that I was about to achieve the one thing I promised my ancestors. I felt excited about becoming a doctor but also disappointed because my grandmother, to whom I owed the drive for the doctorate, would not be present. To make up for my grandmother's absence, I invited her eldest son and my uncle to attend the ceremony. I believe, as Liezel pointed out during the graduation ceremony, that "the ancestors are pleased with this PhD award" and that my grandmother was happy with her son standing in for her.

Our joint journey over six years taught us many lessons. We summarise these under the following headings: understand each other's contexts, mutual kindness as a basis for supervision, the need for compassionate rigour, and the necessity of consulting experts along the way.

Understanding each other's contexts

We came into the supervisory relationship from vastly different places and spaces, as is evident from our dual narrative. Looking back, we realise how fragile the basis was on which our joint knowledge venture was built. We also realise the importance of understanding and respecting each other's contexts in mediating such fragile student-supervisor relationships. Meeting face-to-face on a regular basis at either the university or the study site gave us each the opportunity to understand the other's contexts. These meetings were essential in not only situating the study from both contextual and scholarly perspectives, but also building our mutual trust and understanding. It gave us the opportunity to get to know each other as people, not just disembodied knowledge workers. In previous work, I (Frick 2011) argued that doctoral becoming requires an alignment between how students view themselves in relation to the research process of becoming a scholar (ontology), how they relate to different forms of knowledge (epistemology), how they obtain and create such knowledge (methodology), and how they frame their interests in terms of their values and ethics within the discipline (axiology). This line of argument positions doctoral becoming as an ontological, epistemological, methodological and axiological concern in which supervisors need to help students' transformation to doctorateness (as described by Wellington 2013). But it is not only the student who is transformed – supervisors also need to shift their ontological, epistemological, methodological and axiological positions when they are faced with students who come from non-traditional knowledge systems.

Building mutual kindness and trust

Clegg and Rowland (2010) argue that kindness is one of the necessary but often unremarked aspects of good teaching. However, acts of kindness may also paradoxically be construed as misjudged or harmful to others. Kindness cannot be regulated or prescribed, but forms one of the core aspects of what makes us human (and sometimes it is kindness that makes us carry on despite setbacks or misfortune). We would argue that mutual kindness is one of the core aspects that defined our student-supervisor relationship, and that kindness built mutual trust that facilitated our eventual progress. A mutual show of kindness provided a strong foundation for the otherwise rigorous and sometimes harsh academic critique that characterises doctoral supervisory discourses.

No compromises on quality: the role of compassionate rigour in doctoral education

Doctoral studies are not examined by the supervisors in the South African context, but supervisors play a key role in ensuring that such studies meet the demands of being academically rigorous and making an original contribution. Thus, while mutual kindness and trust lay the foundation for a respectful and humane student-supervisor relationship, it was equally important that the scholarly quality of the work itself not be compromised in any way. Ensuring quality of the doctoral contribution sometimes calls for rigorous debate and a continuous re-interrogation of the merit of the work. Such responses to scholarly work need to be rigorous by necessity, but at the same time compassionate (Manathunga 2005). Compassionate rigour furthermore allows for a more complex understanding of doctorateness, as Wellington (2013) suggests. Such an understanding would allow non-dominant ontological and epistemological positions to enter the doctoral discourse, and make the learning experience richer for both student and supervisor.

Utilising experts

There were other contributors who played a meaningful role in the study. The first was the co-supervisor in this study, who provided expert advice when called upon, and gave us the space to explore the details of the study in our own time. Co-supervision has the potential to complicate the student-supervisor relationship, but it also has the potential to add value – especially if one supervisor is a novice. In our experience, clarifying student and supervisor role expectations upfront is key to building a strong team. Universities further have many support services that may be useful even to students who complete their studies at a distance. In this case, the subject librarian was a key role player in making sources available in a timely manner. Consulting with international experts and scholars when the opportunity arose was also influential in taking the study forward. Such experts may provide different perspectives and insights that can facilitate progress. Our experience has taught us to utilise expertise and support where appropriate and where available to our benefit.

CONCLUSION: THE DUAL NARRATIVE AS AN ON-GOING STORY

Writing a dual narrative about our shared student-supervisor relationship has been a difficult but rewarding endeavour. We had to delve deep within ourselves and into our shared experiences to make sense of our dual narrative, and how it could sensibly be reflected against existing scholarship on doctoral pedagogy. The mutual understanding, trust, kindness and compassionate rigour we built up over a period of more than six years enabled us to approach this task with both sensitivity and academic rigour. We were sometimes surprised by each other's take on our shared story, but agreed that honesty needed to be the hallmark of the contribution we aim to make. We agree that what you have read is a true representation of our shared story.

The purpose of this dual narrative has been to provide a balanced account of how a student-supervisor relationship develops in a complex society such as that of South Africa. We have shown that such a relationship does not develop in isolation of societal factors – neither students nor supervisors can afford to ignore each other's ontological and epistemological positions during a study. We have argued that understanding each other's contexts, building mutual kindness and trust, excepting no compromises on quality through compassionate rigour, and utilising experts when appropriate helped to solidify what started out as a fragile student-supervisor relationship. What postgraduate students and supervisors may draw from this dual narrative is that social factors including the context in which studies are conducted may influence their outcomes. There is, however, room for further interrogation of each of these aspects from both supervisors' and students' perspectives in a (South) African context.

REFERENCES

Clandinin, D. J. & Connelly, F. M. (2000). *Narrative inquiry: Experience and story in qualitative research*. San Francisco, USA: Jossey-Bass.

Clegg, S., & Rowland, S. (2010). Kindness in pedagogical practice and academic life. *British Journal of Sociology of Education*, 31(6), 719-735. http://dx.doi.org/10.1080/01425692.2010.515102

Fataar, A. (Ed.). (2012). *Debating thesis supervision*. Stellenbosch, South Africa: AFRICAN SUN MeDIA.

Foucault, M. (1986). Disciplinary power and subjection. *Power*, 229-242.

Frick, B. L. (2011). *Facilitating creativity in doctoral education: A resource for supervisors*. In A. Lee & V. Mallan (Eds.). Connecting the local, regional and global in doctoral education (pp. 123-137). Serdang, Malaysia: Universiti Putra Malaysia Press.

Frick, B. L., Albertyn, R. M., & Rutgers, L. (2010). The Socratic Method: Exploring theories underlying critical questioning as a pathway in student independence. *Acta Academica, Supplementum* 1:75-102.

Grant, B. (2010a). Challenging issues: Doctoral supervision in post-colonial sites. *Acta Academica, Supplementum* 1(2010):103-129.

Grant, B. M. (2010b). The limits of 'teaching and learning': Indigenous students and doctoral supervision. *Teaching in Higher Education*, 15(5), 505-517. http://dx.doi.org/10.1080/13562517.2010.491903

Grant, B., & McKinley, E. (2011). Colouring the pedagogy of doctoral supervision: Considering supervisor, student and knowledge through the lens of indigeneity. *Innovations in Education and Teaching International*, 48(4):377-386. http://dx.doi.org/10.1080/14703297.2011.617087

Green, B. (2005). Unfinished business: Subjectivity and supervision. *Higher Education Research and Development*, 24(2):151-163. http://dx.doi.org/10.1080/07294360500062953

Holbrook, A. (2014). Doctoral supervision in a cross-cultural context: Issues affecting supervisors and candidates. *Higher Education Research & Development*, 33(3):610-626. http://dx.doi.org/10.1080/07294360.2013.841648

Hugo, W. (2009). Spiralling reference. A case study of apprenticeship into an academic community of practice. *South African Journal of Higher Education*, 23(4):703-721.

Johnson, K. E. (2006). The sociocultural turn and its challenges for second language teacher education. *TESOL Quarterly*, 40(1):235-257. http://dx.doi.org/10.2307/40264518

Johnson, K. E., & Golombek, P. R. (Eds.) (2002). *Teachers' narrative inquiry as professional development*. Cambridge, UK: Cambridge University Press.

Lin, L., & Cranton, P. (2005). From scholarship student to responsible scholar: A transformative process. *Teaching in Higher Education*, 10(4):447-459. http://dx.doi.org/10.1080/13562510500239026

Lusted, D. (1986). Why pedagogy? *Screen*, 27(5):2-16.

Manathunga, C. (2013). Culture as a place of thought. In A-C. R. Engels-Schwarzpaul & M. A. Peters (Eds.). *Of other thoughts: Non-traditional ways to the doctorate* (pp. 67-82). Rotterdam, Netherlands: Sense Publishers. http://dx.doi.org/10.1007/978-94-6209-317-1_11

Manathunga, C. (2009). Supervision as a contested space: A response. *Teaching in Higher Education*, 14(3):341-345. http://dx.doi.org/10.1080/13562510902990242

Manathunga, C. (2005). The development of research supervision: "Turning a light on a private space". *International Journal for Academic Development*, 10(1):17-30. http://dx.doi.org/10.1080/13601440500099977

Mbembe, A. (2015). Decolonizing knowledge and the question of the archive. Retrieved from http://wiser.wits.ac.za/system/files/Achille%20Mbembe%20-%20Decolonizing%20Knowledge%20and%20the%20Question%20of%20the%20Archive.pdf

McKinley, E., Grant, B., Middleton, S., Irwin, K., & Williams, L. R. T. (2011). Working at the interface: Indigenous students' experience of undertaking doctoral studies in Aotearoa New Zealand. *Equity and Excellence in Education*, 44(1):115-132. http://dx.doi.org/10.1080/10665684.2010.540972

Miles, M. B. & Huberman, A. M. (1994). *Qualitative data analysis: An expanded sourcebook*. Thousand Oaks, USA: Sage Publications.

Ollerenshaw, J., & Creswell, J. (2002). Narrative research: A comparison of two restorying data analysis approaches. *Qualitative Inquiry*, 8(3):329-347. http://dx.doi.org/10.1177/10778004008003008

Pavlenko, A. (2002). Narrative study: Whose story is it anyway? *TESOL Quarterly*, 36(2):213-218. http://dx.doi.org/10.2307/3588332

Tierney, W. G. (2002). Getting real: Representing reality. *International Journal of Qualitative Studies in Education*, 15(4):385-398. http://dx.doi.org/10.1080/09518390210145444

Waghid, Y. (2006). Reclaiming freedom and friendship through postgraduate student supervision. *Teaching in Higher Education*, 11(4):427-439. http://dx.doi.org/10.1080/13562510600874185

Waghid, Y. (2015). *Dancing with doctoral encounters: Democratic education in motion*. Stellenbosch, South Africa: AFRICAN SUN MeDIA.

Wellington, J. (2013). Searching for 'doctorateness'. *Studies in Higher Education*, 38(10):1490-1503. http://dx.doi.org/10.1080/03075079.2011.634901

Winchester-Seeto, T., Homewood, J., Thogersen, J., Jacenyik-Trawoger, C., Manathunga, C., Reid, A., & Holbrook, A. (2014). Doctoral supervision in a cross-cultural context: Issues affecting supervisors and candidates. *Higher Education Research & Development*, 33(3):610-626.

3 RESEARCH ETHICS AND ETHICAL DILEMMAS IN THE SOUTH AFRICAN CONTEXT

Simangele Mayisela

INTRODUCTION

While I am not an expert on research ethics, the nature of my PhD study has challenged me to put my ethical standing to the test. This chapter explores the complexities of research ethics in the Social Sciences based on both scholarly insights and my own encounters. I will highlight challenging ethical dilemmas that may seem to threaten the success of the research itself.

To enable you to follow my trail of thought, I need to provide some contextual background information. My study is on "Corporal punishment: Socio-cultural practices of teachers in a South African primary school", with a particular emphasis on a rural village in Mpumalanga as a case study. In this study, I use observations, interviews and document analysis to understand what discipline practices teachers are currently using, how teachers use corporal punishment and how their own childhood experiences influence their views on this practice. I also look at what reasons, if any, teachers give for believing in, or resorting to, corporal punishment, and how learners and parents respond to the practice of corporal punishment. This study has tricky ethical dimensions for both the researcher and the respondents. I therefore use my own study as a practical example from which to explore research ethics as it relates to the researcher's identity, the institution, the participants and the research context.

"WHO AM I?" THE RESEARCHER IDENTITY DILEMMA

The universal values of respect and care for fellow human beings lie central to research ethics. Due to the fallible nature of mankind, these values need to be pronounced and even inscribed, and hence, as researchers, we need to have ethical codes of conduct, like the ethics code for the researchers of the Human Science Research Council (2015). Many professional fields (including teachers, doctors, nurses, engineers and accountants) also have codes of ethics that guide their professional practice.

As a psychologist who is also conducting PhD research, I have become aware of the necessity to define myself as a researcher in a specific profession. For novice researchers this process usually presents an identity dilemma. The crisis stems from conceptualising the research problem – which is usually done from the standpoint of your professional work. For example, in my case, my study is on teachers' use of corporal punishment in South African schools. I conceptualised the research problem while I was working as a psychologist, lecturing and providing counselling to student teachers and teachers. As my study progressed to field work preparation, I needed to reconfigure my position in relation to my research study. This configuration depended on a number of factors: the nature of the study and the research design, my initial relationship with the research field, how I wanted the participants to relate to me during the research process, and the impact that would have on the research outcomes. The two scenarios below clarify my point.

Scenario 1: If I used action research as my research design, introducing myself as a psychologist who is researching the implementation of alternatives to corporal punishment would be appropriate, as the participants would participate in the research process implementing the intervention innovations according to the researcher's professional practice.

Scenario 2: If I used ethnographic observations, emphasising my professional affiliation may impact the observations. For example, if the aim of the study was to determine teachers' use of corporal punishment in the classroom, emphasising my psychologist identity may result in teachers changing patterns of their practice. They may start to engage you, thereby obscuring answers to your research questions. To meet the objective of my study effectively, the emphasis of my psychologist identity may need to be less prominent.

This means there is a fine line to draw in deciding how much one can emphasise a researcher's versus a practitioner's identity. This decision needs to be made before going into the research field to avoid confusing the participants, and yourself. A clear identity definition when you first meet your participants is valuable. It is important to clarify that in the course of the research process, you are a researcher and, therefore, research ethics take precedence. This clarity serves as your point of reference guiding your conduct in the research process, and will help unravel other ethical dilemmas you are likely to encounter. The researcher needs to have clear personal values and skills, and self-regulation that form the internal compass for research ethics. For you to engage in research, the assumption is that you are a professional, a knowledge worker, and by implication you the have research knowledge, skills and values warranting you the freedom to do credible and valid research within your organisational or faculty guidelines.

HAVE YOU OBTAINED ETHICAL CLEARANCE? INSTITUTIONAL ETHICAL REGULATIONS

As a researcher, you may be conducting your research under the auspices of an organisation or a higher education institution. Institutional ethical procedures are a gate-keeping exercise to control the nature of the knowledge produced, and ensure that studies are executed with minimum or no harm to the participants and the organisations involved. Furthermore, institutional ethical procedures protect the reputation of research in the society at large, because some measure of harm done by one researcher is likely to create an entry barrier for future researchers. Considering that a higher education institution is the custodian of a study, the institution would certainly be implicated by association with any of the unforeseen outcomes of the study, be it negative or positive. The foreseeable positive implication is that the institution can use the results of the study to inform the policy and the current discourse. Research ethics help you as a researcher and the university as the custodian of the study to forge appropriate interventions towards accomplishing the policy intent for the benefit of the greater society.

Most higher education institutions ensure that ethics are taken into consideration by the researcher from the research planning stage, hence ethical considerations have become part of the proposal submission, where you need to demonstrate that you have considered all possible ethical implications. Thereafter, you will receive a letter of ethical approval from the institution, stating that the proposed research meets stipulated ethical requirements. Even though procedures you need to follow and how stringently you need to adhere to these procedures differ from one institution to the next, higher education institutions are held liable for ensuring ethical credibility of all studies undertaken under their jurisdiction. Furthermore, some research funders require the fulfilment of ethical processes before funding a study, and some academic journals will not publish (empirical) research unless the authors can provide evidence of ethical clearance from the institutions involved.

Institutional ethical procedures are also linked to the study participants. If the participants belong to some public organisation (such as a school, a hospital or private company) and are identified as entities who belong to the organisation in the study, that organisation is likely to have its own ethical procedures to protect the organisation and its subjects from possible harm that may result from research. For my pilot study, which I have done at a school in the Western Cape, I had to complete ethics forms of the Department of Western Cape Education, and when I was executing the actual research in Mpumalanga, I had to complete similar forms from the Mpumalanga Department of Education. These forms are usually scrutinised by such organisations to ensure that research procedures meet their required ethical standards. This process may take some time, which you would need to configure into the time schedule of your study.

The community as an organised collective, like the case of my research school, also operates as another dimension of ethical consideration. You need to send a letter requesting permission to conduct the study in the community. In some rural communities you may need to negotiate your entry through the chief. It is through this path that you may gain access to your targeted participants. This may seem like a long route but shortcuts may jeopardise your study in the long run. Some South African communities may seem disorganised from the outside, while they are highly organised and sensitive to what may seem exploitative. Ethical dilemmas might arise around how to approach the relevant community. For example, what are the terms of reference for engaging the school in the research? If unforeseen circumstances in the middle of your study change the nature of the study, the terms of reference might change. How would you address that? How do you negotiate going forward?[1] In my study I needed permission from the school governing body to conduct my study. Though schools are the subsidiaries of the departments of education, they also have a level of autonomy. Therefore, the governing body also needed to have a voice in granting the permission for study to take place at the school. Even when the provincial Department of Education gives the researcher permission to conduct the research at a school, the school's governing body and principal may give reasons why the study should not be conducted at their school, in which case the provincial Department of Education has no power to enforce the initial permission given (Wyngaard 2015).

If you are planning to conduct your fieldwork outside South African borders, you may need special permission to enter the particular country as a researcher. You may have to indicate your research intentions when applying for a visa. Different countries have different stipulations and research ethics regulations. For example, when I conducted a study in Finland at an institution situated in the city of Oulu, I had to get ethical clearance from the City of Oulu as well as from the University

---

1 Also see Chapter 20 by Collium Banda, where he discusses the ethics and responsibility to also make research results available to the communities where research takes place.

of Oulu, which was my host university. In short, make an effort to find out what the ethical regulations are of countries where you intend to conduct your research.

"I AM NOT YOUR SUBJECT": ETHICAL CONSIDERATIONS FOR RESEARCH PARTICIPANTS

Access to participants means being in direct contact with the people who may be influenced by your study. Institutional procedures may have conscientised you to ethical research behaviour and principles, but now you have to put these principles into practice. You are expected to display genuine human respect and dignity, and not see participants as mere subjects of your research. One way of showing such respect is by giving participants an opportunity to make an informed choice to participate in the research project and to give their informed consent. You may feel anxious that participants may not give their consent, and this is a valid concern. If this happens, you need to have a plan B at hand.

In researching a sensitive issue like corporal punishment, I was faced with an ethical dilemma of having to decide whether to do full disclosure, partial disclosure, or use deception in gaining access to the participants of my study. While all these approaches may have their place in research, depending on the nature of the study, even stricter ethical regulations are implemented in cases where deception is the only route to be followed. This usually depends on whether the benefits of the research for the society at large supersede the damage of deception, and whether there are procedures in place for later disclosure and methods to deal with the effects of the deception on the participants (Lugosi 2006). In my research, I provided full disclosure of the nature and purpose of the research, even though this could have influenced teachers' willingness to reveal certain information during interviews. I avoided the contradiction of causing some psychological violation though deception while, on the other hand, I addressed the issues of physical violence through the very same research.

While the personal values and the institutional ethics guide researchers' conduct and the relationship they establish with the research participants, researchers are also obligated to adhere to conditions of openness regarding disclosure of the details of the research, anonymity of participants, security and prevention of harm, as well as informed consent by participants including children as laid out in the Protection of Personal Information Act No 4 of 2013. All participants involved in the research have to be genuinely involved regardless of their level of education and possible language barriers between researchers and participants. It is the responsibility of the researcher to ensure that participants fully understand the intentions of the study.

Anderson, Solomon, Heitman, DuBois, Fisher, Kost and Ross (2012) advocate for the establishment of community collaborators who are based in the communities and who work closely with the researchers. They assert that community collaborators have an insider's view. If such collaborators receive an appropriate instruction on ethics, they become valuable to close the gap between the researcher as outsider and the community. In my case, I prepared information letters which explained the details of the research and the nature of participation expected from the participants. In my presentation of the research to the participants, I used isiXhosa in the Western Cape and isiZulu in Mpumalanga. When negotiating consent with the participants, I encouraged them to ask questions for clarity. Once the participants agreed to participate, the concept of consent was also explained to them and they were requested to give a written informed consent for their participation in the study by signing two consent forms. Such a consent form was signed at each research contact with the participants, to allowing participants to continuously review their position and willingness for participation.

"I HAVE A SAY TOO": ETHICAL PRINCIPLES IN WORKING WITH CHILDREN AS RESEARCH PARTICIPANTS

Can children give consent for their participation in research? Children are considered to be vulnerable subjects in research, and there should be special considerations regarding their involvement. Parents or caregivers also need to be involved. Information letters explaining the details of the study and consent letters should be sent to parents or caregivers. Where necessary, parents or caregivers need to be invited to a meeting where the nature of the study and the processes are explained. In my study, parents or caregivers were requested to consent to the participation of their children by signing a consent letter. It may happen that parents are not willing to consent, or that attempts to reach parents to get the consent forms back fail. If this happens, you again may need to have a plan B at hand.

Children who meet the age and maturity criteria can be allowed to provide consent (or commonly referred to as assent in the case of minors) on their own. According to the British Education Research Association (2011) guidelines, such children can provide consent for their own participation if they are willing to participate. BERA (2011) refers to Article 12 of the UN Convention of the Rights of the Child. These proclamations are also articulated in the South African Children's Act 38 of 2005, which states that "every child that is of such an age, maturity and stage of development as to be able to participate in any matter concerning that child, has the right to participate in an appropriate way and views expressed by the child must be given due consideration" (Republic of South Africa 2006:35). Determining maturity is a potential ethical dilemma, but the criteria depend on the conceptual understanding children have about the research topic and the methods of enquiry used for the research. The researcher has to ensure that all child-participants are engaged in an age-appropriate process of informed consent. As David, Edwards, and Alldred (2001) argue, the process of obtaining informed consent from children in itself is a complex one. The researcher should thoroughly consider the methods used to inform children about the research and, therefore, one has to decide whether the process is about "informing" or "educating". Informing participants assumes that the participants have an adequate knowledge base from which to work. Educating participants recognises that children may have gross knowledge gaps about the focus of the study and for that reason there may be a need to have an education session. In the case of my study, it was necessary to conduct a separate, child-friendly process to inform children about the study and its purpose, and explain some concepts in a language that was accessible to them.

"PROMISE YOU WILL NOT TELL": THE ETHICAL PRINCIPLE OF CONFIDENTIALITY

Ethical research demands that the identity and confidentiality of participants are protected. Firstly, this means that if participants do not want to reveal their identity, the researcher needs to respect this and undertake not to reveal the identity of the participants in any distinctive identifying information in reports or any other documents related to the research.

Secondly, the researcher should be transparent about where the research findings will be reported, for example in a thesis, academic papers, and/or seminar and conference presentations. This transparency should be accompanied by the assurance to participants that the principle of confidentiality would be upheld and, where the use of names would be necessary, codes or pseudonyms will be used. Further, field notes and recorded interviews should be exposed only to the researcher (and, where appropriate, the research supervisors), kept safely, and disposed of by deleting the files or destroying hardcopies by fire after completion of the study.

Thirdly, though the key ethical obligation and interest for the researcher is to protect the identity of participants, there is a limitation embedded in this principle. The revelation of illegal practices by participants during a study is a difficult issue (Woodhouse, Potterrat, Rothenberg, Darrow, Slovdahl & Muth 1995). Circumstances may arise where the researcher, for example, is subpoenaed by a court of law to reveal details of the data, including participants' identities. In case of child abuse or the child being at risk, the researcher may be morally and legally obligated to report the issue to relevant support structures (Kirk 2006; South African Children's Act 2006). Although this can offset the outcomes of the data, it is only ethical for the researcher to inform participants about this exclusion on the principle of protection of participants' identity from the beginning. The researcher needs to explain to participants that though the identity of participants will be kept confidential, this confidentiality principle has limitations, for example that it cannot be above the law.

The researcher is likely to encounter an ethical dilemma where participants insist that they want their identity to be revealed, for example children who want their photos placed next to their views. As a researcher, you have the responsibility of weighing the short- and long-term effects of such a revelation of identities in relation to the nature of the study. Conversely, as in my study, the openness of my participants was fundamentally based on the principle of anonymity. They did not want to be associated with corporal punishment since it is an illegal practice in South Africa. Although I maintain that revealing participants' identities maybe risky, once decided to reveal identities, the researcher has to ensure that participants are counselled regarding the future implications thereof. Again, their consent should be sought at every stage of the process, including the last draft before the final publication.

"I CAN'T TAKE IT": POTENTIAL HARM TO PARTICIPANTS

One of the key ethical principles is that of safety of the participants from any harm that can be caused by the research. Though not all studies have such a potential negative impact, it is important to consider the possible psychological effects of your questions on the participants. For instance, corporal punishment constitutes a physical and psychological traumatic experience, therefore interviewing children and teachers about their experiences of discipline including corporal punishment may evoke negative emotions and thoughts of their past experiences which they had forgotten about. It is therefore essential to establish the support services necessary for the participants and ensure that participants have access to such services. In my study, I needed to establish support services in the area to provide debriefing (a preventative short-term counselling process after an event that is likely to cause psychological and emotional disturbance to an individual or a group) and counselling to teachers to ensure that all participants received the emotional support they needed.

During focus group interviews there is a risk of group members revealing details of the interview to people outside the group. Such an occurrence may harm the dignity and image of group members, or it may make them feel vulnerable. To prevent this from happening, at the beginning of group interviews, the researcher has to facilitate an understanding of the group confidentiality clause for members not to share the group discussions with people outside the group.

Publishing the findings and outcome of the research is another area of vulnerability that is often overlooked. Published expressions or observations of participants may be damaging when participants are not given an opportunity to process and understand the findings before they are published (Tracy 2010), especially when participants are not prepared to see their thoughts and verbal expressions in written format. Therefore, the researcher has an ethical obligation to present the findings to the participants first, before they are published. The verification process whereby interview transcripts are presented to participants before publishing the document may mitigate this damage, while it increases the validity of the study (Tracy 2010).

WALKING ON A TIGHT ROPE: LEGAL QUANDARIES AND HARM TO INSTITUTIONS

Tracy (2010) refers to situational ethics as unpredictable, subtle yet important ethical moments that may arise with some dilemma while you are in the research field. In responding to such ethical dilemmas, it is important to be reflective, asking questions on whether the outcome of this study is more valuable than the unavoidable damage that can occur through the research process, should one confront the situation.

It may not be possible to think about all the possible ethical issues that may arise during the research process prior to the actual research activities. Among a wide array of possibilities in my research, a revelation from my observations was that teachers use corporal punishment to discipline learners, which is in conflict with the South African Schools' Act (1996) – an education policy that forbids the use of corporal punishment in schools. In such a situation it was necessary to highlight this infringement to the participants involved and to their superiors (in this case, the principal of the school). In cases where situational ethical dilemmas arise while conducting fieldwork, researchers have to firstly remember their primary professional identity as social science researchers (Hagan 1982). This will enable them to strike some ethical balance by keeping a moral distance to maintain objectivity, while on the other hand, act with moral ethics as human beings and responsible citizens. In my case, it meant notifying the authorities about my observations with the hope that they would do something to abate the situation. This action would not necessarily constitute betrayal of trust of participants if the researchers informed participants from the beginning that they would deal with unethical behaviour in such a manner. Since corporal punishment is illegal and constitutes a form of child abuse, the law requires a researcher and any other adult who observes such actions to report it (South African Children's Act No. 38 2006). My study focussed on the cultural practices that contribute to the persistence of the use of corporal punishment. The intention was not to observe or record incidents of corporal punishment. However, if I observed such actions during the course of the study, I needed to ensure that the school authorities knew about my observations and I needed to warn them about the detriments of such activities while at the same time keep in mind that my role at the school was that of a researcher and not a criminal investigator. However, if the illegal activity continued and placed another person or child's life at risk, I would have had to report it to the relevant law enforcers.

CONCLUSION

While research ethics appear straightforward on paper, this chapter has highlighted possible complexities involved in the actual practice of ethical research. This chapter has also demonstrated how the researcher, on encountering ethical dilemmas, may need to balance internal (personal) values, universal and professional research ethics, while at the same time, ensure credible research outcomes to the benefit of society.

REFERENCES

Anderson, E. E., Solomon, S., Heitman, E., DuBois, J. M., Fisher, C. B., Kost, R. G., Lawless, E., Ramsey, C., Jones, B., Ammerman, A. & Ross, L. F. (2012). Research ethics education for community-engaged research: A review and research agenda. *Journal of Empirical Research on Human Research Ethics*, 7(2):3-19.
http://dx.doi.org/10.1525/jer.2012.7.2.3   PMid:22565579   PMCid:PMC3483026

British Educational Research Association (2011). *Ethical guidelines for educational research.* London, UK: BERA.

David, M., Edwards, R., & Alldred, P. (2001). Children and school-based research: 'informed consent' or 'educated consent'? *British Educational Research Journal,* 27(3):347-362.
http://dx.doi.org/10.1080/01411920120048340

Hagan, F. E. (1982). *Research methods in criminal justice and criminology.* London, UK: Collier Macmillan Publishers.

Lugosi, P. (2006). Between covert and overt research: Concealment and disclosure in an ethnographic study of commercial hospitality. *Qualitative Inquiry,* 12(3):541-561.
http://dx.doi.org/10.1177/1077800405282801

Kirk, S. (2007). Methodological and ethical issues in conducting qualitative research with children and young people: A literature review. *International Journal of Nursing Studies.* 44:1250-1260. http://dx.doi.org/10.1016/j.ijnurstu.2006.08.015   PMid:17027985

Republic of South Africa. (2013). *Protection of Personal Information Act No. 4 of 2013.* Pretoria, South Africa: Government Printers.

Republic of South Africa. (1996). *South African School Act No. 84 of 1996*. Pretoria, South Africa: Government Printers.

Republic of South Africa. (2005). *The South African Children's Act No. 38 of 2005*. Pretoria, South Africa: Government Printers.

Tracy, S. J. (2010). Qualitative quality: Eight "Big-tent" criteria for excellent qualitative research. *Qualitative Inquiry,* 16(10):837-851. http://dx.doi.org/10.1177/1077800410383121

Woodhouse, D. E., Potterat, J. J., Rothberg, R. B., Darrow, W. W., Klovdahl, A. S. & Muth S. Q. (1995). Ethical and legal issues in social network research. In R. H. Needle, S. G. Genser & R. T. Trotter (Eds). *National institute for drug abuse research: Monograph series: Social networks, drug abuse and HIV transmission*. (pp. 131-143). Maryland, US Department of Health and Human Services.

Wyngaard, A. (2015, October). *The ethical implications of applying for research permission*. Paper presented at the Education Student's Regional Research Conference. Cape Town.

PART TWO

A STUDENT PERSPECTIVE ON STARTING A POSTGRADUATE JOURNEY IN SOUTH AFRICA

GETTING STARTED: SURVIVING AND SUCCEEDING DURING THE PRE-DOCTORAL STAGE

Shakira Choonara

INTRODUCTION

Taking the decision to pursue postgraduate studies sets in motion a long-term process and requires a number of important considerations. Registration for postgraduate studies happens quite late in the process, and the application process for further studies may be daunting. This chapter outlines the application stage which is often not covered in literature on postgraduate study. It draws on my first-hand experience of early considerations such as identifying a supervisor, drafting a mini-proposal and securing funding. This chapter also emphasises the importance of having an adequate support structure during these initial stages of one's studies, which is critical especially when dealing with difficulties that may arise during the postgraduate journey.

Pursuing postgraduate studies was a lifelong dream and personal goal to empower myself while contributing to a better South Africa. When first applying for postgraduate studies, I had sleepless nights about how I would afford tuition fees and living expenses, and how I would support my family. It is almost five years later, and despite the lack of funding in the beginning, I continued the journey from an Honour's level all the way to doing a PhD. In this chapter, I reflect on how to deal with the challenges I encountered at the onset of my studies. I argue that it is normal to feel overwhelmed and experience mixed emotions, as well as as to question your decision to pursue further studies but, at the same time, be excited at the prospect of graduation and the benefits which may follow.

FULL-TIME VERSUS PART-TIME STUDY

Pursuing a postgraduate degree is a major decision. Time and funding are important factors that influence the decision to undertake either part-time or full-time studies. There are advantages and disadvantages to both these approaches.

Doing full-time studies can mean that you have fewer competing demands compared to a part-time student who may also be employed. I am based at a grant-funded unit where no salary or benefits apply. Even though I work on projects I am considered to be a full-time student, with only bursaries as a source of income. However, being in a research environment which recognises the importance of advanced study has allowed me some flexibility and I have been able to dedicate a large amount of time to completing coursework and research. A recent report on doctoral studies in South Africa found that in comparison to part-time students, full-time students are able to complete their studies in a shorter period of time (ASSAf 2010). Full-time studies allow for engagement with supervisors, and the attendance of relevant seminars and courses. Another benefit of full-time study is that you are able to interact with other students on a regular basis. It allowed me to draw on the knowledge and experience of my peers, and they assisted in reviewing my work, discussing challenges and brainstorming ideas. A disadvantage of full-time studies is that future employers may argue that you do not have sufficient work experience. I dealt with this constraint by assisting with projects at the unit where I am based and taking on short-term contracts. Full-time studies have also allowed me to be involved in student societies which future employers may consider positively when looking at my overall job application.

A real challenge when deciding to pursue full-time study is the need to secure funding. Funding is considered to be one of the main factors for non-completion of postgraduate studies (ASSAf 2010; Letseka 2008). Financial demands can include tuition fees, living expenses and funds to conduct your research. The financial aid office at a university often lists all the relevant scholarships and bursaries for which a student may be eligible. Specific departments may also offer financial support. It is also a good idea to keep up with funding calls and deadlines. Even if you have funding, I found that the funding is paid out quite late in the year, which means that there can be long periods during your studies in which you don't have funding and this can be quite stressful.

However, the reality is that full-time study is not always an option, especially in the South African context where a high number of prospective students cannot afford steep university fees (Letseka 2008). Pursuing part-time studies is an option to keep a steady income or a job that you do not want to leave, although time availability for postgraduate studies is one of the biggest challenges facing part-time students (MacCann 2012). Many of the part-time students I have spoken to say balancing work and studies is challenging – they find it next to impossible to do study-related tasks and they take much longer to complete their degree[1]. Work demands often keep them from attending a lot of postgraduate activities, including frequent workshops that are offered to students who are on campus. Such students are also more isolated from other students. Some universities do cater for part-time students by posting seminars online or as podcasts.

THE APPLICATION PROCESS

The application stage is often overlooked as an important component of pursuing postgraduate studies. A number of prospective postgraduate students do not expect to face any challenges or difficulties during this stage. The application stage, I found, was crucial to commencing my studies. Being well prepared for this stage proved to be essential. Application processes can be highly bureaucratic and have a number of requirements. My PhD application process was not well defined or outlined on the relevant university's website. I had to complete a separate process to the specific faculty, and then to the university. The entire process took almost six months. When applying for postgraduate studies, look through application forms and requirements well in advance. Doing this allows you to think through the degree you would like to pursue, identifying a potential supervisor and drafting a clear and concise mini-proposal. The application process is quite daunting and there is no guarantee that you will be accepted for postgraduate studies. However, being prepared and informed helped me overcome these challenges.

Selecting a university

South Africa offers a range of universities across all provinces, including both urban and rural universities. Urban universities may be better developed and offer a wider range of courses and degrees. However, universities in these areas tend to be more expensive. These universities can be large, and it may be difficult to interact with lecturers or supervisors. Universities in rural areas are often smaller and offer a fewer number of degrees. However, a rural area is often a more relaxed environment with a smaller student-supervisor ratio, allowing individual attention and interaction with other students, lecturers and supervisors. Your selection of a university will ultimately

---

1   Also see Chapter 7 by Andre van der Bijl that addresses the issues of being caught between work and studies, as well as Chapter 10 by Delia Layton that focusses on achieving a balance between studies and other life responsibilities.

depend on the type of degree you would like to pursue and what university best meets your needs.

South African universities also have multiple links to international institutions. An option that is not often considered is to pursue a joint degree, where you are linked to more than one university. A joint degree allows you to be registered at a South African institution and one of its partner universities in another country. The process is slightly more complicated as you need to apply to both institutions. However, the advantage of a joint degree is that there is an opportunity to extend your research to other countries. Pursuing a joint degree may offer the best of both worlds. There are potentially more opportunities, supervision, resources and extensive networks, particularly in terms of possible employers. As part of joint programmes, students spend time at both universities during their studies, giving them the opportunity to gain access to experiences and research at another university. Supervisors are also able to offer different perspectives based on a specific country context. In addition, there are opportunities for teaching and attending conferences at both universities which allow students to gain experience in both settings. Connecting with other students, especially internationally, allows for further learning and collaboration opportunities in the future.

Application processes

Selecting a university is followed by becoming familiar with the specific university's application processes. Obtain the necessary application forms and guidelines as early as possible. Application forms and procedures differ across universities and faculties in South Africa. Having application forms and deadlines will also give you a goal to work towards, keeping you on track to register for your postgraduate degree.

Brief proposal

During the application stage, a brief proposal is needed which usually covers the proposed topic, justification, problem statement, and a brief literature and methodology section. Before I applied for my doctoral studies, it took me close to a year to prepare my proposal. The process involved an intense review of the literature and finding a novel question to address. The problem statement, or research problem, is quite important as it outlines where the study fits into your subject, and the contribution that the topic will have on the existing body of knowledge. At Honour's and Master's levels the intended topic and research proposal can be relatively straightforward, as it is not yet required to make a substantial contribution to the knowledge field. However, as a doctoral candidate, your proposal would need to indicate that you are contributing something new to the existing body of knowledge. Your topic will need to indicate what you envision your original contribution to be.

Identifying a supervisor

The majority of postgraduate applications require supervisors. I found that a well-thought-out mini-proposal could assist with identifying a potential supervisor. If you are already a student at a university or part of an existing department, it may be quite easy to identify a supervisor. If you are based outside the university or a foreign student, it might be difficult to make contact with a potential supervisor. You can, however, search for supervisors on departmental websites. Supervisors can be quite busy and may not have the time to take on additional students. At Honour's and Master's levels, I was allocated a supervisor. This worked really well, as I did not have to identify a supervisor and merely set up a working relationship with this person. Some students do, however, prefer to select or identify their own supervisor. Should you need to identify a supervisor, it is advisable that you identify more than one supervisor to begin with, contact them as early as possible and have a well-structured idea of your proposed topic. This will enable the supervisor to see if the topic is in line with their work or that of their department and decide whether to take you on.

Identifying a supervisor may be even more difficult if you decide to pursue a joint degree as you will require supervisors from two institutions who have the same interest towards your proposed study. Always bear in mind that co-supervision has its own challenges as the two supervisors might not have the same working habits (see for example Pole 1998 and Wadesango & Machingambi 2011). This process works better when the main supervisor helps select the co-supervisor so that you do not receive contradicting feedback or input. Another option is to have two supervisors that can offer complimentary skills, one with strengths towards your topic and the other with strengths in the methodology or the theoretical framework that you might be using. At the doctoral level, I was fortunate to have my PhD nested within a broader project in which I was involved. When I decided to pursue a PhD, the project heads agreed to serve as my supervisors. Additionally, I have a third supervisor who is based in Canada half of the time and in South Africa the other half of the time. Having three supervisors has certainly been advantageous: each supervisor brings his or her own experience and perspective. I must admit that there are times when the lines of accountability are blurred (with regard to who the main supervisor is) and I often have to deal with conflicting advice. There are even times when I feel I am receiving too much input, which leaves me feeling overwhelmed and wondering whose input to consider. To avoid conflicting advice or input, my supervisors first meet and discuss their input and then provide me with joint feedback, although there are times when this is not always possible. International and local literature emphasise the importance of good student-supervisor relationships for the timely completion of postgraduate studies (ASSAf 2010; Jones 2013; Wadesango & Machingambi 2011). It is vital to have good relationships with your supervisors from the start. The support, advice and input will be invaluable for your postgraduate studies. In reality, good relationships are not always possible. We are often subject to power dynamics where students are required to be submissive, or find it difficult to voice their concerns. When relationships broke down during my postgraduate studies, I felt isolated and found it difficult to keep motivated. In such cases drawing on other support structures (family and peers) definitely makes all the difference.

Funding constraints

Perhaps the most important factor in choosing to pursue postgraduate study is securing funding. I was fortunate to be a recipient of a number of scholarships and bursaries that enabled me to continue with full-time postgraduate studies. Yet when I first came to university, I did not have funds to apply for a degree or pay registration. After I eventually got financial assistance, I still had to take on numerous part-time jobs to supplement my bursary income. Part-time income was imperative to support my family, fund living expenses and pay off my undergraduate student loan. Finding adequate funding has been a challenge for me. Most funding sources only paid out in August, leaving me year after year without any funding for close to eight months in the year[2]. This made pursuing part-time work opportunities all the more important.

An advantage of pursuing postgraduate study in South Africa is that there are a number of scholarships which fund living expenses. A well-thought-out proposal, as discussed earlier, can also assist in identifying relevant funding. Most funding applications are time-consuming, requiring at least a week or two to complete. To have funding when you commence your studies, you would need to apply for funding at least six months to a year prior to commencing your studies.

Further considerations for international students

Foreign students hoping to pursue postgraduate studies in South Africa are likely to face numerous challenges. There are the logistics of organising travel arrangements, accommodation and securing a study permit. The permit process can be lengthy and

---

[2] Also see Chapter 6 by Soraya Abdulatief that addresses issues around funding.

marred by bureaucracy. For more information on applying for study permits in South Africa, go to http://www.home-affairs.gov.za/index.php/types-of-temp-res-permits (the website of the South African Department of Home Affairs). It is important to resolve these practical issues before arriving in South Africa.

Additionally, fees for international students are higher at most South African universities. Most universities in South Africa have a dedicated International Student's Office which offers support during the application process and throughout their postgraduate studies. These offices are easily accessible via university websites and would be able to provide the necessary information. Many prospective international students also experience language barriers or difficulties. English is the standard medium of communication and teaching across the majority of universities in the country. There is minimal language support provided to students as universities expect students to be proficient in English. Speaking to peers may help to gain insights into the student experience at a particular institution.

SUPPORT STRUCTURES

Jones (2013) indicate that during the postgraduate journey, it is critical for students to draw on a range of support structures including family, employers, supervisors and peers[3]. Having friends, family and a supportive work environment can help you to deal with any difficulties which may arise. It is important to be upfront with those around you about the demands of your study. Be honest with friends and family about what you may need from them during this journey. There was a period of four months in the initial stages of my doctoral studies when funding was delayed. My family as well as and the department which hosted me provided financial assistance during this period.

About halfway into my doctoral studies, I experienced the unpredictability of life first-hand when I was diagnosed with arthralgia, causing debilitating pain in my fingers that made it impossible to use a keyboard or a mouse. The stigma and emotional difficulties associated with being disabled added a further toll. The university's disability unit, my peers and family were extremely supportive and helped me to find solutions. I am typing this chapter using voice recognition software (Dragon) which will undoubtedly assist me with writing my thesis as well. Every person will have their own challenges while pursuing postgraduate studies, but having a good support structure will make all the difference and facilitate progress.

---

3 Also see the related chapters by Guin Lourens, Puleng Motshoane and Liz Wolvaardt, Hannelie Untiedt, Mariana Pietersen and Karien Mostert-Wentzel in this book.

IN CONCLUSION

Looking back, my postgraduate journey was anything but easy. There were challenges from the very start, especially during the application stage. I am now in my final year, juggling fieldwork, analysis and writing, as well as inclusion in a broader project. Despite the difficulties, it has been a very rewarding experience. I've presented my research at a number of conferences and gained invaluable work and research experience. Connecting and working with people across the globe have also been very exciting.

Any postgraduate student will face a number of challenges. It is important to keep the end result in mind; the eventual opportunities and rewards. It is not possible to be fully prepared for everything, though having the right attitude and being as prepared as you can from the outset will certainly get you off to a good start and help you to succeed.

REFERENCES

Academy of Science of South Africa. (2010). *The PhD study: Consensus Report*. Pretoria, South Africa: ASSAf.

Jones, M. (2013). Issues in Doctoral Studies – Forty Years of Journal Discussion: Where have we been and where are we going? *International Journal of Doctoral Studies* 8(6):83-104.

Letseka, M. M. (2008). *Policy Brief: High university drop-out rates: a threat to South Africa's future*. Pretoria, South Africa: Human Sciences Research Council.

MacCann, C. F. (2012). Strategies for success in Education: Time managementt is more important for part-time than full-time community college students. *Learning and Individual Differences*, 22(5):618-623. http://dx.doi.org/10.1016/j.lindif.2011.09.015

Pole, C. (1998). Joint supervision and the PhD: Safety net or panacea? *Assessment and Evaluation in Higher Education*, 23(3):259-271. http://dx.doi.org/10.1080/0260293980230303

South African Department of Home Affairs. (2015). Study permits. Available online at http://www.home-affairs.gov.za/index.php/types-of-temp-res-permits

Wadesango, N., & Machingambi, S. (2011). Post graduate students' experiences with research supervisors. *Journal of Sociology and Social Anthropology*, 2(1):31-37.

CLOSE ENCOUNTERS: BECOMING RESILIENT THROUGH COMPASSION AND IMAGINATION

Bella Vilakazi

INTRODUCTION

You are not ready for a PhD. Come back when you are. Your idea will not even amount to a paper.

These are the words that a prospective supervisor uttered when I proposed that he be my doctoral supervisor. A postgraduate study such as a PhD is an emotional journey for which you can prepare only so much. The challenges that come with it are varied and unique for each student. This chapter aims to provide a perspective into postgraduate student experiences and highlights the importance of compassion and sympathetic imagination between a supervisor and a student. My own initial encounter with a supervisor and the implications of these emotions serve as a backdrop of this perspective. I close the chapter with a discussion on the concept of democratic justice that could serve as a guiding notion in South African postgraduate supervision.

COMPASSION IN THE CONTEXT OF DOCTORAL SUPERVISION

The first encounter with your supervisor is crucial when you embark on your postgraduate journey. It comes with a myriad of emotions, one of which is compassion (Nussbaum 1997). Compassion is a reflection of what it means to be human (Waghid & Davids 2013). Compassion can be evoked by how your supervisor senses the depth your academic need, the depth of your study, your prior experience and the capabilities that you bring to the potential study, as well as the potential for personal development through the research and beyond.

Embarking on a postgraduate journey demands something you are passionate about, as well as a gap in current knowledge that can be addressed in the process of becoming a researcher. Your contribution needs to benefit the field of knowledge, as well as your own learning and becoming (Waghid 2006; Barnett 2007; Waghid & Davids 2013). This passion needs to be met by supervisory compassion, which Waghid and Davids (2013:770) call being encouraged by the student's "eagerness to pursue doctoral studies, coupled with her (sic) critical acumen, astuteness and independence of mind". In the context of postgraduate supervision, compassion refers not only to caring about suffering, but also to recognising commonalities that exist between you and your supervisor and how these can shape you as a student or supervisor, the postgraduate journey itself, the supervision process, as well as the possibilities that might emerge from it (Waghid 2010). In the process you will fulfil your academic need with the help of your supervisor, who in turn will produce a doctoral student who will contribute to the discipline and society at large.

Barnett (2007) describes students' work as gifts they present to their supervisors. In the supervision context the pedagogical relationship between a student and a supervisor takes on the exchange of gifts in the form of numerous drafts and critical engagements. These acts of gift giving are mutual obligations between you and your supervisor. Supervisors introduce you to the values and conventions upheld within your discipline of choice, while you develop independence and critical thinking skills. You also become immersed in the academic texts and learn to see patterns in literature, develop an informed opinion, learn how to be coherent, reflective, argumentative and persuasive and – finally – find your scholarly voice (Barnett 2007; Waghid & Davids 2013). Your gift to your supervisors is to respond to each and every feedback they provide, to engage critically with them and meet the agreed deadlines. This mutual exchange of gifts lies central to compassion in the supervisor-student relationship.

You also need to show compassion to yourself. A postgraduate journey has many pitfalls, such as feeling vulnerable and doubting yourself. The challenging aspects of your journey are not going to disappear if you pretend that they do not exist and do not deal with them. Sometimes it may be necessary to take a step back and create some distance between you and your studies. Give yourself space to breathe, think and gain perspective. Treat yourself during these moments. You will come back with a fresh outlook on your studies.

CULTIVATING IMAGINATION IN THE CONTEXT OF DOCTORAL SUPERVISION

Imagination (Nussbaum 1997) is another key emotive element of a supervisory relationship. Nussbaum (1997; 2010) emphasises the importance of having the ability to imagine other people's circumstances. In order for us to do this, we need to imagine what life must be like for other people (Nussbaum 2010). However, imagination does not happen automatically, but develops as supervisors and students get to know each other. Students and supervisors come into the relationship with unequal knowledge, experience and disciplinary speciality – and therefore need to imagine each other's positions in order to build a constructive and productive relationship.

Nussbaum (1997; 2010) supports the idea that supervisors get to know their students and learn about their needs, intentions and circumstances[1]. This does not suggest that you need to reveal your private life to a supervisor. Although life circumstances tend to creep into this pedagogic student-supervisor relationship, imagination may support compassion which – in turn – can enable emotional intellect and ethical deliberation to emerge (Waghid 2010). Your supervisor undertook the same journey during some point of his or her academic career and knows what it is like to be a student. He or she can understand who you are by imagining what it must be like to be where you are at different stages of this journey, especially when you experience challenges. Supervisors are therefore able to support and guide you while expressing compassionate imagination. Compassionate imagination ensures pedagogic interactions that are morally justified and devoid of narcissism (Nussbaum 1997).

My initial encounter with a prospective supervisor may serve as a case in point where compassionate imagination was not enacted. The theoretical explorations of compassion and imagination described above are what might have emerged had his response been different. I will use this experience to argue in favour of compassion and imagination as the basis for developing resilience to survive and succeed during your postgraduate studies.

AN ENCOUNTER WITH A PROSPECTIVE SUPERVISOR: MY STORY

I will use the pseudonym Kopano[2] for the academic whom I first approached with a research proposal to supervise my PhD. Kopano was an accomplished academic and supervisor with a substantial research output and publication record to back it up. Meeting someone of his stature was intimidating for me because I knew about the depth the doctoral study required I wanted to pursue under his supervision, but did not have the words to describe it. Waghid and Davids (2013:776) articulates my

---

1   Also see the second chapter in this book by Zondi Mhkabela and Liezel Frick, where they explore what such a student-supervisor relationship might entail amidst uniquely South African complexities.

2   The name Kopano is a Setswana word meaning "a meeting" or a gathering of two or more people. Setswana is one of South Africa's official languages and is spoken by about 8% of the total population.

feelings of intimidation as "the one constructed on the basis of one knowing much and the other not knowing enough". The interaction left me doubting myself. The difference between what these authors describe and myself was that when she (Davids) encountered her supervisor for the first time, she was "uncompromising" about her idea and knew what it meant to her (Waghid & Davids 2013:776).

I tried very hard not to be too sensitive and read too much into the encounter. However, it was important for me to say what I had come to see him about, be coherent and present myself well. There were awkward and uncomfortable moments, but I gathered up enough courage and requested him to supervise me. I felt vulnerable and no sooner than I knew it, I was out of his office. Dismissed. This was like an "uncompassionate dismissal" that Waghid (2010:19) writes about. While I believe that it was not his intention to treat me that way, I felt violated and disrespected on an academic, professional and personal level. However, Waghid (2006:429) cautions that sometimes we (students) come with "frivolous consumerist logic" and expect supervisors to enable us to obtain a PhD without engaging in a doctoral learning process. He further cautions that we do not take it well when supervisors criticise us. As students, we may become suspicious, feel threatened and make unfounded assumptions about well-meaning supervisors. Doctoral supervision will not always be kind and gentle.

On the same day after this unfortunate encounter I made an inquiry with another professor. I was well received. She gave me space and time to explain what I wanted my study to entail. She confirmed that I was on to something and immediately suggested a doctoral committee for my proposed study. This was a pleasant surprise. However, the doctoral committee included Kopano. I was determined not to be humiliated again and started looking elsewhere for a potential supervisor.

A friend told me about a prospective supervisor at another university. Vulnerable and full of self-doubt, I contacted her. She received me well and I felt respected and appreciated. She also told me that my idea for a postgraduate amounted to a study at a PhD level that could contribute to the needs of my country. Her actions portrayed compassion and imagination. In a short space of time my email inbox was flooded with readings she suggested, and questions that she needed me to answer pertaining to the problem I wanted to investigate. This was followed by a registration for a PhD forum. I never looked back. She has been my supervisor since and I will graduate under her guidance, support, and structured and honest feedback about my work.

CHAPTER 5 • CLOSE ENCOUNTERS: BECOMING RESILIENT THROUGH COMPASSION AND IMAGINATION

DEMOCRATIC JUSTICE IN POSTGRADUATE STUDENT SUPERVISION

Democratic justice, Waghid (2010) suggests, could be a guiding principle in South African postgraduate supervision, especially considering our apartheid past and its legacy in educational settings. I draw on his ideas of mutual attachment, mutual attunement and mutual action as requirements for democratic justice in providing a student perspective.

Following Waghid (2010:51), critical learning is allowing the unexpected or "something new" to emerge. From a supervisory perspective it means that supervisors embody or embrace social justice responsibly in contributing to society by supervising you. As part of democratic justice, your supervisor can use their expertise to contribute to society by taking care of your rights, enabling deliberative engagement and exposing you to critical learning. But the enactment of democratic justice is not a one-way street in the postgraduate supervision context – there needs to be a mutual attachment between supervisor and student.

Mutual attachment is motivated by the work supervisors have done, and their knowledge, experience and level of expertise (Waghid 2010), which inspire students to develop an interest in a particular supervisor. In my encounter with Kopano, I expected him to expose me to possibilities and resources. The relationship became undemocratic and unjust when he dismissed my ideas without any compassionate imagination. I was expecting him to guide me so I could prepare myself for postgraduate study, but his response defeated the potential for mutual attachment that needs to exist in a postgraduate supervision relationship.

You need to recognise the importance of managing and maintaining this fragile yet important pedagogic relationship. You come into the supervision space with having opened up yourself academically and intellectually to your supervisor. You recognise your position as a novice researcher and take into consideration that you must have research questions which need to be well positioned. You become aware of your thoughts and ideas which sometimes can be vague and broad. Supervisors who formatively support you to narrow down all these ideas and make sense out of them enact democratic justice. In the process, you put yourself under their responsibility and, in turn, supervisors become accountable for you. They become the mirror through which you see your strengths, weakness and what you need to learn. They portray democratic justice which is a moral obligation on their part (Waghid 2010).

Your supervisor can also become attached to you because of the attributes or capabilities you might portray. You become your supervisors' mirror that they can use to reflect on their practice. This presents them with an opportunity to learn from and through you. In this way, you broaden their horizons and open unimaginable experiences. Therefore, do not undermine or underestimate your contribution to your supervisors' growth. It is as important as what your supervisor will do for you. It is important to make the most of each supervisory encounter. Mutual attunement therefore underlies the notion of democratic justice (Waghid 2012) and demands compassionate imagination in order for postgraduate students to become resilient.

CONCLUSION

Postgraduate supervision is one of the encounters which forms the cornerstone of your pedagogic experience in higher education. The initial encounter with your supervisor lays the foundation of your postgraduate journey and what may come thereafter. Such encounters are based on compassionate imagination, which may lead to mutual attunement between students and supervisors. These notions form the basis of democratic justice as a characteristic of the postgraduate student-supervisor relationship.

You can show compassion to your supervisor by not taking his or her supervision for granted. You are also showing compassion to yourself by taking your commitments seriously. Compassion calls for you take care of yourself so that you can build up enough resilience and strength to successfully complete your postgraduate journey.

Supervisors, on the other hand, are exercising the lessons learned from their own postgraduate journeys. It is perhaps expected that they give students supervisory advice based on their own experiences. A supervisor will offer you informed choices and you might want to weigh these and choose the one best suited to your study. All this comes from a position of supervisory compassion, imagination and practicing democratic justice values.

REFERENCES

Barnett, R. (2007). *A will to learn: Being a student in an age of uncertainty*. New York, USA: Open University Press.

Nussbaum, M. C. (1997). *Cultivating humanity: A classical defence of reform in liberal education*. London, UK: Harvard University Press.

Nussbaum, M. C. (2010). *Not for profit*. New Jersey, USA: Princeton University Press.

Waghid, Y. (2006). Reclaiming freedom and friendship through postgraduate student supervision. *Teaching in Higher Education*, 11(4):427-439. http://dx.doi.org/10.1080/13562510600874185

Waghid, Y. (2010). *Education, democracy and citizenship revisited: Pedagogic encounters*. Stellenbosch, South Africa: AFRICAN SUN MeDIA.

Waghid, Y., & Davids, N. (2013). Reflecting on a doctoral supervision: From sceptism to friendship. *South African Journal of Higher Education*, 27(4):769-780.

PART THREE

CONTEXTUAL CHALLENGES
IN THE SOUTH AFRICAN
POSTGRADUATE CONTEXT

SURVIVING AND SUCCEEDING: THE FIRST-GENERATION CHALLENGE

Soraya Abdulatief

Viewed from the outside, full-time PhD study seems undemanding and it is only once you are engaged in practices such as doing research, reading for and writing your PhD proposal that you start to learn the underlying rules and covert knowledge of academia. But these are not easy behaviours to learn and practice consistently especially if you are a first-generation PhD student. Lohfink and Paulsen (2005) define first-generation students as those who are the first in their families to attend university and "whose parents had no type or quantity of postsecondary education" (p. 410). They also state that "continuing-generation students were those with at least one parent who had some type or quantity of postsecondary education" (Lohfink & Paulsen 2005:410). Strictly speaking, following Lohfink and Paulsen's (2005) definitions, I am a continuing-generation student since my mother left school at 17 to train as a nurse through a hospital training system. However, I was the first person in my nuclear family to attend university and I am the first person in my family to embark on a PhD, so in this sense, I regard myself as a first-generation student. I write this chapter from the perspective of a mid-career professional who worked in online media and who wanted to reskill after 15 years in the workplace. My PhD is in literacy education, and my place in the PhD journey (I am in the middle of fieldwork as I write this) as well as my experiences shape my ideas and what I express.

At universities and in research, the term "first generation" is used mostly to signal undergraduate students whose class, race and gender differ from what is considered the traditional student, namely white, middle class/wealthy, male, single, young and able-bodied. In South Africa, first-generation students may also be English additional or second language speakers. Cotterall (2013) argues that even at doctoral level – after students have obtained various degrees – the notion that first-generation students are disadvantaged is still prevalent. In reality, PhD students have probably closed most of the knowledge and convention gaps which is said to hamper first-generation undergraduate students. This chapter speaks to those starting the PhD journey and who are unfamiliar with the range of academic practices. It contains suggestions and ideas on how to balance and bridge individual scholarship with belonging to an academic community. I discuss some of the ways you can build or expand your existing repertoire of skills so that you become an emerging academic. I argue that by using Gutiérrez's notion of "Third Space" (2008:148) and by applying it at the level of identity and social practice, you can value your own difference and diversity, and in doing so, create a hybrid model of being that integrates academic practices without excluding aspects of your identity.

LEARNING IN THE THIRD SPACE

My introduction to the notion of Third Space came via Bhabha (1994) at Master's level where our theory module consisted of what I would describe as cultural studies. We learned a mix of Marxist, post-structuralist, postcolonial and feminist theories using the analytical tools of critical discourse analysis. In this chapter though, I use Gutiérrez's (2008:148) conception of Third Space as a learning space "in which students begin to reconceive who they are and what they might be able to accomplish academically and beyond". Gutiérrez's (2008) Third Space is designed and orientated towards empowering first-generation students and via a model of learning that teaches students critical discourse analysis amongst other discourses. Gutiérrez (2008) provides an analysis of an academic programme that consists of curriculum and pedagogy that reposition mainly migrant students as historical actors with a future at a higher education institution. The programme teaches these students to articulate their experiences, to recognise, value and use the resources they have and assists them with bridging the gap between their lived experience and those practices and behaviours required by academia. In the Third Space, the inherited gaps are not treated as a deficit or disadvantage; rather they are acknowledged, historicised, contextualised and treated as missing information. You can learn and acquire what you need to know through guidance or you can teach yourself all the things you need to learn. Gutiérrez's model is not one of assimilation and competition but one of transformation and collaboration where you use your position as outsider and build and maintain a critical lens through which you view your own sociocultural history and context, as well as that of the academy.

Teaching students to value diversity and difference in the South African context is crucial given our apartheid and post-apartheid history. We wish to move away from the subtle but steady pressure to conform to and assimilate into institutional practices that involve the erasure of any type of difference, from language and accent to cultural dress and sexuality. Instead we need to – as the New London Group (2000:18) argues – "recruit, rather than attempt to ignore and erase the different subjectivities, intentions, commitments, and purposes" that students bring to learning. Through embracing the critical discourse of the Third Space, I learned that identities and languages are multiple and part of a repertoire. In the Third Space, seeming conflicting and competing identities can coexist as a subject shifts back and forth daily from a Muslim PhD student to mother, spouse, daughter and part-time employee. Today, for example, I have to rush from fieldwork where I am engaged as a writing mentor for postgraduate students, to fetch my son from school. It is assessment week at my son's school, so preparing for his assessment is our priority when we get home. I am on the organising committee of a student conference being hosted at my academic institution, and I also have to edit this paper. I am editing a document on Special Interest Groups (SIGs) and I am thinking about facilitating one on language in education for the conference. My PhD identity is thus always a negotiated identity and the role I in which I am least comfortable, because it is an area of transition and growth. I have come to realise though that foregrounding and expanding my identity as a PhD student is imperative to completing the PhD within the allocated time.

CREATING A MENTAL THIRD SPACE

Though I have familial support there are no familial role models to teach me how to deal with institutional challenges. Since I have always worked and studied, I could only do the PhD full-time if it was funded, but I was unprepared for the institutional practices regarding scholarships[1]. I was awarded a scholarship, but it was funded by government and only paid out eight months later. Communication from the university around the delay was poor, although I sent numerous emails asking for information. The university has since become more supportive, however, at the time I was one of about twenty-two PhD students who were funded by the same programme. As I felt the financial strain I started doubting my decision to embark on full-time study. I was torn between the tug to return to work and the desire to write and finish my proposal. In an effort to find a space out of this bind, I started to read books on motivation, success and aspiration. Most academics would disapprove of reading motivational books but remain unaware of the thin margin of error and grace under which first-generation PhD and other students exist in South Africa. Gutiérrez, Baquedano-Lopez and Tejeda (1999:286) state that "the use of multiple, diverse and even conflicting mediational tools promotes

---

1   Also see Chapter 4 by Shakira Choonara that addresses issues around funding.

the emergence of Third Spaces, or zones of development, thus expanding learning". These books, in seeming contradiction with the academy, created enough relief so I could continue to work on a proposal for a PhD which at that stage seemed like a fading dream. When I read these books, I relied on my natural scepticism and my analytical training to act as a filter and sift through what I was reading. I learned to distinguish between writers who offer new ways and approaches and those who offer manipulative strategies with short-term results which, if continued, would damage social relationships over time. Now, when I find an author whose writing resonates with me, I write down the ideas that inspire me and that I find meaningful. I have also learned to add my own ideas or affirmations. These ideas normally revolve around projects or writing which I am working on. Motivational books have provided me with options on how to become unstuck and how to train myself to think of ways around obstacles and blocks. I had to learn to downgrade problems to minor challenges instead of elevating them to a crisis. When I made mistakes I had to learn to find the lesson and move ahead, instead of wallowing and becoming bogged down with what I could have done. I have recently started reading books on financial planning and money management as well, because I need a reminder that there is life and there are goals to achieve beyond my PhD. The ideas and stories in these books play a part in staying positive, which is an important aspect of surviving the challenges faced along the postgraduate journey.

FROM SOLITARY LEARNER TO EMERGING ACADEMIC

Gutiérrez (2008:149, in reference to Gutiérrez & Larson 2007) argue that "traditional notions of development generally define change along a vertical dimension", for example moving from a Master's to a PhD, whereas "a more expansive view of development is also concerned with the horizontal forms of expertise that develop within and across an individual's practices". To shape this Third Space of learning and expand my academic practices and identity, I realised that I had to move into new spaces. This realisation was shaped by an experience that I had during my Master's degree. I took a drama course, because part of the curriculum involved visits to the theatre to view and review plays. Our lecturer told us how to dress, what to expect and arranged transport to and from the theatre. Until then, neither my class, race nor gender position had allowed me to consider attending the theatre. I also started attending seminars in my department and in my discipline, and even those at other universities. This gave me a better sense of all the major debates, I learned who the academics were in the departments and discovered that universities favour different theoretical frameworks which are also reflected in the content of the library. My supervisor (who is the course co-ordinator for Master's students) facilitated our introduction to the department by adding all Master's and PhD students to the departmental events list so that we were able to attend lunch-time seminars. This move was a crucial aspect of my transition from solitary learner to joining a community of academics, and was a way of learning the "horizontal forms of expertise" and of extending my "repertoires of practice" (Gutiérrez 2008:149). At these academic events I found people I could talk to and I used the connections I made to build different kinds of networks with students and academics. These networks are important for sharing resources, giving and receiving advice, encouragement, and starting and participating in publishing opportunities. I talked to people whose comments or questions I found meaningful and sometimes I initiated contact with other students by sending them an email containing details of an event or a useful reference. If they did not respond, I respected that and tried someone else – you will find someone you can work with even though the person or persons may be in another department or discipline or at another university.

ASKING AND ANSWERING QUESTIONS

I had to learn to leverage another crucial aspect of Third Space, namely moving from voicelessness to articulation and expression. Attending academic events afforded me opportunities for learning the subtleties of behaviour appropriate to each event such as learning to give presentations, contributing to discussion and practicing asking and answering questions. These practices may seem easy for some, but I grew up in a fairly strict religious home during apartheid, and the way I acted in the world when I was younger was largely shaped by the words "you should" and "you can't". Therefore, learning how to ask and answer questions about my research in a public forum was an important step to finding my voice. A basic building block in creating your academic persona is being able to answer the question, "What is your PhD about?" with knowledge and confidence. You will need two responses: one at a basic level for interested family and friends and one at a complex level for fellow students and academics. Expect to be quizzed by knowledgeable others about your research question, theoretical framework, concepts and methodology. You are already reading in these areas, but a polished response will save you from being tongue-tied and unprepared.

You also need to learn the appropriate way to ask and answer questions in a public forum. You learn to do this by watching those students and academics who manage the questions and feedback at seminars and research events with ease. When faced with a challenging question that they could not answer, they would simply say, "I had not thought of that" or "I'm not sure; I will have to consider that" or "What is your understanding of that?". I saw that this allowed students and academics to keep their composure and gather information because they would write down all the feedback and information they received. Even when they were challenged, they responded by treating the challenge as information and feedback. They would answer by saying, "Thank you for your question", and then say, "That is something I have not considered". I learned to preface my questions with statements such as, "Thank you for that interesting presentation". I learned the practice of conducting question and answer sessions by attending and watching the practice being modelled by students and academics at events.

PUBLISHING AND PRESENTING RESEARCH

Publishing ideas and writing papers are integral to being an academic and it is a means of placing your voice and ideas in the public domain. You need to learn how to choose appropriate journals and it is better to refuse invitations from journals wanting to publish your paper for a fee. You also need to guard against publishing companies that lock you into contracts that allow them to republish your intellectual labour without your consent. You only truly learn the subtleties and rigor of publishing a paper until after it returns from the editor. Then you will learn (like me) that a single paper might go through three or more stages of drafting and just when you thought you ticked all the boxes, you switch editors and you find yourself writing for a person with a different perspective and idea of what is required. This is all part of the learning process and nothing personal I am told. So writing a paper is actually like flinging a boomerang – it will come back faster than you sent it off, and more often than not, whack you on the head to announce its return.

I underestimated the amount of time it takes to redraft and recraft a paper after each edit and to meet deadlines. It can amount to weeks and months of valuable thesis time. You might want to ask your supervisor or fellow students for advice on whether it is wise to write a paper while you're doing your PhD. Some universities do not allow their postgraduate students to publish until after final submission and I can see why. My supervisor suggested that I publish one paper per year while working on my PhD. To guard against fragmenting my time and to remind myself of my primary focus, I created a timeline for my thesis listing the different stages and dates I committed to in my MoU (Memorandum of Understanding) and put it on my wall as a constant reminder of what I am trying to achieve. I even listed my graduation date to make it an achievable goal.

SETTING UP A VIRTUAL STUDY GROUP[2]

For postgraduate students who belong to extended families and close communities, PhD research is often a lonely experience. Since my sense of isolation was shared by other first-generation PhD students, we started an online social group using WhatsApp on our mobile phones. Our social group morphed into a virtual study group that has been running for almost two years. This virtual Third Space is characterised by hybrid language practices where we learn to greet and speak phrases in each other's languages, share our ideas, challenges and different theoretical frameworks and tools. This online space allows participants from Namibia, Zimbabwe or anywhere else in South Africa or the world to participate. We use the structure of a writing workshop that my supervisor created where we write in 25- to 45-minute bursts and then take five- to ten-minute breaks. Group members move in and out of the writing or study sessions as needed, and we have no formal system for starting a study session. Someone would just volunteer to start and keep time and then everyone else would join when they are able to do so. Usually the person to lead is the person with the closest deadline. This study group provides an essential support mechanism and is a source of accountability. We went through a stretch where we were getting up at 4 a.m. to do writing in an effort to balance work and family responsibilities. We also exchanged resources and learned to use electronic resources such as *Edmondo* and *Mendeley*. Those members skilled in an application would provide a learning session for the rest of the group. We exchange information on funding and scholarships, offer encouragement and support for projects, and celebrate when a group member hands in work.

CONCLUSION

Being a first-generation PhD student meant that I had to engage in academic practices in order integrate into an academic community. I had to go through cycles of trial, error and refinement. I had to consciously think about which aspects of my behaviour I wanted to change and which aspects of academia I wanted to learn. I had to find people with whom I could work, which sometimes meant that I had to create a virtual cooperative environment.

Gutiérrez's (2008) Third Space is not only about writing and theory, as she uses a number of modalities to motivate, move and inspire students (such as music, performance art, writing, images and painting). So I suggest that you create a multimodal physical Third Space in which you place objects that inspire you, such as

---

2 Also see Part 5 of this book where various authors reflect on what postgraduate study as a social practice has meant to them.

images of yourself, family or authors and people that you find meaningful. If you do not have the resources, write or type inspirational poetry and messages and place them on your bedroom or study walls, behind the door, on your desk or wherever you do your thesis work. I have stopped trying to fit myself into a template of how I thought an academic should look and act. I believe that academe in South Africa can stretch to accommodate your PhD canvas, and that is why my ideas around surviving and succeeding the PhD experience involve embracing the Third Space. As a first-generation student, I find the notions of hybridity, maintaining a critical lens and staying open to learning on all levels useful in making sense of my new environment.

REFERENCES

Bhabha, H. (1994). *The Location of Culture*. New York, USA: Routledge.

Cotterall, S. (2013). More than just a brain: emotions and the doctoral experience. *Higher Education Research and Development*, 32(2):174-187. http://dx.doi.org/10.1080/07294360.2012.680017

Gutiérrez, K., Baquedano-López, P., & Tejeda, C. (1999). Rethinking diversity: Hybridity and hybrid language practices in the third space. *Mind, Culture and Activity*, 6(4):286-303. http://dx.doi.org/10.1080/10749039909524733

Gutiérrez, K. (2008). Developing Sociocritical Literacy in the Third Space. *Reading Research Quarterly*, 43(2):148-164. http://dx.doi.org/10.1598/RRQ.43.2.3

Lohfink, M., & Paulsen, M. (2005). Comparing the Determinants of Persistence For First-Generation and Continuing-Generation Students. *Journal of College Student Development*, 46(4):409-428. http://dx.doi.org/10.1353/csd.2005.0040

New London Group. (2000). A Pedagogy of Multiliteracies: Designing Social Futures. In B. Cope and M. Kalantzis (Eds.) *Multiliteracies. Literacy Learning and the Design of Social Futures* (pp. 9-37). London, UK: Routledge.

7
CAUGHT BETWEEN WORK AND STUDY: EXPLORING BOUNDARY ZONES AS AN EMPLOYED POSTGRADUATE STUDENT

Andre van der Bijl

INTRODUCTION

Centuries of colonial and apartheid domination divided higher education institutions between world-class universities to institutions of little repute. Staff members have seen their professional identities change from expert practitioner to academic when specialist colleges and technikons were transformed or amalgamated into universities of technology. Since the publication of White Paper 3 (RSA 1997), technikons have become universities of technology and the variety of colleges, including nursing colleges, agricultural colleges and colleges of education have closed down and were incorporated into multi-campus universities. This post-apartheid higher education landscape was envisioned as a transformed space that would redress past inequalities, serve a new social order and, in doing so, meet pressing national needs that would respond to new realities and opportunities.

The processes of restructuring and institutional incorporation left a number of academic staff members unemployed. Those who were employed by the incorporating institutions faced qualification requirements for which they had not been prepared and lacked the skills universities require for employment, notably research skills. A variety of funding mechanisms and, in some cases, recognition of prior learning procedures provided assistance to newly incorporated staff. Differential workload models, social pressures and a lack of research readiness, however, often undermined synchronisation of individual transformation with the planned social and implemented institutional transformation.

My doctoral journey spans this fraught time of transition. My initial teacher education qualification, a Higher Diploma in Education majoring in business and economics, was followed by a Bachelor of Arts in which I was drawn to subjects with a Marxist framework. This was followed by a Bachelor of Education at another university which, at the time, bore vestiges of apartheid education, and finally a Master's degree in educational management. From the educational qualifications I learned about teaching and how to teach. From the Bachelor of Arts I learned about forms of social analysis that, by the turn of the century, no longer appeared relevant. My Master's degree, while in no way linked to my previous qualifications, provided inputs into a research discourse that disappeared soon after I graduated. When I embarked on my doctoral journey, I was wholly unprepared. I needed to face multiple, often conflicting demands and learned to play multiple roles, some required by communities of practice, others tolerated or endorsed as expected of a colleague involved in further studies. This chapter reflects on my journey as both a doctoral student and an employed academic in a newly established university of technology. Using Fairclough's notion of discursive power and boundary zones associated with Engeström's Activity Theory, the doctoral journey of a person employed in higher education is described as a process of, on the one hand, balancing demands of different activity systems and, on the other hand, using power and knowledge from one to influence the other. Understanding the extent of supervisor power relative to that of the power of a student who has an equitable external power base, at least for one doctoral student, provided a key to navigate between studies, work and community.

FRAMEWORKS FOR NAVIGATING DIFFERENT ROLES

The ideological notion of a graduate student being able to conduct a research project under the guidance of a mentoring supervisor may be one experienced by young full-time protégés. This was, however, not my experience. I found that people who, by chance or choice, embark on postgraduate study at a mature age face a number challenges created by the disjunction between their role as academic student and other social roles. While some social roles may assist the study, others obstruct efforts to study. Even where social roles contribute toward the study by, for example, providing a forum for data collection, the relation between postgraduate studies and social roles is seldom linear or simple. My own experience is one of constantly differentiating between roles, understanding the dynamics of each one and behaving accordingly. Two sets of frameworks in particular influenced my role interaction. The influence of one framework was conscious and formed part of my doctoral research framework. The other was subconscious and understood *post facto* when I was introduced to the framework as part of another research project.

CHAPTER 7 • EXPLORING BOUNDARY ZONES AS AN EMPLOYED POSTGRADUATE STUDENT

The framework consciously applied is an application of critical discourse analysis (CDA) developed by Norman Fairclough, particularly his work on language and power (Fairclough 1989:2001), as well as his work on political discourse analysis (Fairclough & Fairclough 2010). Like Fairclough, I was influenced by the work of Michael Foucault. Wodak and Meyer (2001:2) describes CDA as a theoretical perspective based on the analysis of language and semiosis, a perspective Henning, Van Rensburg and Smit (2004:45-46) term a discursive perspective. Meaning is constructed largely through individual and socially-constructed modes of symbolising reality (Henning et al 2004). Discourse is used to make sense of, or comprehend, a social process, as language associated with a particular field or practice, or as a way of "construing aspects of the world associated with a particular social perspective" (Fairclough 2010:230). Discourse analysis provides insight into discourses which she describes as functioning bodies of knowledge (Powers 2007:18). The identification and description of different bodies of knowledge and associated discursive practices was key to navigating, not only between the graduate research project and my other social roles, but, increasingly, between the mix of social roles that included my role as graduate student. Differing social roles imply different norms, practices and requirements for rules of behaviour. Some are determined by means of conscious projection but others are articulated through social symbols.

Navigating between discursive practices required navigation between discursive environments, each with its own structure, division of labour and social rules. Navigating between discursive structures provided opportunities to use information from one discursive environment in another. Navigating between discursive environments provided opportunities to behave as a member of one environment in another. I later discovered that the concept of a community with rules, tools and a division of labour, Engeström (1987:78) called an activity system[1], which I now understand played a role in my scholarly becoming on a subconscious level. Engeström's model has been used to analyse social practice, particularly social transformation under circumstances of conflicting social practice (Uden, Valderas & Pastor 2008). Engeström's (1987) model is commonly represented by a triangle of interacting elements. The key elements of interaction include the subject, the object and the community. The subject processes community demands into objects in the form of outcomes. Rules, tools or instruments and division of labour influence the three key elements. Engeström, Miettinen and Punamaki (1999:31) represent this model as follows:

---

[1] Engeström's (1987) activity theory is also known as Engeström's activity system model, Engeström's triangle (Kaptelinin 2005) or the cultural historical activity theory (Soudien 2013:17).

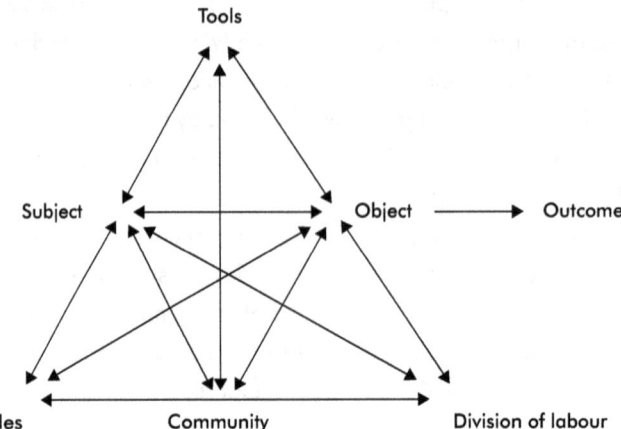

FIGURE 7.1. Engeström's (1987) Activity Theory model as presented by Engeström, Miettinen and Punamaki (1999:31)

Since the 1990s, Engeström's model has been widely used to analyse transformational dynamics of social activities in, amongst others, education and training (Bedney & Meister 1997; Tuomi-Gröhn & Engeström 2007; Bolton & Keevy 2011; Pather 2012; Soudien 2013).

The elements of Engeström's form of activity theory that appeared most relevant to my doctoral journey were roles and division of labour. As a professional academic and leader in a community structure, I was bound by certain rules of behaviour and had become accustomed to a position within them. My doctoral journey started by being subjected to the subordination of my views and position to a proposal format and its defence to a research committee that included experts with whom I was professionally acquainted. The proposal submission process clearly indicated that I was to be subjected to a new set of rules, specific tools and a division of labour that bore little resemblance to those with which I was acquainted.

In its initial form, Engeström's (1987) model focusses on the dynamics of one community, and does not account for interaction between communities, which was addressed in later publications by Tuomi-Gröhn and Engeström (2007), Olvitt (2010), Bolton and Keevy (2011) and others. Each activity system has its own division of labour, as well as sets of rules and tools that regulate both internal activities and systemic inputs and outputs. Rules within activity systems, Bolton and Keevy (2011), using Bernstein's term, suggest act like pedagogic devices with which members recontextualise knowledge, regulate relationships and assess criteria for transmitting knowledge. I, like other graduate students, used knowledge located in one activity system in others. Knowledge gained from work and community involvement was intertwined with my research topic. Some issues facilitated the research process while others did not. Identifying, recontextualising and transferring knowledge between different activity systems is, however, not linear or simple, hence my use of the term navigation. Recontextualising knowledge and situated writing conventions were particularly challenging.

I remember writing at the time, referring to the use of Engeström, adaptations of Engeström's initial model include the idea that more than one activity system can coexist and that the different activity systems interact with each other. Such models include those designed by Uden (2007), Bolton and Keevy (2011), Ludvigsen, Havnes and Lahn (in Tuomi-Gröhn & Engeström 2007:291-310) and Van der Bijl and Taylor (2016). The actions I was involved in were, what Tuomi-Gröhn and Engeström (2007:50) terms, boundary crossing, "a no-man's land", [relatively] free from prearranged routines or rigid patterns. Social objects within boundary zones were used and, at times, adapted to suit objectives; some random, others calculated. Diagrammatically I found myself within a structure of articulated activity systems as illustrated below:

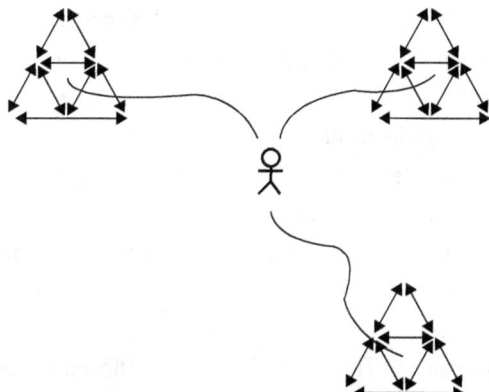

FIGURE 7.2. Articulated multiple activity systems (adapted from Bolton & Keevy 2011:7)[2]

Graduate studies, for a person employed within higher education and heavily involved in community service, require balancing studies with other forms of information gathering and knowledge dissemination in different areas of activity. As

---

2   I adapted Figure 7.2 from one I saw in an article by Bolton and Keevy (2011:7) on their article of the National Qualifications Framework as a relational relational principle. I was later told by Bolton that their diagramme is attributed to the work of Olvitt (2011).

a working graduate student I was active in a number of social environments, each with its own social rules, tools for communication and discursive rules. The transfer of knowledge, Bernstein (in Bolton & Keevy 2011:7-8) noted, is governed by sets of rules involving recontextualisation, a process which involves taking knowledge from one discourse and re-creating it in another. The transfer of knowledge, Bolton and Keevy (2001:8) continued, is regulated by a variety of factors, including "power, social groups, forms of consciousness and practice". Discourse and discursive practice could be added to this list.

At first, navigating within and between the activity systems was extremely difficult, largely because the rules and tools of the newly entered activity system was foreign, but also because my position within the other systems were being realigned. Learning to use the tools of a research activity system was an integral part of the research apprenticeship. Navigating between activity systems and my complying with expected rules behaviour within each system, while taking advantage of the freedom the situation provided, was something that was learned by trial and error. I found Fairclough and Fairclough's (2010:17-18) adaptation of van Dijk's definition of political discourse analysis a useful navigational tool in this regard.

Fairclough and Fairclough (2010) note that political discourse analysis focusses on the reproduction and contestation of power through discourse by actors engaged in processes and events within certain institutional contexts. The extent to which leeway was given to engage in graduate studies, at the expense of involvement in other social activities, depended largely on successful reasoning and argument with people in positions of power. In navigating activity systems, I worked on identifying forms, relations and dynamics of power, the key actors and discursive practices within each activity system. In some cases, I was successful in navigating boundary zones within systems. In others, however, I was less successful and in one community I failed to maintain my position. The key to both navigational success and failure lay in realising the impact of change on me and, in turn, its impact on my relations with others. Some social relations were impervious; others adapted, and a few moved towards incompatibility.

While the oscillation between activity systems had a largely positive influence on the project's completion, at certain key points in the project it was necessary to retract into a single activity system. Key points included times when sections of the dissertation were being concluded, during the project's fieldwork phase and when the final draft was being constructed and corrected. At such times the relevance of knowledge transferred from other activity systems as subordinated to project demands and discursive parameters. At first, subordinating other activity systems was difficult, as the current demands for knowledge that they required appeared to subordinate the project. However, as the project progressed and my own research skills matured, the relative importance of the other activity systems stabilised and serviced the project.

Retraction invariably had implications for honouring commitments in other communities. The success with which retraction from and re-entry into the other communities occurred depended on a number factors of which the most significant appeared to be the relative importance of the project to the community and my ability to influence people in the community who had power over me.

POWER AND KNOWLEDGE

The role of my supervisors in my doctoral journey, as any other, cannot be underestimated. Bradbury-Jones, Irvine and Sambrook (2008) argue that postgraduate supervision is a complex pedagogy involving practices that are uncertain, misunderstood and problematic, to the extent of sometimes being impossible. Supervisors are powerful (Bradbury-Jones Irvine & Sambrook 2008). Not only do supervisors have power, they are perceived as being powerful and are expected to express their power by leading the research process and being the expert in the relationship. The form of power supervisors have, Bradbury-Jones *et al* (2008:83-84) argue, is disciplinary power. The concept of disciplinary power was developed by Michael Foucault (1995) to describe power to punish that flows out of the examination of judgments made from observation. Students, Bradbury-Jones *et al* (2008:86) continue, have expressive power, which they call "power to act". As a result of the expressions of power, the relation between supervisor and student, they argue, is characterised by discourses of unity and detachment.

When reading the article by Bradbury-Jones *et al* (2008), my interest was raised less by their discussion of student/supervisor relations, and more by their use of Foucaultian discourse analysis as part of the conceptual framework of my dissertation. A point not lost at the time, however, was the need to collaborate (unity discourse) and the power to detach. I developed levels of detachment. The first level could be called cognitive detachment, which occurred in meetings when I disagreed with what I was told to do and subsequently ignored the input. The next level of detachment was intellectual detachment, which occurred when I disagreed with conceptualisation or a form of argument. Disagreement tended to require a counter strategy or further research, sometimes justifying my disagreement; other times not. The third level of detachment was physical detachment, which had levels of its own, ranging from putting doctoral work aside, to engrossing myself in professional or community work, using that as an excuse more than a reason to, in the words of my generation, "walk away".

The power to detach is one that all graduate students possess. However, employed, graduate students have a greater level of power to detach when compared to their peers who have taken time off work or have not yet entered the labour market. "I can afford to quit", "I do not really need this", "I can repay the grant" were a few expressions of economic and social power commonly expressed by my employed graduate student peers. Apart from economic power to detach, working graduate students have other activity systems into which they can detach for reasons that are socially justifiable.

A student's power to detach has erosive implications for the expression of a supervisor's power, a power base which could be further eroded when a student brings, real or perceived, forms of social power into the relationship. For unprepared or immature supervisors, student expression of power could hamper or even destroy the project. In my experience, not only as a doctoral student, the supervisor of employed graduate students can therefore not rely on subject-based expert power alone employed by means of a directive discourse. Supervisors of employed graduate students, to a greater extent than their peers who work with younger or full-time students, need to manage and balance students' exploration of the boundary zones within which they operate and from where their knowledge emanates. In my experience, which supports the dual discourse assertion of Bradbury-Jones *et al* (2008), the supervisor of mature working students' needs to rely less on a directive style and adopt a more redirective one. In contrast to directing the use of information derived from rules, tools and the division of labour from an activity system that the supervisor and student share, the supervisor needs to create a boundary zone for, and within, the doctoral study. The boundary zone needs to provide scope for exploration of the student's other activity systems and a space to test the applicability of information brought into the rules and tools required for graduation.

As with any graduate student's journey, the expression of a supervisor's disciplinary power is vital. However, when working with mature employed students, consistently seeking a balance of power is, in my experience, more important than expressing supervisory power. Willingness to balance power requires maturity on the part of both student and supervisor. My doctoral supervisor managed my desire to bring too many concepts into the dissertation by saying "keep it for another publication". Her suggestion not only brought the dissertation into focus, but it provided me with opportunities to detach and explore boundaries in other activity systems. The exploration resulted in publications which informed, and contributed towards, the completion of my doctoral journey.

APPLICATION, TRANSFER AND USE OF KNOWLEDGE

As an employed graduate student in his forties, I felt that I brought a significant amount of knowledge into a project because I had significant knowledge about the project's context. The knowledge, however, tended to be in a format that was not necessarily compatible or aligned with the format required for inclusion in the study. Knowledge accepted without question in other communities and social environments needed to be clarified, sourced and classified before it could be incorporated into a study. Like other mature graduate students with whom I was acquainted, I regarded myself as a specialist in the area of my topic, with notable standing as a professional in the field within which the research would be conducted. Learning to adapt existing knowledge and fit it into the discourse required for graduate writing required a considerable amount of cognitive reconstruction.

The challenge of transferring knowledge between activity systems was aggravated by demands emanating from other systems and its effects on the research project. Some demands complemented the research project, but others were antagonistic. Complementary and antagonistic demands were not necessarily mutually exclusive. Some demands, initiated as complementary, became antagonistic, while some antagonistic demands became complementary. Some demands were both antagonistic and complementary. A notable complementary antagonism emanated from my employment environment. While my employer demanded increased staff qualifications, particularly graduate qualifications, and provided funding for graduate studies, work demands and the interpretation of policies even negated and at times contradicted employer intentions and incentives. In my case, while I was encouraged to study and funds were made available to pay for elements of my studies, my workload increased to an extent that studies was, at times, constrained.

Involvement in the doctoral project had a number of positive repercussions. The most notable is that it served as an account or justification for behavioural quirks, administrative misdemeanours and the transfer of knowledge. Colleagues, friends and family regarded the project as a reason for incongruent behaviour and administrative errors. In meetings, expressions of my opinion were commonly articulated as, or laced with, reference to what "recent research indicates". Operating within a number of activity systems clearly had implications, both for knowledge production and knowledge transfer, and behaviour within the activity systems. The extent to which the implications were positive or negative pedagogic devices depended to a large extent on the tolerance level within the different activity systems. Some social environments were tolerant towards the doctoral project while others were less so.

CONCLUSION: LOOKING BACK, LOOKING FORWARD

In writing this chapter, I have become aware of the lingering, albeit diffused, influence of Marx's writing on my study. Both Fairclough and Engeström's work, and that of Foucault, has its origins in Marx's work and, as a result, so has mine. There were clear patterns of exploitation and oppression within each of the activity systems involved in my study. My situation was unlike the situation facing a young, full-time graduate student in which the student-supervisor relation dominates and the dialectic between studies and social function is a broad one. My situation was one in which the supervisor-student role was but one of a number of competing relations, each with its own dynamic, and oscillating levels of comparative importance. The dialectic was not a broad social one, but a series of contesting, dialectic situations.

The conceptualisation of a mature graduate research study as a dialectic process, rather than the apprenticeship conceptualisation more commonly associated with graduate research, has implications for defining the roles of students and supervisors. Supervisors need to realise that mature students bring a level of expertise and perspective into the project that may not only be unexpected but may result in the revision of supervisor intentions for the student's role in the supervisor's broader research project. Mature students, conversely, need to alter their study intentions, particularly if a student has a specific career or socially oriented reason for doing the study. Subordination of broader intentions for studying is a key not only to study success; it is an important element of successful boundary crossing and survival in boundary zones.

Throughout the writing of this chapter, I have been reminded of the view of Field Marshall Sir William Slim in his autobiography about his involvement as British commander in the Burma campaign during the Second World War. He suggested (Slim 1955:vii) that a general should not write about the battles with which he is involved, but that it should be done by "someone less personally involved". Possibly the proximity of supervisors and graduates to a graduate research journey puts them in a similar position. However, providing an insider's view of the complex system(s) that constitute the postgraduate experience may provide students and supervisors alike with the tools to survive and succeed.

REFERENCES

Bedney, G., & Meister, D. (1997). *The Russian Theory of Activity: Current Applications to Design and Learning*. New Jersey, USA: Lawrence Erlbaum Associates.

Bolton, H., & Keevy, J. (2011). *The South African Qualifications Framework: rational principle in the Activity System for education, training, development, work*. Paper presented at the 7th Researching Work and Learning conference, Shanghai, 4-7 December 2011.

Bradbury-Jones, C., Irvine, F., & Sambrook, S. (2007). Unity and Detachment: A Discourse Analysis of Doctoral Students. *International Journal of Qualitative Methods*, 6(4):14-96.

Engeström, Y. (1987). *Learning by Expansion: An Activity Theoretical Approach to Developmental Research*. Helsinki, Finland: Orienta-Knosultit Oy.

Engeström, Y., Miettinen, R., & Punamaki, R-L. (1999). *Perspectives on Activity Theory*. Cambridge, UK: Cambridge University Press. http://dx.doi.org/10.1017/CBO9780511812774

Fairclough, N. (1989). *Language and Power*. Harlow, USA: Longman.

Fairclough, N. (2001). Language and Power. Second edition. Harlow, USA: Longman.

Fairclough, N. (2010). *Critical Discourse Analysis The Critical Study of Language*. Second edition. Edinburgh, UK: Pearson.

Fairclough, N., & Fairclough, I. (2010). *Political Discourse Analysis A method for advanced students*. London, UK: Routledge.

Foucault, M. (1995). *Discipline and punish: The birth of the prison* (A. Sheridan, Translation). New York, USA: Vintage.

Henning, E., Van Rensburg, W., & Smit, B. (2004). *Finding your way in qualitative research*. Pretoria, South Africa: Van Schaik.

Kaptelinin, V. (2005). The object of activity – making sense of the sense makers. *Mind, Culture and Activity*, 12(1):4-18. http://dx.doi.org/10.1207/s15327884mca1201_2

Olvitt, L. (2010). Exploring contradictions in ethics-oriented learning: activity system influences in an environmental education learnership. *Southern African Journal for Environmental Education*, 27:71-90.

Pather, S. (2012). Activity theory as a lens to examine pre-service teachers' perceptions of learning and teaching of Mathematics within an intervention programme. *African Journal of Research in MST Education*, 16(2):126-140.

Powers, P. (2007). The philosophical foundations of Foucaultian discourse analysis. *Critical Approaches to Discourse Analysis across Disciplines*, 1(2):18-34.

Republic of South Africa (RSA) (1997). *Education White Paper 3: A programme for the transformation of higher education*. Pretoria, South Africa: Government Printer.

Slim, W. (1955). *Defeat into victory*. London, UK: The Reprint Society.

Soudien, C. (2013). *Whither progressive education and training in South Africa?* Address delivered at the South African Qualifications Authority 3rd Ben Parker Memorial Lecture. South African Qualifications Authority, Waterkloof.

Tuomi-Gröhn, E., & Engeström, Y. (2007). *Between school and work: New Perspectives on transfer and boundary-crossing.* Bingley, UK: Emerald.

Uden, L. (2007). Activity theory for designing mobile learning. *International Journal of Mobile Learning and Organisation,* 1(1):81-102. http://dx.doi.org/10.1504/IJMLO.2007.011190

Van der Bijl, A., & Taylor, V. (2016). Nature and dynamics of industry-based workplace learning for South African TVET lecturers. *Industry and Higher Education,* 30(2):98-108.

Wodak, R., & Meyer, M. (2001). *Methods of critical discourse analysis: Critical discourse analysis as a method in social scientific research.* Sage Research Methods. Available online at http://srmo.sagepub.com/view/method-of-critical-discourse-analysis/d8.xml

8

THE INCLUSION OF VISUALLY IMPAIRED STUDENTS IN POST-GRADUATE PROGRAMMES: A PERSONAL AND POLITICAL PERSPECTIVE

Heidi Lourens

INTRODUCTION

Over the last two decades, the ideology and practice of inclusive education gained momentum across the globe. In 1994, 92 governments adopted the well-known Salamanca statement, whereby they agreed to include disabled children and students in regular learning environments (UNESCO 1994). Following this statement, inclusive policies provided the necessary impetus to include, amongst others, disabled students within institutions of higher learning (Beauchamp-Pryor 2012; Taylor 2004). As Taylor (2004:46) writes, "the number and experiences of students accessing HE will invariably be influenced by changes in legislation". Following in the footsteps of this global agenda, the South African government formally stated their commitment to welcome and accommodate disabled students in higher education through the introduction of Education White Paper 6: Building an Inclusive Education and Training System (Department of Education 2001). So, when South African tertiary institutions started opening their doors to disabled students, it was not a matter of granting them a favour; it was a matter of equal rights and quality education for all.

But what does "accommodate" and "welcome" really mean? How will universities know that they have adequately welcomed and accommodated disabled students on their grounds? Firstly, a welcoming and accommodating environment will translate into more disabled students crossing the borders of university campuses (Howell 2006). However, simply being there is not merely a sufficient measure of true inclusion. True inclusion will echo in the day-to-day experiences of disabled students when their equal participation is facilitated through adequate support and reasonable accommodations (Bantjes *et al* 2015; Howell 2005, 2006; Lourens &

Swartz 2016a). The responsibility does not rest on students to make the environment accessible or to adapt to an unwelcoming university climate; the onus rests on institutions of higher learning to facilitate the equal participation of all students entering their campuses (Department of Education 2001; Department of Higher Education and Training 2013; South African Government 2015).

This responsibility of universities does not end once disabled students obtain their first degree (Farrar, Young & Denicolo 2007). When disabled students enrol for a postgraduate programme, they maintain the right to reasonable accommodations. This right is neatly captured in the recent White Paper on the Rights of Persons with Disabilities (South African Government 2015). One of its measures of inclusion reads, "[e]nsuring that persons with disabilities are able to access general tertiary education, vocational training, adult education and lifelong learning without discrimination and on an equal basis with others by, among others ensuring that reasonable accommodation is provided to persons with disabilities" (p. 83). It goes without saying that post-graduate support is included in the reference to lifelong learning.

In this chapter, I reflect on some of my experiences as a visually impaired doctoral student. I highlight the challenges I encountered, as well as those aspects that made the journey a bit easier (the latter I often stumbled upon by chance). Looking through a rights-shaped lens, I provide a brief overview of relevant factors that moulded my doctoral journey. Firstly, I explore the emotional and psychological underpinnings of the decision to ask for necessary support during postgraduate research. Hereafter, I reflect on practical accessibility difficulties and successes that I have encountered during this part of my educational career, such as (a) access to reading material; (b) access to participants and supervision – matters of transport; and (c) attending academic conferences. Lastly, I offer a reflection on the supervisor-student relationship and the importance of flexibility. The thread that runs through all these sub-themes is the right to reasonable accommodations.

Unfortunately, there is no one-size-fits-all model to accommodate and include all disabled students in postgraduate programmes (Farrar, Young & Denicolo 2007). This work provides a mere glimpse into my specific experiences as a visually impaired doctoral student. Yet it is my hope that, through my experiences, disabled students and disability-support staff might start to gain some insight into the rights and challenges of post-graduate studies for disabled students.

CHAPTER 8 • THE INCLUSION OF VISUALLY IMPAIRED STUDENTS IN POST-GRADUATE PROGRAMMES

ENTITLEMENT TO SUPPORT: THOUGHTS ON IMPOSTERS AND STRUCTURE

The decision to disclose an invisible disability is often not easy. For many disabled students, the anticipated social and academic costs of disclosure are simply too high. They often fear discrimination and exclusion by teaching staff and peers (Beauchamp-Pryor 2013; Elliot & Wilson 2008; Foundation of Tertiary Institutions of the Northern Metropolis 2011; Kranke et al 2013; Lourens & Swartz 2016b; Magnus & Tøssebro 2013; Ngubane-Mokiwa 2013). Even though being open about their disability entitles them to reasonable accommodations, the very real fear of discrimination and exclusion sometimes outweigh the benefit of adequate support.

Since I am completely blind, it is almost impossible for me to pass as "normal" (Goffman 1963). I never had the option of concealing my disability and, partly because of this visibility, I comfortably requested reasonable accommodations during my undergraduate years. But, when I embarked on a doctoral study in 2011 – my first dissertation-based university programme – I lost the confidence to ask for support. My disability was still visible, but I felt less entitled to admit that I still needed reasonable accommodations. Farrar (2006) comments on the difficulty of disclosure during postgraduate studies, as the stakes are higher at these levels in terms of time, energy and intellect invested, as are the expectations of both students and staff involved. There were two aspects to the doctoral journey that lead to my reluctance to request support. Firstly, the unstructured nature of writing a dissertation blurred the scope and boundaries of reasonable accommodations. Secondly, I carried with me the erroneous assumption that I would not deserve a doctoral degree and the title that comes with it if I asked for support. In the following few paragraphs, I will briefly elaborate on these two aspects.

Usually, an undergraduate programme is highly structured. My three-year Bachelor of Arts Humanities degree was no exception. I attended lectures, completed assignments and wrote examinations. It was often the latter that hurriedly urged and "allowed" me to request support. Examinations that loomed around the corner felt like solid grounds for requesting accessible course material and extra time to complete assessments. Because I had to write examinations, it felt reasonable and legitimate to ask for reasonable accommodations.

And then I enrolled for a doctoral programme. Suddenly there were no formal lectures, no immediate assessments and no imposed deadlines. I mostly worked from home and, while drinking one steaming cup of coffee after the next, I brewed over my next sentence or paragraph in solitary confinement. While I clearly needed some level of support, I rarely thought about my need for reasonable accommodations. At the time, it was unclear to me why and for what I needed any form of support. As previously mentioned the lack of intermittent examinations and frequent assignments clouded my judgment on this matter. But, as it will become clear in this chapter, the presence or absence of frequent examinations does not measure the urgency or need for reasonable accommodations. Even though my doctoral programme was unstructured and the examination was, for the most part, in the distant future, I nevertheless needed accommodations. A doctoral candidate in a study by Farrar (2006:176) captures this need for support beautifully when she remarks, "[i]n theory research study with a physical-mobility impairment should be easier than undergraduate study. ... However, and it's a big however, in practice it is much, much harder. Research study is a lonely, isolating and anxious experience at the best of times. Doing it with an impairment multiplies those factors".

Having said this, I strongly believe there was something that weighed heavier; something that spoke louder than the structure of the doctoral degree programme. It was my beliefs around entitlement and worthiness. I firmly believed that the less I asked for assistance, the more the university, the academic department and my supervisor would recognise that I really deserve the title of "doctor". I believed that asking for too much support would be a clear sign that I was not worthy of this title. True to the imposter syndrome, first described by Clance and Imes (1978:241), I was scared to be "found out" for my "intellectual phoniness". This syndrome is not uncommon amongst doctoral students who could be considered different from their university counterparts (Gardner & Holley 2011).

As all other postgraduate disabled students in South Africa, I undoubtedly had the right to request support. This right is clearly stipulated within inclusive policies such as White Paper 6 on Inclusive Education (Department of Education 2001), the White Paper on Post-school Education (Department of Higher Education and Training 2013) and the White Paper on the Rights of Persons with Disabilities (South African Government 2015). As I gradually made my way through my doctoral journey, I learned that neither the university nor my supervisor would have thought less of me if I asked for help. Ironically, it was the insight and understanding of my research supervisor that, in many regards, gradually provided me with the confidence to request accommodations.

In the following sections, I will reflect on the specific accommodations I needed to successfully complete my doctoral degree. The gaps in provision and the facilitating factors that aided my journey will be illuminated. I will also show the ways in which my uncertainties and reluctance to request reasonable accommodations permeated various practical parts of my journey.

CHAPTER 8 • THE INCLUSION OF VISUALLY IMPAIRED STUDENTS IN POST-GRADUATE PROGRAMMES

ACCESS TO THE WRITTEN WORD: POVERTY IN THE CURRENCY OF RESEARCH

Access to the written word, even in this electronic age, remains a challenge for visually impaired persons (Watermeyer 2014). In one of his recent articles, Brian Watermeyer (2014) critically dissects the phenomena of the "book famine" and the psychological ramifications thereof. Growing up with a degenerative visual impairment, he experienced the acute pain of losing the ability to feast on any book he wanted to read. He movingly writes, "[t]he words were slipping away, and with them my periscope into the world. Losing the words felt like being left behind, left by myself. … Suddenly I had to survive on a little less each day, and then none at all. … When one's soul has experienced a banquet, it is hard to be thankful for scraps from the kitchen door" (Watermeyer 2014:3).

These words of Watermeyer echo my disappointing experiences with the written word. From a very young age, I was left with no choice but to choose from a small collection of accessible books. My experience of the "book famine" was brought into sharp focus during my doctoral research – books mattered, not just because I loved them, but because I needed them. Obtaining a doctoral degree required intensive and extensive reading (Farrar, Young & Denicolo 2007). I was no longer able to carefully and strategically select course materials to successfully complete assignments as I did during my undergraduate years. For my doctoral studies, I had to ensure that I read as much as possible to cover my field. In this section, I will briefly discuss some challenging encounters with printed and online texts. I will also provide a brief overview of those factors that actually facilitated, and those factors that could have facilitated my access to the written word.

A physical book, the printed pages of a readable text, remains unreadable to me. The promise of secrets within unreadable pages evaporates into nothingness in my hands. Almost nowhere is this awareness more acute than in the labyrinth of a university library. I usually asked friends to accompany me to the library and help me browse through books. All the while I remained fully aware of the time-consuming nature of this exercise, leaving me unable to shake off the guilt I felt towards my helpers. Once again, I fully agree with Watermeyer when he writes, "I remember wandering down a library corridor around the beginning of my first year, with a surreal awareness that I could not extract knowledge from even one of the millions of items that surrounded me. I was supposed to be able to read, and my illegitimacy made me fearful" (Watermeyer 2014:3).

Scanning printed material into an accessible, digital format remains one of the ways in which visually impaired persons can access written text. While there was an excellent scanning service at the university where I studied, textbooks for undergraduate students were their first and most urgent priority. The urgency of undergraduate examinations, coupled with the reality of limited staff, overshadowed my need for access to research material (Ngubane-Mokiwa 2013; Seyama 2009). In the end, I scanned most of my own texts. Of course, this endeavour took up a tremendous amount of precious research and leisure time. I remember that plummeting sensation in my stomach when I realised that a book that took hours to scan was not useful for my research. On the fortunate occasion when I discovered that a text was indeed useful, I had to make sense of badly scanned material.

Online materials were, and still are, more accessible than printed texts. Browsing the university library database was a far more pleasant experience than navigating through the hard copies of books in the physical library. Yet not all online materials are equally accessible. For example, my screenreading software, *Jaws for Windows*, is incompatible with .pdf image files (Mokiwa & Phasha 2012; Ngubane-Mokiwa 2013). When the software unyieldingly announced, "page is empty" I had to print the document and scan it before I was able to read it.

Given all these struggles with the written word, it might seem like finding accessible reading materials will always be an insurmountable hurdle for visually impaired students. While this may be partially true, there are some factors that made this challenge a bit easier. The insight of my research supervisor was one of them. To a large extent, he expertly narrowed down the scope of my reading and pointed me to the most essential texts for my research. And, in those areas where he was unable to assist, he put me in contact with people who were able to help me such as the university librarian. Perhaps he suspected that I found it difficult to ask for help, because he took it upon himself to request support from the university librarian.

Having said this, it was not always possible for my supervisor to fill in the blanks of my silences. My reluctance to ask for appropriate and much-needed support sometimes simply meant that I had to continue without it. After I completed my doctoral research, many disabled students informed me that they requested, and was granted, an assistant to help them with reading-related challenges. I regret never requesting for this reasonable accommodation – someone to help me browse library books, scan reading materials, ask for electronic books from publishers and browse the internet. Simply asking for an assistant would have saved me valuable time.

In short, I found it challenging to comfortably navigate my way through postgraduate research, since I often lacked the currency for it, namely readable texts. The insight of my supervisor often steered me into the right direction and narrowed the scope of my reading, while an assistant would have made my journey a little bit easier.

GETTING THERE: NOTES ON SUPERVISION AND RESEARCH INTERVIEWS

Access to transport is often an inherent requirement of the research process. Data often needs to be collected on various sites and within different towns or cities. And, since a doctoral programme is in most instances not a residential degree, it might also be necessary to drive to the university to attend supervisory meetings. This nature of a doctoral programme might pose some obvious challenges to students with a visual impairment. In South Africa, public transport is far from ideal. While the larger cities have some public transport options, the university where I studied was in the countryside where public transport is mostly unreliable and unsafe (Lourens 2016). I believe that some pre-doctoral planning and the flexibility of my research supervisor circumvented most of my potential transport challenges.

The research design of my study was carefully planned and strategically selected (Farrar 2006). To a large extent, the question, "would I be able to physically reach my target population" guided and filtered my research topic and design. In the end, I decided to collect data from disabled students at the university where I studied. In this regard, transport was not an issue. Unfortunately, I was unable to shape my research entirely around my transport difficulties; I was also required to interview students at a nearby university (approximately 30 kilometres away). Reaching this destination contributed to many sleepless nights. I anxiously called family members, friends and acquaintances to ask for their support. In the end, several people offered to take me to the university and I refunded them from study bursaries. (Fortunately, there are many bursaries available for disabled students. For example, the National Research Foundation offers an extensive bursary for disabled postgraduate students.) Requesting an assistant with a driver's license would have spared me the long and anxiety-provoking search for a driver. In addition, it would have lessened the guilt I felt towards people who volunteered their support.

After I conducted all my research interviews, I thought that my transport challenges were something of the past. It was not. During the write-up phase of my research, I had to move to another town for my husband's work. However, during the same year, my research supervisor took a one-year sabbatical and suggested that we have telephonic supervisory meetings. This eliminated the need for me and my supervisor to travel to the university for meetings.

In summary, potential transport difficulties were largely circumvented through the flexibility of my research supervisor, adequate and careful planning of research design and sufficient study bursaries. Once again, I firmly believe that I was entitled to ask disability support staff to assist me with some of these challenges, for example assigning an assistant to help with transport.

TRAVELLING ABROAD: NOTES ON ACADEMIC CONFERENCES

Presenting research findings at national and international conferences is often a component of postgraduate research (Farrar 2006). With me it was no different. In 2013, halfway through my doctoral research, my research supervisor encouraged me to present at an academic conference in Austria. I had mixed feelings. On the one hand I was grateful and overwhelmingly excited about the prospect of travelling abroad and meeting academics with the same research interests as myself. But I was also nauseatingly worried about the prospect of being alone in a foreign country with a visual impairment my only familiar travelling companion. Who would assist me during the flight? Who would assist me from one flight to the next after a stop-over? Who would take me to the hotel, to the conference venue and to different rooms within the venue? How would I know where to go? As the date of my departure drew closer, these questions feverishly raced through my mind. Thankfully everything went smoothly. I indicated my disability on my flight ticket and the assistance was flawless. On the first day of the conference, I met someone who offered to help me throughout the conference week. In hindsight, hoping for the best is not the ideal way of approaching an upcoming conference.

Now, three years later and with many trial and errors behind me, I finally know how to approach the prospect of an academic conference. Firstly, as I have done on that very first flight to Austria, I indicate my disability on my flight ticket. Secondly, I email the conference organisers and explain the extent of my impairment. I always enquire whether they could provide me with someone who would assist me during the conference. Not once did a conference refuse to provide me with such assistance. Looking back, I think it would have been helpful to enquire to what extent university disability staff members would have been able to assist me. Helpful advice would have spared me many anxiety-provoking conference attendances.

A LAST NOTE ON THE RESEARCH SUPERVISOR

Disabled postgraduate students in the United Kingdom identified their relationship with the research supervisor as the most important vehicle for success (Farrar, Young & Denicolo 2007). I wholeheartedly agree. Throughout this chapter I have continually emphasised the ways in which my research supervisor's insight, flexibility and empathic understanding contributed to the successful completion of my doctoral studies. He narrowed down the scope of my research, insightfully offered support and was flexible enough to allow telephonic supervisory meetings.

Possibly the most important advice I could give to disabled students who want to pursue doctoral research would plainly be to choose the right supervisor. This would entail a predoctoral meeting with the potential research supervisor. Even if supervisors are not familiar with disabilities, a mere willingness to meet, learn and adapt is probably a good indicator that he or she will be a good team member.

CONCLUSION

Embarking on postgraduate research is often a challenging journey for disabled students. While the support needs of disabled students take on a different shape and size during this phase of their studies, their right to reasonable accommodations remains unchanged. The responsibility still rests on universities to facilitate the lifelong learning of disabled students.

I have shown, through reflections on my own research journey, the ways in which I had to adapt to the research process. I had to scan many of my readings, organised transport for data collection and hoped for a pleasant and accessible stay at conference venues. I missed out on many supportive structures, simply because I never asked for it. Having said this, I believe that some formal gesture from disability support staff would have given me a higher sense of entitlement and would have strengthened my voice to ask. While they may maintain an unwavering commitment to support disabled students, the latter might not be aware of this continual support and their right to ask for it. I believe that a small but formal reminder could make a significant difference in the lives of disabled postgraduate students.

ACKNOWLEDGEMENT

I would like to thank my research supervisor, Prof Leslie Swartz, for his unwavering support throughout my doctoral research. Thank you for making this potentially lonely process feel like teamwork.

REFERENCES

Bantjes, J., Swartz, L., Conchar, L., & Derman, W. (2015). "There is soccer but we have to watch": the embodied consequences of rhetorics of inclusion for South African children with cerebral palsy. *Journal of Community and Applied Social Psychology,* 25:474-486. http://dx.doi.org/10.1002/casp.2225

Beauchamp-Pryor, K. (2012). Changes in the political and policy response towards disabled students in the British higher education system: A journey towards inclusion. *Scandinavian Journal of Disability Research,* 14(3):254-269.
http://dx.doi.org/10.1080/15017419.2011.574840

Beauchamp-Pryor, K. (2013). *Disabled students in Welsh higher education: A framework for equality and inclusion.* Rotterdam, The Netherlands: Sense Publishers.
http://dx.doi.org/10.1007/978-94-6209-344-7

Clance, P. R., & Imes, S. A. (1978). The imposter phenomenon in high achieving women: Dynamics and therapeutic intervention. *Psychotherapy: Theory, Research, and Practice,* 15:241-247. http://dx.doi.org/10.1037/h0086006

Department of Education. (2001). *Education White Paper 6 Special Needs Education Building an Inclusive Education and Training System.* Pretoria, South Africa: Department of Education.

Department of Higher Education and Training. (2013). *White paper on post-school education and training.* Available online at http://www.dhet.gov.za/SiteAssets/Latest%20News/White%20paper%20for%20post-school%20education%20and%20training.pdf

Elliot, T., & Wilson, C. (2008). *The perceptions of students with hidden disabilities of their experience during transition to higher education.* East of England Research Project. Available online at http://www.impact-associates.co.uk/hidden_disabilities.html

Farrar, V. (2006). Equal to the task: disability issues in postgraduate research study. In M. Adams & S. Brown (Eds.), *Towards inclusive learning in higher education: Developing curricula for disabled students* (pp. 176-187). London, UK: Routledge.

Farrar, V., Young, R., & Denicolo, P. (2007). *Supervising disabled research students.* London: Society for Research into Higher Education.

Foundation of Tertiary Institutions of the Northern Metropolis (FOTIM) (2011). *Disability in higher education project report.* Available online at http://www.uct.ac.za/usr/disability/reports/progress_report10_11.pdf

Gardner, S.K., & Holley, K.A. (2011). "Those invisible barriers are real": The Progression of First-Generation Students Through Doctoral Education. *Equity and Excellence in Education,* 44(1):77-92. http://dx.doi.org/10.1080/10665684.2011.529791

Goffman, E. (1963). *Stigma: Some notes on the management of spoiled identity.* Harmondsworth, Penguin.

Howell, C. (2005). *Higher Education Monitor. South African Higher Education Responses to Students with Disabilities.Equity of Access and Opportunity?* Monitoring and Evaluation Directorate (CHE). Pretoria, South Africa: Council on Higher Education.

Howell, C. (2006). Disabled students and higher education in South Africa. In B. Watermeyer, L. Swartz, T. Lorenzo, M. Schneider, & M. Priestley (Eds.), *Disability and social change: A South African agenda* (pp. 165-178). Cape Town, South Africa: HSRC Press.

Kranke, D., Jackson, S. E., Taylor, D. A., Anderson-Fye, E., & Floersch, J. (2013). College student disclosure of non-apparent disabilities to receive classroom accommodations. *Journal of Postsecondary Education and Disability,* 26(1):35-51.

Lourens, H., & Swartz, L. (2016a). Experiences of visually impaired students in higher education: bodily perspectives on inclusive education. *Disability and Society,* 31(2):240-251. http://dx.doi.org/10.1080/09687599.2016.1158092

Lourens, H., & Swartz, L. (2016b). 'It's better if someone can see me for who I am': stories of (in)visibility for students with a visual impairment within South African Universities. *Disability and Society,* 31(2):210-222. http://dx.doi.org/10.1080/09687599.2016.1152950

Magnus, E., & Tøssebro, J. (2013). Negotiating individual accommodation in higher education. *Scandinavian Journal of Disability,* 16(4):316-332. http://dx.doi.org/10.1080/15017419.2012.761156

Mokiwa, S. A., & Phasha, T. N. (2012). Using ICT at an open distance learning (ODL) institution in South Africa: The learning experiences of students with visual impairments. *Africa Education Review,* 9(1):136-151. http://dx.doi.org/10.1080/18146627.2012.755286

Ngubane-Mokiwa, S. A. (2013). *Information and communication technology as a learning tool: Experiences of students with blindness.* (Unpublished doctoral dissertation). University of South Africa, Pretoria: South Africa.

Seyama, L. G. (2009). *Information seeking behaviour of students with visual impairments: A case study of the University of KwaZulu-Natal, Pietermaritzburg.* (Master's dissertation). University of KwaZulu-Natal, Pietermaritzburg: South Africa.

South African Government (2015). *White Paper on the Rights of Persons with Disabilities.* Available online at http://www.gov.za/documents/white-paper-rights-persons-disabilities-official-publication-and-gazetting-white-paper

Taylor, M. (2004). Widening participation into higher education for disabled students. *Education and Training,* 46(1):40-48. http://dx.doi.org/10.1108/00400910410518214

The United Nations Education, Scientific and Cultural Organization (UNESCO) (1994). *The Salamanca Statement and Framework for Action on Special Needs Education.* World Conference on Special Needs Education: Access and Equality. Paris: UNESCO.

Watermeyer, B. (2014). Freedom to read: a personal account of the 'book famine'. *African Journal of Disability,* 3(1):1-6. http://dx.doi.org/10.4102/ajod.v3i1.144

BEING A POSTGRADUATE WOMAN: RELATIONSHIPS, RESPONSIBILITIES AND RESILIENCY

Guin Lourens

INTRODUCTION

Female students face particular constraints when pursuing postgraduate degrees. The challenges they may face regarding the timing of their studies in relation to lifeline events such as childbearing years and the constant tension between academic and family responsibilities is a reality across the world. Therefore, women's education is shaped by personal and structural gendered forces, including family, economic and workplace issues. The culmination of such studies I have found to be a career-altering experience, which develops personal resiliency, but tests your reserves for relationships and responsibilities. This chapter discusses the educational pathways of postgraduate female students in higher education, possible barriers and sources of support.

GENDER AND EDUCATION

Gender issues are not unique in the South African context and are located in history and in the heady cultural mix of a country that holds a population rich in ethnic diversity with a wide range of cultures, languages and religious beliefs. The focus at most universities in South Africa prior to 1994 was the struggle against the apartheid regime and racial inequality. The gender inequality struggle, however, gained momentum during this time to set the agenda for women's issues and champion women's liberation. The socalled academic arm of the women's movement took this articulation of a feminist agenda into the universities and created space for debate (Gouws 2012). Gender mainstreaming as part of South Africa's National Gender Policy has given rise to commonplace phrases such as gender equality, women's empowerment and gender transformation. This process should question policy to rectify gender disparities, but success has been hampered by the masculinised organisational cultures and deeply patriarchal institutions in which women's interests are in some cases met with hostility (Gouws 2010).

Education for women is regarded as fundamental to the empowerment of women and to achieve gender equality. The South African government has produced a number of policies and equality legislation in pursuit of women's empowerment. For instance, the Constitution includes Section 9 which promotes equality for all persons and freedom from discrimination and the Employment Equity Act, No 55 (1998), which strives to achieve equity in the workplace by promoting fair treatment in employment. The African Union (AU) declared 2015 as the Year of Women Empowerment and Development. The declaration is a display of AU's renewed political commitment and support for the women's empowerment and the gender equality agenda. So while other parts of the world may have moved on from focussing on the disadvantages and difficulties of women pursuing post-basic degree programmes (Acker 2014), the advocacy for the female agenda still rages on in Africa.

Statistics South Africa (2010) reveals a social profile in the country of fractured families, rising numbers of children orphaned by HIV and AIDS in child-headed households or being raised by female relatives, and single motherhood as a widespread norm. Gender-based violence, sexual harassment and assault, as well as the objectification of women are still commonplace, as reported in the status of women and girls in SA report (ONE 2015). Most racial and ethnic groups in South Africa, historically segregated, have distinct cultural long-standing beliefs concerning gender roles. Some are based on the premise that women are less important or deserving of power than men and that women's contributions to society should be sanctioned by men. This includes some traditional Afrikaner and African social organisations which are male-centred and dominated. Urban and rural cultures continue to differ, but a generational shift in cultural expression towards a more interracial, multi-ethnic, enlightened, inclusive and cosmopolitan slant is slowly weaving a new South African social tapestry (StatsSA 2016).

Gender has shaping effects in the South African societal context and to a large extent many of us simply live the subtle subordination of women. A continued gendered domestic division of labour and obligations leaves women students remaining responsible, as it was in my case, for most of the routine physical and emotional care for children (Leonard, Becker & Coate 2010). Housework includes caring for men as husbands or partners, housekeeping, shopping, preparing meals and laundry, and cleaning up. Motherhood is a combination of seeing to children's nutritional, hygiene, health, environmental, as well as social needs and relevant educative activities. Acker (1994), a seminal author on gendered education, found that married female students – especially those with children – face impossible demands on their time and energy, with which I would concur. They also experience the expectation that the husband/male partner's career will have priority in case of conflict. Family work for female students is not only confined to housework and childcare. It also includes care for the elderly, disabled, fostered or orphaned children, working on maintenance of kinship ties and spending quality time with partners and significant others. Other constraints encountered by female students as found in literature include domestic problems, concerns about suitable childcare, less freedom to travel than men, a lack of fair access for women to and unresponsiveness of academic institutions (Evetts 2014), exorbitant study fee costs against a backdrop of limited financial stability and no forthcoming financial aid or suitable accommodation near campus, resulting in gruelling commutes (Murray 2014). Authors such as Acker (2014) ask if higher education is fair to women in finding a path towards their academic aspirations.

In the World Economic Forum's Global Gender Gap Report (2013), South Africa ranks well in terms of women's political empowerment, economic participation and opportunity, yet the status of women in the country remains complicated. The higher education levels and qualifications, the more likely a woman is to be employed while studying. Work-life articulation therefore requires more attention. Career success and studies are affected as even full-time employed women usually retain the major responsibility for caring and domestic work (Crompton & Lyonette 2011).

Nevertheless, women as a group is a collection of individuals making choices about taking options, seizing chances and seeking opportunities. Access to better quality secondary education and tertiary education opportunities for previously marginalised women in South Africa has increased (ONE 2015). This has been partly enabled, I believe, by dedicated academic bursaries for women, something I have been involved in and benefitted from myself. It is encouraging to note a 42% to 58% female versus male postgraduate trend in South Africa (Cloete, Mouton & Sheppard 2015), with a significant annual growth in female students.

Female postgraduate students are by no means a homogenous group. When this group is viewed through a South African lens, we see a kaleidoscope of variety in terms of age, background, urban or rural origin, economic, work and family responsibilities. However, a discourse on gender equity and activism in higher education academic communities would benefit a broad base of women in this country. There is a difference in having substantive and procedural equality in the gendered nature of citizenship, and living it. The way in which rights and gender are constructed in discourse and implemented in reality, makes the difference in the complexities of women's lives (Gouws 2005). I have written this chapter from my own narrative perspective as a part-time postgraduate student, working full-time with demanding work and family responsibilities, while remaining cognisant of the multi-layered gendered perspectives that may require individual exploration.

DEVELOPING RESILIENCE

According to Dole (2014) resilience, which is conceptualised as a group of traits enabling individuals to withstand and to recover quickly from adversity, differs from academic resilience. Academic resilience is defined as "the process and results that are part of the life story of an individual who has been academically successful, despite obstacles that prevent the majority of others with the same background from succeeding" (p. 144). Your postgraduate journey as a female student will require a fluid process of acquiring resilient qualities which strengthen over time[1].

Women's career aspirations are often influenced by the fact that they are female. Gender-specific notions of pursuing an education are socio-culturally and psychologically deeply rooted in traditional values and traditions. The paths for simultaneous career and professional development for a woman may seem unclear and to combine the two, exceptional intrinsic motivation and determination to overcome obstacles is needed (Bhalulesesa 2010). Dole (2014) identifies protective factors that contribute to resiliency in order to overcome the barriers women encounter on their paths to academic success. The factors include strong personal characteristics, such as perseverance and positive relationships in the family and community. These serve as sources of support to ameliorate the effects of difficulties.

In my predominantly female profession in South Africa, only around one percent of professionals obtain a doctorate opposed to 23,54% of academics holding PhDs (Van Rooyen, Ricks & Morton 2012). These are the type of statistics which, for me, can cultivate a steely determination to beat the odds and foster goal directedness. As in the poem, *The Road Not Taken* by Robert Frost, which is often read at graduations, I can relate to the doubt and apprehension of taking the route of postgraduate studies less travelled by my female colleagues. It has, however, made all the difference in career self-actualisation. I would regard a strong sense of self-belief as a vital ingredient to success.

---

1 Also see Chapter 5 where Bella Vilakazi writes about the lived experience of developing resilience.

THE ROLE OF FAMILY AND FRIENDS

The postgraduate student does not study in isolation. Family and friends have to put up with a lot while you are working on your research. Even when not working late or over weekends one may often be pre-occupied with your study in time that they may view as belonging to them. As Cryer (2006) suggests, it is useful to tell family and friends what to expect from the outset, negotiate ways of meeting their needs as well as yours, and get their support (Cryer 2006). Family support appears to be one of the most important factors in succeeding as a student (Dole 2014), and it is therefore essential to get family and significant others on board.

Family responsibilities are often seen as an inseparable commitment around which a career must be built. The need to fulfil typical caretaking roles can be a distraction for self-actualisation in postgraduate studies. When families and academic communities both value the dual roles that having a family and an academic pursuit entail, women are better able to balance their roles and cope with the stress of postgraduate studies (Bhalalusesa 2010). I would consider work and family demands realistically when setting deadlines for completing a degree.

Role conflict or the simultaneous, incompatible demands of family and being a student can lead to role overload (Rowlands 2010). Achieving a balance between social roles, relationships and responsibilities and the interface between that and academic expectations of the postgraduate student often require some support with domestic and childcare duties. Women in families are more likely to be called upon and expected to help with extended family crises involving siblings or the care of aging parents. These types of commitments, although they inevitably caught me off guard, need to be factored into study plans.[2]

I concluded my doctoral studies while working full-time as a manager in the health sector and doing part-time postgraduate lecturing at a distant university. In addition, I had a husband and two school-going children. I would not have been able to complete my studies without the support and encouragement of my close female friends. If you have young children, you can ask your network of friends who stay at home to help you with transporting children and play-dates when you need to focus on your studies. I will always be indebted to these selfless friends. Mobilising grandparents to assist with childcare is helpful, but not always geographically possible. Planning for more than one child to go on play-dates with friends at the

---

[2] See also Chapter 12 by Langutani Masehela that is focussed on the notion of Ubuntu, as well as Soryaya Abdulatief's chapter on dealing with first-generation challenges.

same time can also give you pockets of uninterrupted time, though you would need to reciprocate these favours.

As a working mother with multiple commitments, you may not always be at liberty to put your studies first. Sometimes you may need to first focus on your work and family commitments and then work on your studies at night when your family is asleep, or get up early if you are a morning person. Similarly, the best use of time must be made when family members are not at home over weekends. Prioritising, sharing responsibilities with a partner, procuring all the labour-saving devices you can afford (Hart 1997), as well as hiring domestic assistance may help you achieve your academic goals. Having a system to organise the family diary and an effective household filing system can help reduce chaos. Organising menus, buying in bulk and preparing meals in advance can be useful. Reducing domestic clutter goes a long way to enable an environment conducive to study completion. Having administrative support at home can also help you make progress. Outsourced administrative support services are available to create order in your research filing system or study space. Assistance is also available for transcription, statistical analysis, as well as proofreading and formatting of your thesis according to the university guidelines. Seeking out and engaging with such support services, as I did, may be invaluable in surviving and succeeding your postgraduate studies.

THE INFLUENCE OF EMOTIONAL PRESSURES ON FEMALE POSTGRADUATE STUDENTS

Complex emotions associated with balancing family and scholarly commitments and having to choose between "head" and "heart" are experienced. Family relationships can be both places of solace and generators of stress in terms of lost time and opportunities. Conflicted feelings can emerge over the impact of studies on the family and feelings of guilt over prioritising your own needs over children, partners and extended family or friends. These emotional pressures can be overwhelming and erode at one's confidence, resilience and productivity. Sustained tensions between the two key emotional flashpoints of study and family relationships may have a debilitating impact on your studies (Aitchison & Mowbray 2013).

The research process itself comes with patterns of emotions and while each stage of the research process is inclined to start in a positive way, inevitably obstacles arise. Each stage from planning, to data collection, to analysis, to reporting and even publication has its own set of difficulties, sending one on a tumultuous emotional passage. The researcher experiences a changing emotional state over time, something I have experienced myself. As an emotive woman, I can personally relate to the dejection of having periods of writing block, getting corrections and rejections, and struggling with delays. Persistence and problem solving are tested to the utmost.

Sometimes, you may experience bouts of energy, but these should be treated with care. Harnessing the energy can be productive, while on the other hand, it can fire an emotional war of scorching proportions and lead to burnout. I found that these short bursts of energy gave momentum in writing my thesis, but had to be countered by making room for rest and limiting sleep deprivation. It is understandable to me that the ways women knowledge workers cope usually involve working harder and sleeping less, but it must be questioned to what extent this can be considered empowering (Acker & Armenti 2004).

Connecting with my personal energisers such as poetry and music helped drive creativity in the writing process. Amidst the domestic clatter, consciously creating personal spaces for sanctuary, rest and relaxation in my home allowed for some revitalisation. Other approaches to deal with the tension of postgraduate study include yoga, relaxation exercises, taking time out, meditation, prayer and writing a daily gratitude journal. Journaling can be useful to ventilate your feelings and thoughts (Ban Breathnach 2005) or mind-map your concepts. The idea of morning pages, which is free writing of a couple of pages about whatever comes to mind first thing in the morning, can stimulate creativity (Cameron 1995). Flores (2015) suggests seeking out sources of inspiration and feedback, saying no to distracting activities, not neglecting your physical health, budgeting some money for time away from your studies, fighting perfectionism and having a supportive friend or family member as ways of counteracting emotional pressures. Join supportive networks with other students[3].

WORK ARRANGEMENTS

Despite the changing demographics of the South African workforce which includes more women, driven by the economical need and employment equity legislation, flexible work options are not common. The South African workplace is still largely inflexible for the working female student. The Labour Relations Act (Act 66 of 1995) does not single out flexible workers, but includes all employees that work more than 24 hours per month. There is, however, a swell rising in the country towards working from home, flexible hours with more productive time and less time spent in traffic. Change is very slow and most women still have to comply with rigid office hours, full responsibilities and commuting while doing postgraduate studies. The Centre

---

3   See chapters 16 and 17 in this book for discussions on the benefits of such interactions.

for Economics and Business Research, Citrix and Productivity SA concur that flexible working hours would be beneficial to productivity, the economy, for employees who are parents and reduce the risk of burnout (Leshoro 2015). Flexibility to adjust work time or workplace when your study needs are in conflict with your work schedule would allow female post graduate students to function better.

Flexible work arrangements are ideal while conducting postgraduate studies. Working and studying while managing a home life is challenging and tiring, but can also be interesting and rewarding. Seen in a positive light, the studies do add to the mental stimulation a job offers, personal development and furthering your career in numerous ways. A workplace which provides research opportunities for women, and especially one which allocates dedicated protected time for postgraduate research (White 2004), is conducive to successful studies. It is not always possible to get study leave or a sabbatical. It might be viable to sacrifice some of your annual leave, as I did, to get ahead with research activities and writing. If you are serious about completing your studies, this kind of sacrifice is well worth it.

BUILDING A SOCIAL SUPPORT SYSTEM

Isolation is identified as one of the key factors associated with non-completion of postgraduate studies (Mouton 2009). Concluding a thesis is often an independent and lonely journey. White (2004) cites isolation, lack of confidence, minimal mentoring, limited informal networking, inflexible and unsupportive university environments, as well as negative attitudes towards women pursuing postgraduate studies as reasons for not completing research degrees. As a woman you may grapple with a lack of understanding amongst family and friends for your drive to attain a postgraduate degree and this may compound the feeling of the loneliness.

Loneliness can, however, be cultivated to allow your thoughts to grow. It was often in these lonely spaces where I found the time to reflect on my doctoral work, interrogate my aims to reach increased insight, and develop the intervention strategy of my study. Graduate support groups, friends and partners can be sources of impetus to counter personal and academic pressures that may cause stress and anxiety. Linking up with like-minded women on the same journey has the potential to propel you forward. Correspondence with female authors in the field of your study can also be inspiring. Emulating leading female academics and finding female mentors can help you to transition the thresholds of postgraduate study completion. I belong to a local business network which meets weekly and I drew a great deal of inspiration from the other professional women in the network who are successfully combining career and family.

Social networks can be instrumental for women in providing emotional and informational assistance while studying. Actively seeking strong social network ties or postgraduate study support groups can impact on meeting your psychosocial needs and developing resilience. This can take different forms, depending on personal preference, and can include physically meeting on a regular basis, an email discussion or online group, or even a mobile phone based group.

Social and academic integration can help to ensure academic postgraduate success (Koen 2007). This integration can be achieved by means of joining quality academic support groups for connected learning and developing strong student to student relationships. I joined a PhD support group late in my doctoral studies but even then it gave me that final push to reach the finishing line. It was beneficial to network with other female health professionals and take some courage away from each session. Joining such a group will allow you to benefit from the shared experiences, lessons learned, process guidance and the collegiality which these groups offer. It fuelled my ambition and drive to finish[4].

INSTITUTIONAL SERVICES AND SUPPORT

Generic support provided by higher education institutions may not be suited to the specific support needs of the postgraduate woman, especially those whom study part-time and/or at a distance. Institutional administrative support can also make a difference in your success. Universities that offer flexible options for even mundane aspects such as parking disc collection, or registration options and accurate information on fees, bursaries and thesis requirements are much easier to navigate. For a working postgraduate student, flexibility in the format or structure of the course is key due to potential time constraints during office hours.

Seek out a higher education environment which includes tailored support, collegiality with other postgraduate women and an acknowledgement of stresses linked to gender. Acknowledgement of the duality of demands most women face in the journey towards achieving doctoral level studies could be insightful in navigating the pursuit of postgraduate study through enhanced access to appropriate educational provisions and services (Grenier & Burke 2008). Most universities offer free counselling services to students. A sounding board may be required if you grapple with issues of being a professional career woman, wife, caretaker, mother, daughter, sister and student with an academic identity. With progress towards completion of postgraduate qualifications comes consideration of career path changes. I view

---

4   Also see Part 5 of this book that explores postgraduate study as a social practice.

student counselling and support services positively, as they hold the possibility of access to advanced career coaching.

Obers (2014) describes mentoring as a supportive, nurturing process of providing psycho-social support and coaching to facilitate growth. Mentoring programmes can address social connectedness. It is, however, not always optimally utilised in higher education as a transformation strategy for building women's self-esteem in academic environments and developing a professional network structure of women academics.

Choosing a university and supervisor wisely can have a determining impact on your ultimate success. Support and facilities should be of such a calibre that you would want to invest your money and your valuable time there. The peer support and academic development culture is something to scrutinise. The needs of women for a social learning environment, comfortable postgraduate learning spaces, and support in the development of academic research and writing skills should influence choice of institution (Whisker 2008).

A healthy supervisor-student relationship is characterised by mutual respect (McMillan 2002), dignity, courtesy and honesty (Cryer 2006). Boundaries in terms of privacy and personal space may need to be set in terms of accessibility to each other. In negotiating deadlines, disclosure upfront about your responsibilities at home and work can be done without burdening your supervisor with all the personal challenges you face while juggling to learn. Discuss demands on both parties' time and how you feel about after hours' contact. Well-defined boundaries help both student and supervisor to be clear about where they stand and encourage clarity and progress. I found getting into a rhythm of monthly meetings with my supervisor conducive to momentum. We opted for no after hours' contact, but I did most of the academic work at night, and sent electronic correspondence or made telephonic contact during office hours.

Among the interventions that may assist more women to enrol and successfully complete higher degrees, White (2004) lists excellent information, financial support, flexibility in study mode to include full-time to part-time transition, active encouragement from lecturers, mentoring schemes and a research culture to facilitate postgraduate networking and student support groups. Policy innovations should move from a homogenous approach. Innovation should stem from acknowledging that women are increasingly "time poor" and helping them cope with this by new modes of working and considering what to do to enable women to study. A postgraduate study journey gains emotional, intellectual and vocational ground for female students but requires careful consideration in terms of the institutional approach (Leonard, Becker, & Coate 2010).

TIME MANAGEMENT

Writing up a study from the proposal phase through to the individual chapters and finally the completed thesis requires substantial blocks of time – time for preparation, reflection, searching for relevant information, reading, writing, data gathering and analysis, and meetings with your supervisor. I find the theory of time management fascinating and useful but often obliterated by reality. It is often more realistic to use short bits of available time daily than trying to find several hours at once.

Time management in postgraduate studies is marked by being realistic about what is involved and about the volume of work, as well as what is humanly possible within your multiple responsibilities, and planning for some periods of rest and recreation. Life events may force you to modify your plan, and through this process, I had to learn the lessons of flexibility, acceptance and self-kindness. Talking to other postgraduate students with similar family, work and/or study responsibilities in terms of how they structure their time may help set realistic goals for completion with clear, concrete outcomes. Dividing up tasks and activities, using a to-do list for each section or applying time management software can be helpful approaches. It is rewarding to keep track of your academic progress and there are some electronic software applications geared towards this end.

CONCLUSION

Unfortunately, there is a dearth of literature on the experiences of female postgraduate students in the South African context. The value of this chapter lies in its contribution to the emerging debate in this field in South Africa and the implications for our society and academic institutions. The need for all stakeholders to play an active role in detailed planning for facilitation of female postgraduate teaching and learning to promote academic success is apparent.

The dual worlds of research writing and juggling job and family demands are often challenging for female postgraduate students. The need to be self-directed in learning and passionate about your topic to find the courage to continue and sustain academic impetus is evident. Intrinsic motivation, as well as developing self-confidence as a student, and tenacity in commitment to your studies can contribute to your eventual success.

When you finally come to the end of a postgraduate study, you may vacillate between elation and a sense of anti-climax. As you re-shift your focus from your thesis, take a moment to reflect. There is a host of transferable skills you have learned in terms of problem solving, project mapping and management, planning, balancing priorities, time management, communicating and presenting. Find creative ways of sharing your life lessons and approaches with other women who are headed on this road. Encourage other women with academic ambitions – it is now your time to be a role model and mentor.

REFERENCES

Acker, S. (2014). A foot in the revolving door? Women academics in lower middle management. *Higher Education Research and Development,* 33(1):73-85. http://dx.doi.org/10.1080/07294360.2013.864615

Acker, S. (1994). *Gendered education.* Buckingham, UK: Open University Press.

Acker, S., & Piper, D. (1987). *Is higher education fair to women?* Surrey, UK: Society for Research in Higher Education.

Acker, S., & Armenti, C. (2004). Sleepless in Academia. *Gender and Education,* 16(1):3-24. http://dx.doi.org/10.1080/0954025032000170309

Aitchison, C., & Mowbray, S. (2013). Doctoral women: Managing emotions, managing doctoral studies. *Teaching in Higher Education,* 18(8):859-870. http://dx.doi.org/10.1080/13562517.2013.827642

Ban Breathnach, S. (2005). *Simple abundance.* New York, USA: Bantam Books.

Bhalulesesa, E. (2010). Women's career and professional development: Experiences and challenges. *Gender and Education,* 10(1):21-33. http://dx.doi.org/10.1080/09540259821078

Cameron, J. (1995). *The artist's way: A course in discovering and recovering your creative self.* London, UK: Pan Books.

Cloete, N., Mouton, J., & Sheppard, C. 2015. *Doctoral Education in South Africa: Policy, Discourse and Data.* Cape Town, South Africa: African Minds.

Crompton, R., & Lyonette, C. (2011). Women's career success and work-life adaptions in the accounting and medical professions in Britain. *Gender, Work and Organization,* 18(2):231-254. http://dx.doi.org/10.1111/j.1468-0432.2009.00511.x

Cryer, P. (2006). *The researcher student's guide to success* (3rd ed.). New York, USA: Open University Press.

Dole, S. (2014). Voices of resilience: Successful Jamaican women educators. *Journal of Ethnographic and Qualitative Research,* 8:144-156.

Evetts, J. (2014). *Women and Career; Themes and issues in advanced industrial societies.* New York, USA: Routledge.

Flores, L.A. (2015). Dissertation finish line. Available online at

https://www.insidehighered.com/advice/2015/04/10/easy-bow-reach-phd-dissertation-finish-line?hootPostID=eaa9d82861aa00a151c9cf0ec8fbddddd

Gouws, A. (2005). *(Un)thinking citizenship. Feminist debates in contemporary South Africa.* Aldershot, UK: Ashgate.

Gouws, A. (2010). Feminism in South Africa today: Have we lost the praxis? *Agenda,* 24(83):13-23.

Gouws, A. (2012). Reflections on being a feminist academic/academic feminism in South Africa. *Equality, Diversity and Inclusion: An International Journal,* 31(5/6)"526-541.

Grenier, R., & Burke, M.C. (2008). No margin for error: A study of two women balancing motherhood and PhD studies. *The Qualitative Report,* 13(4):581-604.

Hart, M. (1997). *Mothers at work.* London, UK: Michael 'O Mara Books.

Koen, C. (2007). *Postgraduate student retention and success: A South African case study.* Cape Town, South Africa: HSRC Press.

Leonard, D., Becker, R., & Coate, K. (2010). Continuing professional and career development: The doctoral experience of education alumni at a UK university. *Studies in Continuing Education,* 26(3):369-385. http://dx.doi.org/10.1080/0158037042000265953

Leshoro, D. (2015). *Most South Africans would love flexible working hours.* SABC News. 27 August.

McMillan, W. (2002). *The postgraduate student's survival guide.* Bellville, South Africa: University of the Western Cape.

Mabokela, R.O. (Ed.) (2007). *Soaring beyond boundaries: Women breaking educational barriers in traditional societies.* Rotterdam, Netherlands: Sense Publishers.

Murray, M. (2014). Factors affecting student dropout rates at the University of KwaZulu-Natal. *South African Journal of Science,* 110(11/12):1-6. http://dx.doi.org/10.1590/sajs.2014/20140008

Mouton, J. (2009). *How to succeed in your Master's & doctoral studies: A South African guide and resource book.* Pretoria, South Africa: Van Schaik.

Obers, N. (2014). Career success for women academics in higher education: Choices and challenges. *South African Journal of Higher Education,* 28(3):1107-1122.

ONE. (2015). *Status of women and girls in SA.* Available online at https://s3.amazonaws.com/one.org/pdfs/Status-of-women-and-girls-in-South-Africa-2015.pdf

Rowlands, S. (2010). *Non-traditional students: The impact of role strain on their identity.* (Unpublished Master's dissertation). Department of Workforce Education and Development in the Graduate School, Southern Illinois University, Carbondale, IL, USA.

Statistics South Africa. (2010). *Social profile of South Africa.* Pretoria, South Africa. Available online at www.statssa.gov.za

Statistics South Africa. (2016). *Mapping diversity:an exploration of our social tapestry.* Pretoria, South Africa. Available online at www.statssa.gov.za

Van Rooyen, D., Ricks, E., & Morton, D. (2014). Status of research related activities of South Africa's University Nursing schools. *Trends in Nursing,* 1(1):29. http://dx.doi.org/10.14804/1-1-29 http://dx.doi.org/10.14804/1-1-30

White, K. (2004). The leaking pipeline: Women postgraduate and early career researchers in Australia. *Tertiary Education and Management,* 10:227-241. http://dx.doi.org/10.1080/13583883.2004.9967129

Wisker, G. (2008). *The postgraduate research handbook.* New York, USA: Palgrave MacMillan.

World Economic Forum. (2013). *The Global Gender Gap Report* 3:12-13.

10 BEING MY OWN COACH: ACHIEVING BALANCE IN THE FOUR DOMAINS OF LIFE

Delia Layton

INTRODUCTION

Postgraduate study is so much more than just a cognitive journey. There are other equally important aspects of our lives. To succeed and, more importantly, survive your postgraduate study, you also need to have a reasonable quality of life throughout the journey. As human beings we are in relationship with and to the world. We have a relationship with our own inner world of thoughts, feelings and ideas, we have a relationship to our own bodies, we have relationships with other people, and with the world we live in. While cognitive competence is certainly important, from my experience, postgraduate study can be greatly supported by having a certain level of competency in all these other key areas of life and relationships as well.

Since completing my doctorate I have come across many people, who were (or still are) struggling to complete their doctorates after many years, and who expressed curiosity as to how I was able to complete my doctorate in three years while working full-time. At the time, I did not really reflect on this achievement and put it down to my hard work and application. It was only later that I realised that I had developed what Murphy (2013:24) called "strategies to survive and maintain wellness" while doing my PhD. Murphy (2013) highlights the importance of finding ways to enjoy the doctoral journey by achieving balance in one's life. The "kisses between paragraphs" she made sure happened with her husband, were described by her as "one small step in a much larger and calculated strategy to surviving a PhD, maintaining wellness and completing it" (2013:25). Her advice to those on the PhD journey – to avoid negativity and to surround oneself with positivity – reflects a holistic approach to well-being, which is essential if you are to survive and succeed in postgraduate study.

Finding an integrated way to develop well-being in all aspects of one's life is one of the aims of self-coaching — a self-directed activity in which an individual seeks to gain success in thoughts, actions and outcomes in life. Luciani (2005), a clinical psychologist and author of *The Power of Self-coaching*, developed three basic "self-coaching truths":

- You must challenge the myth that anyone else can "rescue" you. Professional help can have huge value (and is essential for many struggling with severe depression), but you have to do the work.
- You must accept responsibility for personal change.
- You must be convinced that you really have a choice.

With the understanding that self-coaching involves much self-reflection to develop a deeper understanding of ourselves in terms of how we are in life, I have found the Four Human Domains model, used in the practice of Integral Coaching®, to be a useful way to ensure balance and wellness in life while undertaking postgraduate study. This model was developed by James Flaherty (2016, forthcoming), drawing on the work of the German philosopher, Habermas. It is used in integral coaching to assess what is happening in a person's life by mapping out and examining closely the different areas or domains in which life is being experienced.

The principal idea contained in this model of human experience is that it is important to live an integrated and balanced life that gives equal attention to all of the different domains that constitute our lives as human beings. I was introduced to this model after I had already completed my doctorate, so it was in retrospect, by applying my experiences to the four human domains, that I have come to realise that I was largely supported in all of these different areas of my life, and that this contributed greatly to my ability to survive and achieve success in my postgraduate study, as well as in "maintaining wellness" (Murphy 2013:26).

There has been much research conducted on the implications of work-life balance in the lives of graduate students. For example, Stimpson and Filer (2011:69) concluded that achieving balance with regard to one's family, work, studies and personal life was especially challenging for women[1]. While a study by Martinez, Ordu, Della Sala, and McFarlane (2013) on how doctoral students strived to achieve school-life-balance found that the predominant need that all participants expressed was for well-being, which included "maintaining their health, managing stress, and creating personal time" (Martinez *et al* 2013:54), and that these doctoral students (of both

---

1 Also see the previous chapter by Guin Lourens that focusses on surviving and succeeding your postgraduate studies as a woman.

genders) were able to achieve this to a large extent by managing their time, roles and responsibilities, managing their stress levels, as well as their physical and mental health, seeking financial and emotional support from various sources both in their institutions and privately, and by making "trade-offs" with regard to time spent with family and time for themselves (Martinez et al 2013 p. 44). Furthermore, Harrison (2012:279), whose doctoral study focussed on the development of doctoral identity, argues that the common feature of a successful doctoral journey seems to be "the position of taking the time for oneself, of having the doctoral space as an escape rather than its being an additional burden in a busy life (and) refusing to feel guilty about taking time for ourselves".

This chapter will discuss these various aspects of human experience with regard to postgraduate study. I will discuss each of the four human domains in turn, providing specific questions that you can ask yourself as a form of self-coaching. The answers to these questions will be different for every person, but they can demonstrate ways in which different life experiences fall into these different domains. In reflecting on the answers to these questions there may be greater levels of support in one domain than in another, and different people may have more interest in or devote more energy to certain areas, giving less attention to or completely ignoring other areas. Awareness of what is happening in the different life domains may enable the identification of where changes may need to be made, such as giving more attention to certain neglected areas or making some adjustments within a particular domain. From my own experience, I believe that gaining this kind of self-awareness can greatly help your ability to survive and succeed in your postgraduate study. It may help, as it did for me, to shift your perspective to adopt a more positive outlook. As Harrison (2012:279) writes, "the most effective position to take is that learning is fun, and that one's own thinking is interesting".

THE FOUR HUMAN DOMAINS

According to Flaherty's (2016, forthcoming) model, all events happen in and impact on four domains of life: the "Inner I" (inside me), the "Outer I" (body and behaviour), the "We" (group membership) and the "It" (the environment). The "Inner I" domain deals with our thoughts, beliefs, emotions, intentions and feelings. The "Outer I" domain focusses on our body and behaviour. The "We" domain has to do with our social context such as the language(s) we speak, the culturally specific practices we engage in, the relationships we are part of, and the history of the groups to which we belong. The "It" domain describes our relationship with the physical environment (including both the natural and the technological). While in life these domains are naturally interlinked and overlapping, to become competent in all of them, it is useful to separate them for analytical purposes. This analysis facilitates an awareness of what may be enabling or constraining our ability to succeed. I have found that by asking yourself questions relevant to each domain, it is possible to get a fairly accurate picture of what your world of postgraduate study looks like. For me, this kind of self-questioning and self-reflection has been really helpful in locating how I was positioning myself with regard to my doctoral journey. It has indeed been suggested that this kind of self-reflective activity can enable one "to be reflexively oriented towards improvement, personal or social, through a more realistic and nuanced understanding of a phenomenon" (Harrison 2012:4). The phenomenon here being the development of one's doctoral identity.

THE "INNER I"

This domain relates to your individual inner experience and consciousness. It is not observable by others and has to do with your private inner world. Questions you can ask yourself here are:

- What are my thoughts and ambitions about my study?
- What assumptions am I making about my study and myself?
- What are my feelings and current emotions about my study?
- What is my predominant mood with respect to my study?
- What are my wishes and dreams about my study?
- What do I picture when I think about my study and the outcome of it?

Feelings tend to be tied in with emotions that may be triggered in the moment by some specific thing and may be quite fleeting. Moods, however, are emotions that may have accumulated and tend to remain more consistent over a period of time. Moods often determine the way we engage in our everyday lives and the actions we take (or do not take). So you may need to explore what your over-arching mood is around your study. For example, are you overwhelmed or anxious about your ability to succeed? In other words, what are you telling yourself about your study, and what are you paying attention to? As Foot *et al* (2014:113) argue, "doctoral students need to investigate their ways of being in the world and how this influences their daily practice". This study found that there was great benefit in self-reflection as a way to address self-doubt and fear of failure, which the findings highlighted as common themes related to a sense of "self-inefficacy" (Foot *et al* 2014:111-112). For me, even though I was able to complete my study in a relatively short time, I also had the occasional voice of doubt and even sometimes asked myself why I was doing a doctorate. It was therefore useful for me to become aware of this voice, because the more I was able to tune into it, the more I could consciously engage with it rather than just letting it negatively impact the quality of my thoughts and ability to take action.

THE "OUTER I"

The notion of the "Outer I" relates to your body and outer observable behaviour. This domain asks you to assess how doing your postgraduate study is affecting your body, behaviour and well-being. Questions to ask yourself are:

- What is my relationship to my body generally, and how aware of it am I in my day to day life?
- Where do I hold tension in my body?
- Which part of my body do I tend to react from?
- How is my study impacting my body?
- What physical sensations do I experience when I am busy working on my study?
- How is my posture and breathing when I am working?
- What is my daily study routine?
- How am I taking care of my body?
- What physical activity am I doing?

In this domain, you would think about your awareness of and your relationship to your body generally. Your study may be impacting your body in various ways, such as affecting your sleeping and eating patterns, for instance. You may be holding tension in certain places in your body because of the way you sit at your desk or the length of time you spend at your desk. You may need to pay attention to this domain because it is easy to forget that you have a body as well as a brain, and you can become quite trapped in the cognitive space while working hard on the concepts and complexities related to your study.

During my doctorate I realised the importance of finding a balance in life and engaging in some form of physical activity – even just stretching or taking a walk. A change of scenery and pace would often give me the energy boost that was needed to release a feeling of being "stuck" and at the same time give a feeling of "re-charging my batteries". Getting enough sleep and exercise should help with your ability to think and be creative. A lack of sleep not only impacts on your productivity, but also negatively affects your mood and emotions. When I was tired or feeling physically or emotionally stressed, it was easy to start feeling irritated or overwhelmed. However,

I found it was really worthwhile addressing the tensions I was holding in my body by making frequent visits to the physiotherapist, massage therapist and chiropractor. In addition, my daily practice of meditation, while often "thought-filled", brought much-needed time for me to be still.

THE "WE"

This is the domain that comes into play with regard to your membership to groups or your relationships with others and the community. Your background and upbringing, history, culture, religious affiliations, social and familial relationships, as well as relationships with colleagues at work all have an influence on you and your postgraduate journey[2]. Questions you could ask yourself with regard to this domain are:

- What language do I most typically use when I talk about my study?
- What sorts of conversations do I have around my study?
- How is my upbringing and cultural history impacting my study and how I see myself?
- How does my role and obligations as a parent, family member, member of a community, or religious group impact on my study?
- Who is supporting me with my study?
- What requests do I make of others?
- How is my study impacting my relationships and my ability to be present to others?
- How am I taking care of my relationships while focussing on my study?
- Which relationships are supportive of me and my study?
- Which relationships are unsupportive of me and my study?

The kind of language you use and how you generally speak about your study can often bring into clear focus the way you view yourself in relation to the study itself. For example, if you find yourself often saying in conversation, "this study of mine is such a pain" or "I'm sick of my study" or words to that effect, it might be that you are really doubting your ability to succeed or you are finding the study is taking up too much of your time and affecting your relationships. Issues from this domain can link directly with your inner world in domain one (the "Inner I"). In my study, for

---

2 Various chapters in this book highlight the importance of postgraduate study as taking place within a larger social realm. See, for example, the chapters by Shakira Choonara (Chapter 4), Soraya Abdulatief (Chapter 6), Andre van der Bijl (Chapter 7) and Guin Lourens (Chapter 9).

instance, I recall using a fair amount of negative language about a particular theorist whose writing style I was initially finding to be rather impenetrable. This impacted negatively on my engagement with the theory and my ability to gain the necessary conceptual understanding of the work. It was only after I became conscious about how negatively I was speaking about this issue that I was able to take a different approach and eventually find a way around the initial blockage.

Perhaps you find that in your culture or family, postgraduate study is not valued much or perhaps is seen to be taking too much of a priority in your life at the expense of your other social roles such as being a parent, family member, or member of a particular community. Alternatively, your success or failure with regard to your postgraduate degree may be putting you under strain because it means so much to your family. It may be worth looking at the level of support you are getting from others with whom you have a relationship. This could include members of your family, your friends, your supervisor or even work colleagues. Do you feel, for instance, that others are giving you the kind of support or the space you need, or do you feel your study is having a negative impact on your ability to be present and available to them? What requests are you making of others? What requests are others making of you? Do you even think about the impact on you agreeing to the requests made by others? What offers are you making to others that no one is even asking for? These are really important questions to be asking yourself, because doing this kind of study is demanding and it is important to find balance in your life. If you're not being conscious about making requests and thinking about your capacity, it could easily add to your feeling of being overwhelmed if you are not creating enough space for your own needs. Also important to ask is which relationships are nourishing you and which ones are being unsupportive or undermining of you and your study?

I am well aware of how fortunate I was in that I was well supported both at home and at work in my "being-on-the-doctoral-journey". This all-encompassing kind of support played a key role in my ability to successfully complete my PhD. Of course, the relationship and support of your supervisor cannot be underestimated. In my case, I had a productive and supportive relationship with my supervisor. I am also grateful that I was able to form a connection with a group of postgraduate scholars doing their doctorates and regular contact with this "community of practice" (Lave & Wenger 1991) certainly made the journey a less lonely one[3].

---

3   See also chapters 15, 16 & 17 in Part 5 of this book that positions postgraduate study as a social practice.

THE "IT"

The "It" aspect relates to the external world and asks how does your relationship with the natural and technological world impact your study. Questions that can be asked of this domain are:

- How do my physical surroundings impact my study?
- What are the systems, processes and procedures that I am using for my study?
- Am I making optimal use of the resources I have?
- What additional skills might I need to make better use of systems and processes?
- How do I manage my time?
- How do I go about learning new things?
- When I am working, how much do I connect to the natural world?
- Where do I find beauty and meaning in my life while doing my study?

Is your physical environment (where you work or perhaps your office) conducive to your study? Sitting on an uncomfortable chair at a cluttered desk could result in physical discomfort and irritation. Similarly, working in a noisy place with constant distractions can affect your capacity to concentrate. This domain also has to do with systems, processes and procedures, and you may need to ask whether you are using these systems, processes and procedures in an efficient way or whether you could improve your skills to make better use of them? You may need to learn how to better use a computer program or some other technology to assist you with your study. Are you managing your time well? Are you making the best use of the resources you have at hand? The "It" domain also relates to the natural environment, so it may also be useful to look at how you are interacting with the natural world while doing your study. Do you take time to connect to nature, even spending just a few minutes in your garden or outdoors?

In my doctoral study, taking time out to commune with nature often provided a much needed respite from the busy-ness of my internal world of work. Technologically, I was fortunate to have easy and reasonably reliable access to the internet, and found that email and *Skype* conversations with my supervisor could be conducted without too many problems. However, I had to learn how to use certain types of technology as I went along, for example how to use a software program to help me analyse parts of the data that I had transcribed from interviews. There were also some rather heart-stopping moments when I forgot to back up the latest or correct version of my drafts, or when I got confused over which saved version was the "final", "very final" or "absolutely final" one. Having reliable systems can be useful in being organised and meeting deadlines, as well as reducing version anxiety.

CONCLUSION

Bandura (2006:165) argues that "most human functioning is socially situated" and so we are affected not only by our own self-reflections but also by the people we interact with and our environmental context. The concept of the four human domains, by situating a person in terms of both the inner and outer aspects of individual and group life, as well as that of environmental influences, can provide a useful way to self-coach by getting a comprehensive view of how you are living through your postgraduate study. If you are able to reflect (by giving your own honest responses to the various questions that I have posed), there may be areas receiving too much or too little attention. Being aware of possible imbalances can be a first, but crucial, step towards surviving and succeeding.

REFERENCES

Bandura, A. (2006). Towards a psychology of human agency. *Perspectives on Psychological Science*. 1(2):164-180.   PMid:26151469 http://dx.doi.org/10.1111/j.1745-6916.2006.00011.x

Flaherty, J. (2016 forthcoming). *Integral Coaching*. San Francisco, USA: New Ventures West.

Foot, R., Crowe, A. R., Tollafield, K. A. & Allen, C. E. (2014). Exploring doctoral student identity development using a self-study approach. *Teaching and Learning Inquiry: the ISSOTL Journal*, 2(1), 103-118. http://dx.doi.org/10.20343/teachlearninqu.2.1.103

Harrison, L. (2012). *PaperHeaDs: Living Doctoral Study, Developing Doctoral Identity*. Oxford, UK: Peter Lang. http://dx.doi.org/10.3726/978-3-0353-0276-9

Lave, J. & Wenger, E. (1991). *Situated learning: Legitimate Peripheral Participation*. Cambridge, UK: Cambridge University Press. http://dx.doi.org/10.1017/CBO9780511815355

Luciano, J. (2005). *The power of self-coaching*. Available online at https://experiencelife.com/article/the-power-of-self-coaching/

Martinez, E., Ordu, C., Della Sala, M. R., & McFarlane, A. (2013). Striving to obtain a school-life-work balance: The full-time doctoral student. *International Journal of Doctoral Studies*, 8:39-58.

Murphy, C. (2013). Kisses between paragraphs: Strategies to maintain wellness during the PhD journey. *Early Education*, 53:24-26.

Stimpson, R. L. & Filer, K. L. (2011). Female graduate students' work-life balance and the student affairs professional. *Empowering women in higher education and student affairs: Theory, research, narratives, and practice from feminist perspectives*, 69-84.

PART FOUR

POSTGRADUATE STUDY
AS IDENTITY WORK:
THE SOUTH AFRICAN EXPERIENCE

11 SEEING YOURSELF IN A NEW LIGHT: CROSSING THRESHOLDS IN BECOMING A RESEARCHER

Sherran Clarence

INTRODUCTION

Undertaking doctoral study is a transformative act. Doctoral students develop from "becoming-researchers" to scholars through the process of researching and writing. The transformation of the novice doctoral scholar into a capable, confident and independent researcher is a process, often fraught and challenging, that asks such candidates to cross many thresholds. You primarily think your way through your study, and it is the changes in the way you think and what you think about that hold the greatest transformative potential for you as a "becoming-researcher". Transformation – change – is tough, but almost always worth the effort. Aitchison and Mowbray (2013), Barnacle and Mewburn (2010), Mewburn (2011) and Barnacle (2005) have written about the emotional, personal and identity-related challenges that those undertaking doctoral study encounter. What their work highlight, in relation to this chapter, is that a doctorate is not just a qualification alone, and a thesis is not just something we write to get a qualification. Undertaking doctoral study changes the way we think about ourselves, our research and the world around us. The process, in all its struggles, triumphs and challenges, transforms us into something other than what and who we were when we started out, and this is not an easy or comfortable process. It must, therefore, be something that, as a postgraduate student, you ultimately want, even if you do not know exactly what you are getting into when you start out.

In this chapter, I reflect on the emotional or identity shifts that I felt happening within me as I crossed three key thresholds in my journey from a "becoming-researcher" to a full-fledged researcher. As I crossed these three thresholds, my conceptions of my own researcher identity changed, in profound ways, and the way I viewed my research changed too. In what follows, I will look critically at my own research journal and blog writings, and offer some useful insights into how doing a PhD, or indeed any significant postgraduate research project, can enable a new way of seeing yourself as a "becoming-researcher", and related career possibilities.

THREE THRESHOLDS TO CROSS

I reflect on three thresholds I crossed during my PhD by drawing on the work of Kiley (2009), and Kiley and Wisker (2009). They adapt and use as an analytical tool Meyer and Land's (2005) threshold concepts, with Turner's (1979) concept of liminality. Essentially, a threshold is a doorway into a new space. Crossing a threshold changes the way you understand the concept and its relationship to other concepts, theories or problems, as well as the way you see your research and/or yourself in relation to the world around you (Meyer & Land 2005). The key to understanding a threshold concept is that you cannot "unsee" once you have seen, and although the threshold concept will not uncover all the relationships of the whole, crossing one threshold enables you to cross further conceptual, epistemological and ontological thresholds as you progress (Kiley 2009). Threshold crossing is thus transformative (Land 2014) – it changes you as a scholar, as a researcher and as a person.

Kiley and Wisker (2009) and Kiley (2009) connect the concept of thresholds with that of liminality – thus dealing with uncertainty while being transformed (drawn from Turner 1979). Turner describes three stages in a transformative process: separation, where you have to move away from what you already know or believe; margin or limen, where you are in a liminal space between not knowing and knowing; and aggregation, where you are transformed as the threshold is crossed and new understanding or clarity is achieved. Liminal spaces tend to be uncertain in nature; you feel that you are on the cusp of change, but even if that change is welcome you do not always know what is on the other side, and what you will have to leave behind in order to move forward. Moving through a PhD involves moving across thresholds, through liminal spaces of uncertainty, anxiety and sometimes fear. Liminality is part of the journey, perhaps the most challenging part. Change and transformation are difficult processes, as they require us not only to gain something, but also often to leave something behind – ideas we have long cherished, or a way of seeing the world we have become comfortable with, for example (Land 2014).

The following sections outline three major thresholds I crossed during my PhD, and how they changed the way I saw myself as a researcher in terms of my changing scholarly identity. These thresholds involved acts of writing – either formal (such as chapter drafts) or informal (for example, field notes and research journaling) – and these three points mark significant shifts in many PhD scholars' endeavours.

CHAPTER 11 • SEEING YOURSELF IN A NEW LIGHT: CROSSING THRESHOLDS IN BECOMING A RESEARCHER

Designing your "Theoryology": A house can only stand on firm foundations

"Theoryology" is a term I created during my PhD to help me understand what I was creating in my theoretical and conceptual framework – one of the key threshold concepts Kiley and Wisker's (2009) research identified as being challenging for PhD scholars. This was the most challenging part of thinking and writing my thesis as I really had no idea what this kind of framework was in the abstract, how to build one for my own study, and what to actually do with it once built.

I spent the better part of a year working on the theory chapter. It was a year in which I wrote several drafts, trying to find my voice and build a framework that would enable me to take the next steps into methodology and data analysis. It was frustrating in large parts because it did not really feel like I was doing very much. Taking a whole year out of three years in total to work on one chapter (out of six or seven chapters) seemed overly indulgent, and dangerously slow. I was, for a long time, in a series of smaller liminal spaces around my theoretical concepts, knowing something and then losing it again, letting go of older understandings as newer meanings made more sense to me. I was also in a larger liminal space around this bigger threshold of finally having a conceptual framework, and having my gaze become clearer as I moved forward in my research.

I can track a small sense of shifting in three entries taken from my research journal, all written in 2012 (the theory year).

> *No real sense of how the theoretical bits I am writing will blend into a coherent structure yet, but this is as far as my headlights are reaching right now* (11 May 2012).

To:

> *I am restructuring, building, rethinking my framework – I feel like this process will go on for a while yet!* (9 August 2012).

And then to:

> *The BIG thing I need now, for me to feel like I'm on top of this, is to find examples that will explain all of this dense + complex theory or pictures, or both. I'm feeling a little more clear and a little more lost.* (22 September 2012).

What these comments indicate to me now, looking back, is a sense of a non-linear and layered writing and thinking process, and a sense of my own ideas and thinking changing along the way. From May to August there is a sense that I had new insights into the connections between the concepts I was using and how they fitted into the framework, necessitating rethinking and restructuring. In August, compared to May,

I sounded a little more confident in my sense of creating something more coherent, indicating that I was starting to see how things were fitting together. By September, I had worked out a fairly coherent structure, and needed examples to illustrate the theory to readers so that they would understand how I was using it all and why.

The comment about being both lost and found is how I felt throughout most of my PhD journey. As I found my way to something new, I felt like I lost my grip a little on something else, especially when I had to move away from the theory for a while to generate my data. This feeling of being lost and found and then lost again signals, I believe, movement through liminal spaces from one side of this threshold to the other. This image I drew (on 9 August 2012) represents the cyclical, but progressive thinking and writing process that I felt was pushing me over thresholds – from being a novice researcher, to becoming a less novice researcher over time. Each point or arrow in the spiral is a theoretical or conceptual threshold crossed, slowly moving me towards the centre – a clearer, tighter account of what my study was about[1].

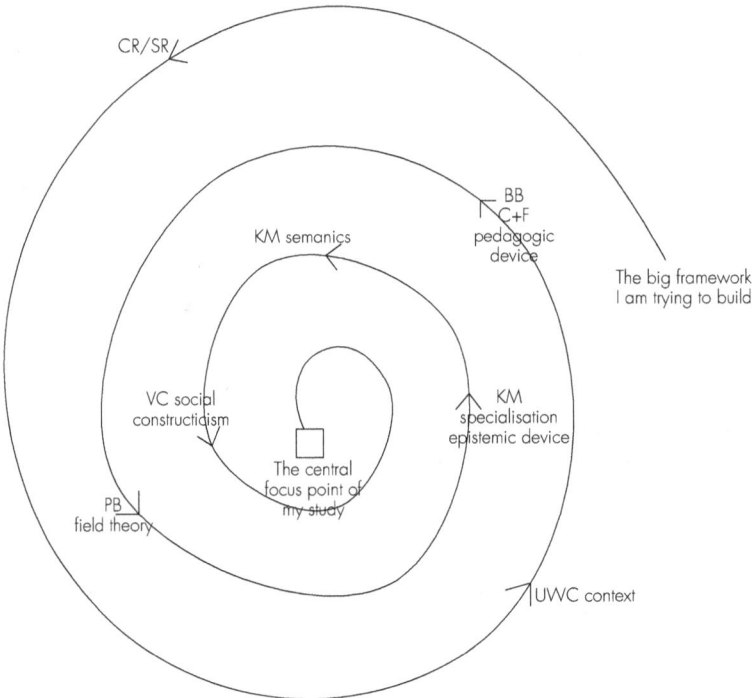

FIG 11.1. Pushing thresholds

---

1 This image seems in a way similar to Catherine Robertson's progression towards her conceptual framework (see Chapter 13 of this book).

Towards the end of the year I wrote, "I have too much theory" but then a day later, after a conversation with a colleague, I wrote,

> No theory pruning yet. Leave what is there, hone, refine and finish, and move on. Prune later. Need data first. (29 October 2012)

I did not really feel completely ready at that point to generate data, but I knew I had to move on from the theory. I had sufficiently crossed theoretical and conceptual thresholds such that I had a gaze – I had a way of looking at the part of the world my research was interested in, and I needed to start looking at it. I needed to move beyond the theory thresholds towards the next set of thresholds and liminal spaces: the field, and the generation, organisation and analysis of my data. In the South African context, within the social sciences and humanities, most postgraduate research seems to require students to immerse themselves in reading, both their field and theory, to find and firm up their research questions and a focus for the study, before the study itself can be enacted. If you are working in this way, you may find yourself at this threshold feeling similarly hesitant: with a tenuous gaze that needs to be further tested, refined and developed through getting stuck into your study, whether this includes fieldwork, archival work or other forms of empirical research.

Moving into the field: Out of the theory clouds into the data swamp

For any researcher who has never really done an empirical study before, the step that moves you from theory to data can be a big and intimidating one. But as thresholds go, this is a vital one to cross in terms of your development and growth as a researcher. It is another of the threshold concepts identified as being a potential stumbling point for doctoral students (Kiley & Wisker 2009).

Bernstein (2000) argued that theory and empirical data have an important and necessary relationship: theory informs the generation of empirical data, but empirical data, in turn, speaks back to and can reshape, challenge or push the theory in new ways. They have a dialectical relationship, and one that should not be underestimated. Without data, theory is rather meaningless (and without theory, data is just information). This threshold, then, is important on two levels: on the first level, it moves your study from going around in circles telling yourself what you probably already know about the theory in an abstract way towards making sense of the theory in empirical contexts that speak back to it, situate it, and bring it to life. On the second level, it moves you as a researcher from seeing yourself as being a researcher in a more abstract, perhaps "bookish" sense to actually *doing* the role of researcher in a more physical, active sense.

I had never felt like a "proper" researcher before I did my PhD. I had not designed a study, put it into practice and seen it through from beginning to end. My Master's research project was a policy analysis, and all my data were documents. I had done a small empirical study before I started my PhD, but I did not really feel like I knew what I was doing in terms of research design or data generation, and I certainly did not understand the connections between theory and data, and the need for a "theoryology" that would influence what data I would generate and how I would analyse it. The liminal space around this threshold was a lonely one for me, in spite of my supervisor's support. I had to go out into the field on my own, and I had to work out how to connect the data, once generated, back to my "theoryology" in a relevant dialectical and generative way.

Excerpts from my research journal attest to some of the struggles and also moments of realisation in making my way across this particular threshold in my PhD:

> I need to think a bit about ... what is theory? Clearly [my framework] is influencing my choices, but I can't just restate my 2nd chapter. What do I need to include ... to create a theoretical discussion about why I have chosen my particular research design? What is my research design? Oh dear. I have a lot of work to do here. (19 February 2013)

> What is ER + SR in my data may not fit very neatly into the way these are portrayed in the theory. I will need to use the theory as a guide but then explain my analysis using my data, making it speak back to or respond to the theory. But this is good, because this is the ... language of description ... linking theory to empirical data. (17 May 2013)

> Theory not being realised in the data as it looks in the theory has been quite alarming. Big thing is already seeing how CH2 (theory chapter) needs to be revised but also waiting until I have made more sense out of the data ... Climbing my way up data mountain – trying to avoid falling off into the valley of despair. (11 July 2013)

Moving from theory to data, and then eventually back again, in an iterative organisation and analysis process formed a series of smaller thresholds that, once crossed, changed me as a scholar and researcher. These excerpts show a process of realising that theory and data do not always line up perfectly to speak exactly the same dialect. The ways in which I had to create a relationship between the two in my study and show this to my readers have changed the way I see myself, as well as what I am now capable of in terms of future research. I moved closer, with each trudging crossing, to a completed PhD thesis, and to more fully taking on a new doctor-researcher identity.

CHAPTER 11 • SEEING YOURSELF IN A NEW LIGHT: CROSSING THRESHOLDS IN BECOMING A RESEARCHER

The first draft: "It's a thesis!" (but there's work to be done)

The final threshold is the submission of the first full draft. Until I pressed "save" and sent the first draft to my supervisor, I did not truly believe that I could finish my PhD or that I could be a researcher-doctor. I could not see my argument as a whole, or how all the pieces had come together underpinned by what Trafford and Leshem (2009:305) call "doctorateness". Doctorateness refers to a deeper ontological stance that enables the researcher to take all the parts of a PhD and create a thesis that is more than the sum of its parts, and that makes a contribution to knowledge in its field.

A PhD is written in chunks, bursts and multiple drafts. It takes its form slowly, and this bit-by-bit way of writing and thinking means that it can be very difficult to see the wood from the trees, as it were, in terms of the transformations in yourself, or those in your writing and thinking. You cannot see that first full draft with all the bits and pieces brought together into a coherent whole, because all you really see are the bits and pieces.

One of the most challenging parts of producing the first full draft was the revisions that came after I submitted it. This was a painful threshold for me, full of self-doubt and worry about the quality of my work. But it brought about further shifts in my thinking, and in my subjectivity as a scholar. Once I received all the feedback, I put off the revisions for as long as I could. I was just too tired to go on. At times, I longed for someone to come and cross this particular threshold – from first to examination-ready draft – for me:

> Revisions suck ... I am so tired now. Why can't this draft just be done? I wish I was like the cobbler in The Elves and the Shoemaker who would wake up in the morning and find that sweet little shoemaker elves had come and helped him to finish all his work because they saw how tired he was and how much he needed to get the work done. But there are no sweet little PhD-writing elves to help me. I wake up every morning and my to-do list for the revisions I have to do seems longer rather than shorter. (Blogpost, Revisions Suck, 21 September 2013)

But I also realised that if I did have someone, like my supervisor for example, to do the revisions for me – and we know from the research Clare Aitchison and others (2010) have done that this often happens – I would feel cheated. I would not have actually done the threshold-crossing myself, and could therefore not have felt, gained and also legitimately claimed the rewards I ultimately did. So, at the end of this same blogpost I wrote:

> I am realising that, while some days (like today) I really wish the elves were real, I actually would feel a bit cheated if someone did this bit for

> me, even though it sucks. So much of this PhD-writing is more about the
> journey and the learning along the way than it is about the destination
> (Blogpost, Revisions Suck, 21 September 2013).

Getting to the point where the draft was ready to submit for examination was a long struggle – some of it thrilling and exciting, much of it difficult and exhausting as I balanced work, home, children and my PhD. Handing in the first draft was a huge threshold crossed – it transformed my sense of myself as a researcher far more than handing in the revised draft for the examination process or the final draft to the library before graduation. This was the point at which I knew that I would indeed be able to claim my new identity as a researcher, a doctor, a peer.

REFLECTIONS: SEEING YOURSELF IN A NEW LIGHT

Looking back, I think that the ways in which doing my PhD has changed me – as a writer, researcher and scholar in my field – is less about the "big book" I have written, and more about the thresholds I crossed along the way. Crossing these thresholds enabled me to experience and develop a new scholarly identity. Working in liminal spaces, where you feel you are changing in terms of the ways in which you think, read, write, speak and interact with other PhD scholars and researchers in your community can be thrilling. It can also be terrifying and filled with self-doubt, anxiety and feelings of being an imposter. But, as Land (2014) and others (Kiley & Wisker 2009; Trafford & Leshem 2009) argue, if we are able to push through these discomforts and worries, and challenge ourselves to look on the thresholds in whatever form they come as opportunities for transformation and growth, we will be able to see more clearly what they have to offer, instead of focussing on the struggle and giving up. We can see the potential for ourselves – intellectually and emotionally – to be different, and hopefully different to be more than what we were.

As a scholar and researcher, I am certainly different and more capable, confident and sure of myself than I was before. This self-assuredness is not always easy to hold onto in the face of challenges to my research, or new thresholds in the form of extensions and developments of that research. But the PhD has taught me that if I "trust the process", it will come. If I do the work – and I now know that I can – the project will unfold, and the thinking and writing work will yield interesting answers and new knowledge. The PhD – all those liminal, scary, anxious spaces and challenging thresholds – has transformed me into a scholar, a researcher, who believes that even when I cannot see the answers, I can work on a process that will eventually show me what these answers could be.

CONCLUSION

This chapter offers a way to think about the research journey as a series of thresholds you can cross. If you are able to think more reflectively about the ways in which your thinking, writing and speaking about your research are changing and shifting in relation to the thresholds you may cross, you may be able to see yourself in a new light; as more than just a student doing a PhD or Master's degree. You may see yourself as a "becoming-researcher" and therefore begin to own that identity and harness it – not only pushing you through your own liminal spaces and across uncertain thresholds, but also re-imagining your career and work prospects, and possibilities for future research and writing endeavours.

REFERENCES

Aitchison, C., Catterall, J., & Ross, P. (2010). *Learning doctoral writing: Pain and pleasure*. Paper presented at the WDHE Conference, London, United Kingdom, 21-23 July 2010.

Aitchison, C., & Mowbray, S. (2013). Doctoral women: Managing emotions, managing doctoral studies. *Teaching in Higher Education*, 18(8):859-870. http://dx.doi.org/10.1080/13562517.2013.827642

Barnacle, R. (2005). Research education ontologies: Exploring doctoral becoming. *Higher Education, Research and Development*, 24(2):179-188. http://dx.doi.org/10.1080/07294360500062995

Barnacle, R., & Mewburn, I. (2010). Learning networks and the journey of "becoming doctor". *Studies in Higher Education*, 35(4):433-444. http://dx.doi.org/10.1080/03075070903131214

Bernstein, B. (2000). *Pedagogy, symbolic control and identity* (4th ed). New York, USA: Rowman and Littlefield, Inc.

Clarence, S. (2013, 21 September). Revisions suck [Web log post] Available online at http://wp.me/p3VNfn-e

Kiley, M. (2009). Identifying threshold concepts and proposing strategies to support doctoral education. *Innovations in Education and Teaching International*, 46(3):293-304. http://dx.doi.org/10.1080/14703290903069001

Kiley, M., & Wisker, G. (2009). Threshold concepts in research education and evidence of threshold crossing. *Higher Education, Research and Development*, 28(4):431-444. http://dx.doi.org/10.1080/07294360903067930

Land, R. (2014). *Liminality close-up*. Keynote paper presented at Higher Education Close Up (HECU) 7, Lancaster, United Kingdom, 21-23 July 2014. Available online at http://www.lancaster.ac.uk/fass/events/hecu7/docs/ThinkPieces/land.pdf

Mewburn, I. (2011). Troubling talk: Assembling the PhD candidate. *Studies in Continuing Education*, 33(3):321-332. http://dx.doi.org/10.1080/0158037X.2011.585151

Meyer, J., & Land, R. (2005). Threshold concepts and troublesome knowledge (2): Epistemological considerations and a conceptual framework for teaching and learning. *Higher Education*, 49(3):373-388. http://dx.doi.org/10.1007/s10734-004-6779-5

Trafford, V., & Leshem, S. (2009). Doctorateness as a threshold concept. *Innovations in Education and Teaching International*, 46(3):305-316. http://dx.doi.org/10.1080/14703290903069027

Turner, V. (1979). Betwixt and between: The liminal period in rites of passage. In W. Less & E. Vogt (Eds.). *Reader in Comparative Religion* (pp. 234-243). New York, USA: Harper and Row.

12 AGENCY AND UBUNTU: EXPLORING THE POSSIBILITY OF COMPLEMENTARITY IN POSTGRADUATE STUDY

Langutani M. Masehela

INTRODUCTION

Doing research for the purpose of postgraduate study is a challenge in developing countries, in this case, with specific reference to South Africa. Mutula (2009) shares the challenges of doing postgraduate studies in Africa, while Magano (2011) reports on the experiences of female postgraduate students in South Africa. These researchers confirm the existence of challenges encountered by students when studying towards a postgraduate degree in the African context. I share some of the sentiments in this chapter. Such challenges may be intensified when Africanised socio-cultural approaches that emphasise the collective (for example, the notion of Ubuntu) and westernised academic demands that elevate the notion of student agency clash. Thus postgraduate students in Africa often find themselves operating in a multiplicity of systems which tend to obscure the development of true student agency due to the dominance of westernised discourses. As such, the social exigencies of cultural or family demands are often not compatible with the postgraduate project that is shaped by western ideologies, values and norms[1].

This chapter is mainly motivated by my experiences as an academic, wife, mother, and extended family and community member. Though I understand the idiosyncratic nature of each postgraduate student's experience, I believe my experiences might find relevance to that of a wider range of African postgraduate students. In this chapter, I highlight hindrances that make it difficult for me, during my postgraduate studies, to exercise agency due to clashes in the multiple systems that I operated in as a human

---

[1] Also see the second chapter by Zondi Mkhabela and Liezel Frick that speaks to this notion of knowledge construction.

being[2]. Furthermore, my intention is to make a contribution towards strengthening relationships between supervisors and students. Experiences that I share may assist African and non-African supervisors to understand their students and appreciate them as social beings[3]. Students may also benefit from alternative ways of dealing with challenges that might delay the completion of their studies.

In this chapter, I focus on how postgraduate demands and African practices of Ubuntu in a South African context may clash. The chapter first elaborates on the notion of agency as explicated by Margaret Archer's (Archer 1995, 1996 and 2000) theory of social realism, which is rooted in Roy Bhaskar's (1979) philosophy of science known as critical realism. This background is followed by a description of the meaning of postgraduate study as it is embedded in the westernised, individualised notion of agency. The chapter then continues to explore the notion of Ubuntu in the African context, which imbibes the idea of collectivity as opposed to the individualistic westernised notion of agency. But instead of juxtaposing these notions, I argue that the two concepts can be complementary if supervisors and students can draw on the strengths of both agency and Ubuntu in an African context.

AGENCY AS A DRIVER OF THE POSTGRADUATE PROJECT

The notion of agency necessitates the existence of agents, in this case, postgraduate students and their supervisors. For Archer (2007), agents are social beings born with a sense of self who occupy social roles over time. She argues that this sense of self is not socially constructed because it comes into existence prior to our socialisation. Although the development of the sense of self takes place in the individual, this does not mean that structure (for example policies, social systems, organisations or institutions) and culture (norms, values, ideologies or beliefs) are not acknowledged, but only that sociality or the society is not key to this process. This implies that the sense of self is superior to that of the social. It is interesting to note that although Archer emphasises the primacy of this sense of self, she also provides an account of agency in socio-cultural contexts (Archer 1996).

Archer (1996) identifies three layers of agency: the person, the agent and the actor. The person relates to the sense of self with which we are born. The agent and the actor then emerge as a result of interaction with social contexts. Within an African

---

[2] Being caught between conflicting systems is also addressed by Andre van der Bijl (Chapter 7) in relation to work and study, Soraya Abdulatief (Chapter 6) with regards to being a first-generation student, and Guin Lourens (Chapter 9) on being a studying working mother.

[3] In this regard, also see the chapter by Bella Vilakazi (Chapter 5) that addresses student-supervisor relationships.

social milieu, it appears that the latter two layers of agency (the agent and the actor) may obscure the person (sense of self) to an extent of losing it due to the dominant (western) discourses that emerge in a postgraduate student's study context. I realised during my studies that I was losing my "personhood" in one way or the other to the actor in an African social context, for example a neighbour, mother and aunt. Many a time I have to put others first and my needs and concerns last. Archer (1996) furthermore distinguishes between two types of agents: primary and corporate agents. According to Archer (2000:263), primary agents are "collectivities sharing the same life chances". A group of black working-class students from rural backgrounds enrolled at an institution could thus be considered primary agents. Primary agents can transform themselves into corporate agents in pursuit of change. They would do this by exercising the personal emergent powers and properties accorded to them in interaction with the cultural and structural emergent powers and properties they encounter. Archer (1995:258) defines corporate agents as groups "who are aware of what they want, can articulate it to themselves and others, and have organised in order to get it, can engage in concerted action to re-shape or retain the structural or cultural feature in question." Later in the chapter, I illustrate how I evolved from being a primary agent in my context and became a corporate agent by partnering with other individuals in order to practice the African collective practices in the solitary westernised academic exercise of studying towards a postgraduate degree. This I did through joining a study group that aims to catapult progress of its members' studies despite our clashing ideologies and systems[4].

The final concept used by Archer (1996) in her account of agency is that of the social actor. Social actors are individuals who occupy roles which themselves have powers and properties that cannot be reduced to those of the person who occupies them. In an academic context, the supervisor, head of department or dean would all be examples of such roles. Although the roles have powers and properties, social actors exercise their incumbency of roles in different ways, depending on their own powers and properties. In the case of postgraduate supervision, supervisors have roles that are coupled with powers and properties that influence their supervision style and choices. Therefore, while supervisors acknowledge their powers and properties they can also exercise their agency, the sense of self. Supervisors could, for instance, establish a mutual relationship between themselves and their students in such a way that there is flexibility that enable students to meet both study and family demands.

---

4   Also see Part 5 of this book that highlights the value of such social practices during postgraduate study.

Given this background on the notion of agency, the link between the westernised culture of studying for yourself and Archer's notion of agency as the sense of self is noticeable. Postgraduate study, which is rooted in the western education system, is founded upon dominant discourses that may influence the relationship between supervisor and student. The issue of student agency becomes critical in that the student has to contribute in setting up terms and conditions of the student-supervisor relationship and take ownership of the research project. A prospective student might exercise agency by finding out how many successful Master's or doctoral students were supervised by the potential supervisor. How long did these students take to complete their studies? What are the potential supervisor's research interests, and how does this match the prospective student's research interests?

However, agency not only lies with the student – both universities and supervisors also have agency within the postgraduate system. Universities use postgraduate programmes to develop research capacity and generate the high-end skills required for a functional economy and to address complex issues (Mutula 2009). However, both students and supervisors may encounter challenges that prevent them from achieving this end when societal and academic demands clash. I therefore argue that student agency in postgraduate studies is not an option but a condition with which every student needs to engage.

Agency within the student-supervisor relationship plays a critical role in completing a study successfully. The way in which postgraduate programmes are structured in the South African context encourages students to work in silos as the apprenticeship model is still the dominant form (ASSAf 2010:64). As a result, students may have limited chances of interacting with their peers, especially in non-laboratory fields of study. Therefore, the experience of doing postgraduate studies can be intimidating to the student who is being inducted into a culture of studying independently without the involvement of family and peers following a similar study programme. Westernised systems of knowledge production furthermore promote and encourage student agency, which are often in conflict with traditional African ways of being. As a result, postgraduate studies in the African context may present challenging experiences to the student. The notion of Ubuntu, which promotes the idea of doing things collectively or operating as a collective, provides some insights into how to understand this alternative way of being.

THE NOTION OF UBUNTU

Le Grange (2012:331) describes Ubuntu as a concept that is derived from proverbial expressions (aphorisms) found in several languages in Africa south of the

Sahara. Ubuntu is not only a linguistic concept, but it has a normative connotation embodying how we ought to relate to each other and our moral obligations towards each other. Du Toit (2011:253) views the concept of Ubuntu as a humanist African philosophy indispensable to African socio-ethical reflection. As such, Ubuntu elucidates the joint rootedness and interdependence of persons, which is often not well pronounced in western traditions of knowledge production. In this section, I share possible circumstances that I personally encountered during my postgraduate studies rooted in the Ubuntu tradition that might be in conflict with such westernised forms of education, particularly as it relates to the notion of agency.

Postgraduate study is constituted by the western epistemological idea of "education-for-me" which is in conflict with "education for us" (Du Toit 2011:253). Postgraduate supervisors therefore need to have an understanding of their students' heritage and belief systems if they want to help these students develop their agency. I found my supervisor acquainted with such because of the noticeable flexibility I observed during our interaction. African postgraduate students, especially those that live in rural communities such as myself, belong to communities that continue to strongly uphold the idea of sharing, which could be sharing of pain, pleasure, food, chores or any other activities. This is evident in the way people greet – not only inquiring about your well-being but also about the well-being of the rest of the family. For instance, in my tribe we say, *"minjhani"* (the literal translation of "how are you" in Xitsonga). The *"mi"* in *"minjhani"* is the plural of "you" and also signifies respect. One is always attached to other members of the family (who may not necessarily be your husband, children, siblings or parents). Cousins, for instance, first or second, are equally close to one and deserve one's attention as much as any other close family member. This form of connectedness might impact directly or indirectly on postgraduate study progress because students are often expected to compromise their time and space due to the setup in a family environment. For example, it is customary to be fully involved in funeral and wedding preparations of not only your closest family members, but also that of your neighbour, second cousin, or friend. Ubuntu can become a "spider web" relationship when the student finds it impossible to escape the circumstances. A typical spider web makes it very difficult for you to escape because of the nature of its form and its ability to trap you when you want to rescue yourself from it. I realised that, as an actor or agent in my community, I ran the risk of losing my sense of self as described by Archer (2000). In the next section, I share how I found the middle ground between agency and Ubuntu to save myself from losing myself in either my studies or community life.

FINDING THE MIDDLE GROUND: AGENCY AND UBUNTU AS COMPLEMENTARY PERSPECTIVES IN POSTGRADUATE SUPERVISION

My experience of doctoral studies has brought about a strong-willed resolve to deal with circumstances where my studies and family responsibilities have competed for my attention. I would suggest three key ideas that I adopted in my journey to complement Ubuntu with agency.

Firstly, I joined a study group. Study groups connect colleagues with similar interests to form a special interest group where they agree to share research-related challenges among themselves. If there is one in your circle, consider joining it. If there is none, become the pioneer of such a group. Do not think about the financial implications for such a group – you will only be required to agree on the frequency of your meetings and the venue could be in someone's home on a rotational basis. More often than not I would find myself unable to attend these meetings because of the physical distance between my home and my group members. I then resorted to joining them through social networks. Social networks can be very useful for this purpose. Recognise that knowledge transfer is key in your journey towards completing your study as it helps you to understand what you are learning even better. Share the study material that you might come across no matter how short an article may be or how big a book might be. As you share and discuss study materials with your study group, you will notice that it also detangles some of those threshold concepts that you have been grappling with in your own research. At the institution where I completed my doctoral study, there were structured "doctoral weeks" that I found beneficial. These doctoral weeks were coupled with an active online learning site where the coordinator of the doctoral programme regularly engaged with everyone by providing relevant sources, sparking debates about a common topic of interest, and keeping candidates in the loop around issues related to higher education at national and international levels. I found this approach to be a powerful tool to eliminate loneliness during my postgraduate journey. Not only did they provide me with the opportunity to develop my own agency in the postgraduate environment, the interaction with other postgraduate students and scholars built a sense of Ubuntu within the study group itself. Study groups may therefore help students and supervisors to find the middle ground between the notions of agency and Ubuntu.

Secondly, I had to vehemently develop basic research skills, such as proposal-writing workshops where topics such as crafting research questions and identifying a research problem are discussed. This is especially important if you are not working in an academic environment. If the department where you are enrolled does not offer such skills development workshops, ask your supervisor to suggest such opportunities.

Developing your research skills will help you become more eloquent in your field of study, and improve your agency when you need to consult with your supervisor or other experts. Well-developed research skills gained at the onset of your study will save you much time in the long term, which may, in turn, enable you to engage with your family and community when the need arises.

Thirdly, I developed a planned study schedule. I would decide how long the next study session should take and what I would be reading or writing about. In case I wanted to start a new chapter, I tried to sketch a rough outline of that chapter and then decide which subsection I would work on next. This made my study sessions much more productive. Part-time students are pressurised to juggle work, family, societal and postgraduate responsibilities. I had to use my annual leave days to get uninterrupted study time. Supervisors also need to provide space within supervisory relationships and study schedules to accommodate unforeseen circumstances students might face during the course of their studies. Involvement in such activities remains an act of Ubuntu for the student, but it is important to decide how involved you should be considering your study obligations. You will have to prepare family members and neighbours that you will be less visible at such occasions for the duration of your studies. Also communicate openly and regularly with your supervisor so that they may have a greater understanding for your circumstances (which might be different to theirs). Such communication is a form of agency, while at the same time recognising the need for Ubuntu in the South African context.

CONCLUSION

In this chapter I explored the possibility of complementing two contrasting notions, that of Ubuntu and the notion of student agency during a postgraduate journey of African students. Finding the middle ground between the two notions has potential to levelling the ground between supervisor and student challenges. It is possible for such students to meet social demands and responsibilities with a stronger sense of agency, while supervisors could benefit from having a better understanding of their students and accordingly devise more effective supervisory strategies.

REFERENCES

Academy of Science of South Africa. (2010). *The PhD study: Consensus Report*. Pretoria, South Africa: ASSAf.

Archer, M. S. (1995). *Social realist theory: The morphogenetic approach*. Cambridge, UK: Cambridge University Press. http://dx.doi.org/10.1017/CBO9780511557675

Archer, M. S. (1996). *Culture and agency: The place of culture in social theory*. Cambridge, UK: Cambridge University Press. http://dx.doi.org/10.1017/CBO9780511557668

Archer, M. S. (2000). *Being Human*. Cambridge, UK: Cambridge University Press. http://dx.doi.org/10.1017/CBO9780511488733

Archer, M. S. (2007). *Making our way through the world*. Cambridge, UK: Cambridge University Press. http://dx.doi.org/10.1017/CBO9780511618932

Bhaskar, R. (1979). *The possibility of naturalism. A philosophical critique of the contemporary human sciences*. Brighton, UK: Harvester.

Du Toit, C. (2011). Off-campus education as a "we-ness": A Case for Ubuntu as a Theoretical Framework. *HURIA Journal of The Open University of Tanzania Volume, 13 August, 2012 ISSN 08566739*. Special Issue: Edited Proceedings of the Third ACDE (African Council for Distance Education) Conference Held in Dar es Salaam, Tanzania on 12-15 July, 2011.

Le Grange, L. (2012). Ubuntu, ukama, environment and moral education. *Journal of Moral Education*, 3(41):329-340. http://dx.doi.org/10.1080/03057240.2012.691631

Magano, M.D. (2011). The Social and Emotional Challenges of Female Postgraduate Students in South Africa. *Journal of Social Sciences*, 29(3):205-212.

Mutula, S. M. (2009). *Challenges of postgraduate research: global context, African perspectives*. Keynote address delivered at the University of Zululand, 10th DLIS Annual Conference, from 9-10 September 2009.

13 WHOSE VOICE IS RIGHT WHEN I WRITE? IDENTITY IN ACADEMIC WRITING

Catherine Robertson

INTRODUCTION

Paré (2010:40) relates a story of a student who sees the postgraduate journey as being on a bus and says, "I'm not quite sure yet where it's going. The scary part is that I am the one driving the bus." I, on the other hand, as a mature student who returned to an academic pursuit after many years, saw my postgraduate journey as far more arduous than a bus trip. I felt as if I had to summit a mountain, the peak of which remained shrouded. Every inch of my climb produced further challenges (not to mention the heady rush of vertigo I experienced most of the time). Sometimes, I had to retrace my steps to find a safer, easier way to keep up the momentum. At other times, I was ready to admit that I was no mountaineer and that I had taken on the impossible. What I found to be the most difficult was to get started; to settle down and write. Something kept blocking me. It did not mean that I had not read sufficiently, that my data was inadequate, or that I did not know what I wanted to say; I simply found starting to write challenging. There is a great deal of advice available to people who have writer's block. "Just start writing", people say cheerfully, "and it will all come to you". Others advised, "Write early and write often" (Lee & Aitchison 2009:94). The problem is that it is only once you have found your way on the mountain, which you eventually do, that this advice makes sense to you.

The reason why students may find writing difficult at first is because they realise that they are not only writing about some subject matter which they feel knowledgeable about, but that they are communicating something about themselves. Private thinking becomes public when it is written down (Aitchison 2010). The writer therefore has to think carefully and deliberately about ideas before committing them to paper. Paré (2010:32) contends that writing is not merely a means of expression but a type of learning and "thinking made tangible".

Academic writing does not mean that you can automatically remove the person you are from your writing and replace it with the new scholarly you. To be able to write like a scholar when you are still learning to be one is very difficult. You need an insider's knowledge to become a member of the academic discourse community. To be able to write well, you need to know what is meant by "well structured" and that your arguments are "well supported". At the same time, you need to find your own, authentic voice. The term "voice" as used by Bakhtin does not refer only to an "auditory signal", but includes the notion that "human communicative practices give rise to mental functioning in the individual" (Wertsch 1981:13). Students often feel intimidated by these expectations and even experience an identity crisis, as they feel that they have to become someone they are not, or that they simply do not fit in (Ivanič 1998). In the following sections, three identities of the writerly self, as identified by Ivanič (1998), will be explored and located using my own experience.

THREE IDENTITIES OF THE WRITERLY SELF

Ivanič (1998) suggests that writing can be seen as a site of struggle in which the writer negotiates three types of writer identity: an "autobiographical self", a "discoursal self" and the "self as author". These three identities are generally chronological but interrelate with one another. All three identities negotiate socially available possibilities for, what Ivanič (1998:23) calls, "self-hood". People's identities (or selfhoods, to use Ivanič's term) "are affected if not determined by the discourses and social practices in which they participate" (Ivanič 1998:10). Identity is thus socially constructed and not left to individual choice. Identity is a "complex of interweaving positionings" (Ivanič 1998:10).

Boud and Lee (2009) point out that doctoral education is a form of social practice that is shaped by the broader economic, political and intellectual agendas which shape knowledge production and exchange. All the activities involved with doctoral studies are thus forms of social practice which are shaped by the same influences. Writing is an activity of doctoral work. There has been a shift from seeing language (and by implication writing) as an independent skill, divorced from social and cultural practice. If language can be influenced by its social and cultural context, the construction of language must be recognised as being complex and heterogeneous (Ivanič 1998; Aichison 2009; Boud & Lee 2009). The ability to master academic writing goes beyond knowledge of one's subject or discipline and includes an understanding of what examiners will be looking for, what discourse is taking place in that discipline and to what extent you have mastered what is expected of you. It is in this realm of expectation that you realise that academic writing is not without elements of power and authority, neither of which is yours as a student.

CHAPTER 13 • WHOSE VOICE IS RIGHT WHEN I WRITE? IDENTITY IN ACADEMIC WRITING

The "autobiographical self"

The first identity to be brought to the act of writing referred to above is the "autobiographical self". This means that writers bring their experiences from their life-history, their encounters with people, their interests, ideas, opinions and commitments to their writing. Experiences are a dimension of who you are; your consciousness. You are not a neutral writer writing objectively about your research. You bring a variety of values and beliefs to your writing, as well as a range of literary practices learned throughout your life. You have a "multiple social identity", but in the course of your studies, you have to become a member of the academic discourse community (Ivanič 1998:1). You need to become familiar with institutional and disciplinary writing conventions and develop an appropriate voice while learning to adopt an authoritative stance in your writing (Cotterall 2011).

Identities are also defined by their historical context. The way people think and behave change over time. Today, people are far more comfortable speaking and writing about topics that were regarded as controversial fifty years ago. This means that your identity constantly has to be redefined and changed to keep up with time. Your identity is thus located in events and experiences that you interpret as you move through time. Ivanič (1998) suggests that there is a three-way interplay between the writers' life-experiences, their sense of self and the reality that they construct through their writing. There is thus a connection between the writer's biographical narratives and his or her writing. There are also critical events in your life that redefine your identity, such as becoming a parent. All these moments "foreground" change in identity (Ivanič 1998:16). Mature students, like me, often embark on their postgraduate studies after an interruption which most probably means that academic writing does not come naturally at first. Learning to write well is often a matter of observation, trial and error (Lee & Aitchison 2009). All students must learn the many traditions, expectations and unspoken rules of the academic world. Ivanič (1998) notes that mature students entering the academic world after some time away from it struggle with conflicts of identity since they feel strange in their new environment and lack confidence in this unfamiliar world. Students also enter the academic world with a wealth of personal experience which may mean that they have multiple and conflicting identities.

As a result of my earlier postgraduate studies in Critical Linguistics, as well as the nature of my work, I wrote a great deal and regarded myself as a competent writer. However, I soon realised that a large amount of my writing, albeit grammatically correct, was emotive and had been based largely on my opinion. Having my own opinion was not wrong, but I quickly learned that it had to be grounded. I had to learn to see things through other lenses. In order to speak with authority, I had to borrow someone else's voice before I knew what I was doing. My autobiographical writing self also brought with it many entrenched habits. I had to rid myself of the habit of modifying most of my adjectives with adverbs of degree, especially where I felt strongly about a topic, for example by using words such as "extremely", "exceptionally", "huge", "very" and many others. The use of these words might add colour to descriptions, but it breaks one of the ground rules of academic writing, namely writing objectively and neutrally. I also had a tendency to start my sentences with pronouns which were vague in locating their antecedents, such as words like "this" and "it", without qualifying what these words referred to in the previous sentence.

It is also valuable to remember who your reader(s) are. Your identity includes how you relate to others. It is important in doctoral studies to learn how to write for specific audiences (Murray 2010). Postgraduate students know that they are not writing for a single person but their audience consists of a supervisor or two, as well as their eventual examiners. The readers, too, have different interests and knowledge, and form opinions of the writer as they read, trying to find the writer's identity in the writing. Identity is evident in the choice of words that are used, the sentence structure and the syntax. There is thus a complex relationship between the writer and his or her identity, and the readers. Mature students often feel that they have to change their identity to fit in with or accommodate the dominant values and practices of their institutions (Ivanič 1998). Writers can decide to accommodate or resist conforming to readers' expectations, but Thesen (2014) points out that where writers are unable to make sense of their intended audiences the notion of voice can also be silenced or erased. As a mature student I therefore needed to learn how to capitalise on my autobiographical self, but also move beyond it in order to engage my readers.

The "discoursal self"

The second identity that a writer develops is called the "discourse identity". Ivanič (1998:17) defines "discourse" as "the mediating mechanism in the social construction of identity". This can take place through speaking or writing. Discourse is the site where identity is manifested. Discourse provides the framework for thinking about identity. In writing a thesis or dissertation, the writer develops his or her "discoursal self". The writer thus constructs this identity through writing.

A writer's "discoursal self" is the impression that writers create of themselves through the discourse choices they make as they write or speak; the way in which they align themselves with "socially available subject positions" (Ivanič 1998:32). This is done either consciously or unconsciously. The position we hold in society, our ethnicity, gender and what we can or cannot do are indicators of who we are. Ivanič (1998) states that writing is an act of identity, as well as a form of discourse. The way we write is a result of the way we are.

The characteristics of the discoursal self are created by the values, beliefs or power relations in the social context in which they are written. In the discipline or field of the writer, there are special conventions of writing. The discoursal self tries to adopt these conventions and to fit into this environment as much as possible, adapting it to the specific genre which constitutes the purpose of writing, such as writing a thesis or dissertation, writing a paper for a conference, or writing an article for publication. Discoursal selves can thus change as people engage in different discourses. Writers' identities can differ considerably depending on the demands made by the occasion for which they write. Ivanič (1998) maintains that while it is sometimes difficult to find traces of a writer's autobiographical identity in academic writing, the only real evidence of an author's identity can be found in the writer's discoursal self. According to Ivanič (1998:18) the self cannot be "studied in isolation but as something that manifests itself in discourse".

Murray (2010) mentions that in early doctoral writing, the critique of others' work is overstated in literature reviews. Ivanič (1998) also notes that in the early stages of discoursal identity, students are apt to imitate or depend upon the ideas contained in their readings, often without citing their sources or failing to use their own words when paraphrasing. They often fail to mark these statements with quotation marks, indicating their source. They also incorporate many of the ideas that they read about into their own thinking processes so that the lines between their ideas and those of other sources become blurred. The student writers' "own" discourse often consists of a conglomeration of discourses with which they are familiar and which they have adopted in the absence of having a voice of their own. The way in which writers use these other discourses establishes a discourse identity of their own. However, Ivanič (1998) points out that there is a fine line between intertextuality and plagiarism. She also points out that it is sometimes difficult to distinguish between a novice writer trying to establish a discoursal self and plagiarism. The dilemma students face is that all the ideas and words they encounter come from what they read. They admire the way some writers write and, in trying to emulate them to become part of the discourse, they are in danger of copying writers verbatim instead of signalling when they use other people's voices by using quotation marks or by means of attributing an idea to another author.

My discoursal self branded me as someone who took far too long to make my point. Reading widely comforted me. The more I read, the more knowledge I built up about the subject. This left me with a large amount of information that had to be assimilated, synthesised or discarded. In the early stages of my studies, I had not developed the self-discipline to select the information that I needed for my argument without wanting to include at least something from all my sources. Trimming a chapter down to what was regarded as acceptable by my supervisors remained a challenge. I developed a ruthless attitude in my writing and deleted pages of it. This was a painful but necessary process. My long-windedness could partially have been attributed to my tendency to paraphrase other writers' writing and, instead of synthesising their ideas, I retained their discoursal voices instead of developing my own.

Ivanič (1998:28) points out that there is not a range of possibilities to writers in constructing their "discoursal self", as it depends on the "possibilities of self-hood supported by the socio-cultural and institutional context in which they are writing". Thus, "negotiating a 'discoursal self' is an integral part of the writing process: there is no such thing as 'impersonal writing'" (Ivanič 1998:32).

Cooper (2014) points out that there is little research on the role that experiential learning plays to enrich academic practices. Yet when many mature students return to an institution to take up their studies, they bring a wealth of experience with them – not only from their personal lives, but also from their working lives. The dilemma is: to what extent can prior knowledge be referred to or incorporated into research writing since the truth value accorded to this type of writing cannot be the same as that found in formal knowledge. The solution to this quandary has many implications for mature students acquiring acceptable writing conventions.

One of these implications is that scientific knowledge traditionally belongs to a western (or northern), metropolitan and masculine knowledge practice[1]. Different social and cultural groups' autobiographical selves vary considerably. The autobiographical self influences the discoursal self. An African worldview, for example, is different. Conceptions of knowledge in the African context are based upon cooperation and collective responsibility, corporateness and interdependence (as opposed to competition, individual rights, separateness and independence) (Cadmon 2014). In other words, the well-being of others and striving towards a common good rather

---

1   Also see Chapter 2 and Chapter 12 in this book that both speak to how African knowledge systems often get subverted to a westernised epistemic point of view. Chapter 12 in particular addresses some of these issues by highlighting the possible tension African students might experience when working across these knowledge systems.

than that of the individual are of primary importance. This is known as Ubuntu: "I am because we are, and since we are, therefore I am". Any form of knowledge other than the traditional form of knowledge tends to be lost or discarded. Cadmon (2014) argues that the power relations that are underpinned by Eurocentric discourse should be challenged. Internationalism has meant that universities have become multi-cultural and multi-ethnic. These students do not always have the traditional or "accepted" knowledge perspective and struggle to find their academic voice in research conversations as their experiential knowledge forms a barrier. Academic writing consists of a set of practices, but these practices are socially constructed and so may be contested and challenged.

Deyi (2014) points out that in her writing, she needed to use more proverbs and idioms because in isiXhosa, writers or speakers never make their point in the beginning but first present many examples and use many synonyms to explain an issue. African languages have a natural rhythm and if the text has to be cut, this breaks the rhythm. This type of academic writing in the western world would be regarded as repetitious since the language should be used as a vehicle and not as an end in itself. While writing her thesis, Deyi (2014) felt that by confining the thesis to the writing standards imposed by convention created a distance between her and the research, and filled her with a sense of loss. This loss was as a result of the feeling that the postgraduate thesis did not belong to her but was determined by the intended audience, the external examiner and other possible readers. It would also be difficult for the writer to find his or her own voice, the voice of authority, under these circumstances.

The "authorial self"

When the writer finds his or her own "voice", the writer becomes "self as author". This is the third of Ivanič's (1998) writer identities towards which every student strives. According to Ivanič (1998), this aspect of writer identity is concerned with the writer's beliefs, the position the writer takes and the opinion the writer holds. It is a different sense of voice to that of the discoursal self. It is less tentative, less searching and more confident. This is when writers can claim authority in the content of what they are writing and establish an authorial presence in their writing. They can take responsibility for their authorship. This does not always happen as some writers credit all their work to the ideas of others, thereby hiding their identities. Ivanič (1998) maintains that the "authorial self" is a product of the autobiographical self and to write with authority is an aspect of the discoursal self. Although this identity is not separate from the other two identities, it is distinctly different.

The process of developing the self as author is complex as it works on many levels. Murray (2010:102) points out that becoming authorial involves "learning about the structures of written academic argument, developing a sense of audience requirements, increasing their understanding of how to construct the case for 'contribution' to the field, gaining insights into the politics of academic writing and developing confidence and resilience to dealing with critique". Murray adds that this process involves students moving to a position where they can see their field as a debate and how they can position themselves in that debate.

Even though it might be widely acknowledged that writing plays a focal role in academia, relatively little is known about the development of writing practices in doctoral writing (Aitchison, Catterall, Ross & Burgin 2012; Ferguson 2009; Kamler & Thomson 2008; Cotterall 2011). Many students struggle to find their authorial voice which causes them a great deal of anxiety and distress. Traditionally, the supervisor/student dyad remains "the primary location for learning" (Lee & Aitchison 2009:94). This finding is supported by Aitchison et al (2012). Chihota and Thesen (2014:132) suggest that however good the student/supervisor relationship is, "there are inevitably times of isolation and confusion, with emotions of loss, blame and frustration". Lee and Aichison (2009) point out that some supervisors are not properly equipped to deal with their students' linguistic needs. There are other ways in which students can hone their writing skills and discover their writer identities, for example by attending writing workshops or consulting self-help books. Even though students need support and guidance, Lee and Aitchison (2009) and Kamler and Thomson (2008) warn that while many of these books stress the importance of writing well, they tend to be too prescriptive and do not take writers' changing identities and needs into account. Lee (2010) believes that it is developmental to talk about your research and about your writing. Talking can clarify what you mean and what you do. The flaws that you have become blind to, will be pointed out by others. Aitchison (2010) regards the process of discussion and feedback as vital to developing writing. A writing group (or writers' circle) provides a safe rehearsal space where students can use their peers to bounce off their ideas before submitting their work to their supervisors. Many of the students who join writing groups are international students (Chihota & Thesen 2014).

In my experience, I was given the opportunity to introduce my research to other postgraduate students in a five-minute presentation. I had to explain my research and answer questions. I was also asked to explain my research to various groups of post-graduate students and to describe how, as a mature student, I experienced my return to academia. I also explained my methodology at workshops. This meant that

I joined the "ongoing conversation" in my disciplinary community (Paré 2010:34) and the experience was of inestimable value.

I regarded discovering the "self as author" stage of my writing identity as an epiphany. I first encountered it when I managed to view my research through the lens of the conceptual framework that I had chosen. I realised that the choice of framework was a challenge, yet I had an inkling that it would provide the necessary theory to explain my research. I agonised for weeks as the way in which the theoretical framework could be used in the context of my research remained elusive. I tried to verbalise my ideas to a colleague and fellow student, drawing a visual representation of how I thought it could work, when I suddenly realised I "got it", confirming Lee's (2010) contention that to talk about your research can be helpful. It was a eureka moment as I saw the mist clear for a fleeting moment – before it covered the summit once again. However, I grasped the theoretical application at last and where there is understanding, the writing can go on.

This epiphany was not a singular event, but also occurred after the third or fourth re-writes of my literature review. I had just read something that suddenly made sense to me, and I realised that nothing that I had written up to then would ever satisfy me in that chapter. It meant that I had to start over and rewrite the chapter, discarding months of work and piles of resources, and missing my deadline to hand in so that I could graduate that year. However, it was a worthwhile sacrifice. I suddenly found that, at last, I was in charge: occupying the subject position in my writing in an authoritative way. I had found my voice and discovered my "self as author". This surge of confidence continued into the writing of my final chapter. It was the easiest chapter to write because it was as though I finally understood what I was writing about. The mist had lifted and the path to the summit was suddenly clear. Everybody deserves that epiphanal moment as a reward for sticking to the arduous task of writing a thesis or dissertation to the bitter end.

My "self as author" also manifested itself fully in my methodology chapter. I had the satisfaction of working with a methodology that suited who I was; my autobiographical and discoursal identity. This good fit gave me the confidence not only to explain a complicated methodology to the potential readers of my dissertation, but to describe and analyse my data with relative ease. My authorial self helped me to fit the various pieces of the jigsaw into the complex whole. I realised that I had discovered my scholarly self.

FINAL REFLECTIONS

Aitchison et al (2012:438) asked a group of doctoral students and their supervisors to describe how they experienced the writing part of their doctoral candidature. Both groups spoke in extremes, of the "joys and pleasure" or of the "pain and frustration" of writing. No one found it easy, even when they found it stimulating or rewarding. These findings mirror my experience. For me, there is no doubt that doctoral writing is "emotional work".

Thinking about identity and writing can be of use, even have a liberating effect on us as we write, as well as helping us to write in an institutional context. This comes about through thinking about why we write the way we do and understanding why we make the choices we do. Ivanič (1998) believes that critically reflecting on your own experiences as you write your thesis or dissertation makes a researcher out of you.

REFERENCES

Aitchison, C. (2010). Learning together to publish: Writing group pedagogies for doctoral publishing. In C. Aitchison, B. Kamler, & A. Lee (Eds.). *Publishing pedagogies for the doctorate and beyond* (pp. 83-100). London, UK: Routledge.

Aitchison, C., Kamler, B. & Lee, A. (Eds.) (2010). *Publishing pedagogies for the doctorate and beyond*. London, UK: Routledge.

Aitchison, C., Catterall, J., Ross, P., & Burgin, S. (2012). 'Tough love and tears': Learning doctoral writing in the sciences. *Higher Education Research and Development*, 31(4):435-447. http://dx.doi.org/10.1080/07294360.2011.559195

Boud, D., & Lee A. (2009). *Changing practices of doctoral education*. Oxon, UK: Routledge.

Cadmon, K. (2014). Of house and home: Reflections on knowing and writing for a 'Southern' post-graduate pedagogy. In L. Thesen, & L. Cooper (Eds.). *Risk in academic writing: Postgraduate students, their teachers and the making of knowledge* (pp. 166-200). Bristol, UK: Lavenham Press.

Chihota, M.C., & Thesen, L. (2014). Rehearsing 'the postgraduate condition' in writers' circles. In L. Thesen, & L. Cooper (Eds.). *Risk in academic writing: postgraduate students, their teachers and the making of knowledge* (pp. 131-147). Bristol, UK: Lavenham Press.

Cooper, L. (2014). 'Does my experience count?' The role of experiential knowledge in the research writing of post-graduate adult learners. In L. Thesen, & L. Cooper (Eds.). *Risk in academic writing: postgraduate students, their teachers and the making of knowledge* (pp. 17-47). Bristol, UK: Lavenham Press.

Cotterall, S. (2011). Doctoral students writing: Where's the pedagogy? *Teaching in Higher Education*, 16(4):413-425. http://dx.doi.org/10.1080/13562517.2011.560381

Deyi, S. (2014). A lovely imposition: The complexity of writing a thesis in isiXhosa. In L. Thesen, & L. Cooper (Eds.). *Risk in academic writing: Postgraduate students, their teachers and the making of knowledge* (pp. 48-56). Bristol, UK: Lavenham Press.

Ferguson, T. (2009). The 'write' skills and more: A thesis writing group for doctoral students. *Journal for Geography in Higher Education,* 33(2):285-297.

Ivanič, R. (1998). *Writing and Identity: The discoursal construction of identity in academic writing.* The Netherlands, Amsterdam: John Benjamins Publishing Company.

Kamler, B., & Thomson, P. (2008). The failure of dissertation advice books: Toward alternative pedagogies for doctoral writing. *Educational Researcher,* 37(8):507-514.

Lee, A. (2010). When the article is the dissertation: Pedagogies for a PhD by publication. In C. Aitchison, B. Kamler, & A. Lee (Eds.). *Publishing pedagogies for the doctorate and beyond* (pp. 12-29). London, UK: Routledge.

Lee, A. & Aitchison, C. (2009). Writing for the doctorate and beyond. In D. Boud, & A. Lee (Eds.). *Changing practices of doctoral education* (pp. 87-99). Oxon, UK: Routledge.

Murray, R. (2010). Becoming rhetorical. In C. Aitchison, B. Kamler, & A. Lee (Eds.). *Publishing pedagogies for the doctorate and beyond* (pp. 101-116). London, UK: Routledge.

Paré, A. (2010). Slow the presses: Concerns about premature publication. In C. Aitchison, B. Kamler, & A. Lee (Eds.). *Publishing pedagogies for the doctorate and beyond* (pp. 30-46). London, UK: Routledge.

Thesen, L. (2014). Risk as productive: Working with dilemnmas in the writing of research. In L. Thesen, & L. Cooper (Eds.). *Risk in academic writing: Postgraduate students, their teachers and the making of knowledge* (pp. 1-24). Bristol, UK: Lavenham Press.

Thesen, L. & Cooper, L. (Eds.) (2014). *Risk in academic writing: Postgraduate students, their teachers and the making of knowledge.* Bristol, UK: Lavenham Press.

Wertsch, J. V. (1991). *Voices of the mind: A sociocultural approach to mediated action.* Cambridge, Massachusetts, USA: Harvard University Press.

14 THE PHD PROCESS: DOCTOR OR DOCTORED?

Kasturi Behari-Leak

INTRODUCTION

The doctoral journey has been the most profound and intense intellectual and emotional engagement I have had in my academic life. It is fitting that the PhD graduation ceremony, which is the culmination of years of intellectual endurance and perseverance, is filled with tradition and ceremony. The four-year doctoral journey is similar to the four-minute walk across the stage to be capped and hooded. Stepping onto the stage is like stepping into the doctoral space. Walking across the stage requires that you are mindful of the audience – as you have to be with the reader of the thesis. Being acknowledged by the university through its conferring of the degree is synonymous with academic peer review. Finally facing the academic community is like coming through the examination process. All these physical movements during graduation embody the stages in the doctoral journey from conception of the research question, to the final submission of the thesis for examination, and then to graduation.

Standing there, finely kitted out in academic gown and regalia, the more pressing and immediate task was walking across the stage. What if I tripped over myself in my eagerness to make it to the other end as Doctor Behari-Leak? I had just completed an intellectual marathon to the finish line, so the short "walk to freedom" could not be that involved, could it? As I made my way to the chancellor to be capped, I faced a huge dilemma. If I knelt down onto the low stool, would I be able to stand up again given that I was wearing a *saree*, which is a traditional Indian outfit? Would my cultural trappings result, literally, in my downfall? If my *saree* did get caught, would I be stuck there, frozen in time, half capped, not hooded? The weightier issue was that submitting or kneeling down to anyone was not something I did very well, so how would I succumb and humble myself before this esteemed chancellor of the university?

Although initially annoyed that these questions had found their way into my celebratory minute of fame, this challenging of your assumptions is the very skill needed in a doctoral project. Through this, you learn that it is important to insert and assert your own questions, voice, beliefs, values and attitudes into the process of *becoming* a doctoral scholar and researcher. After all, who you are and what you as researcher bring to the doctoral endeavour influence and shape the type of research questions you ask and the rigour with which you carry out your investigation. The whole thesis, by its very nature, does not simply emerge by itself. The research question itself is driven by your own passion, commitment and engagement with a topic that has come to mean something important to you. It is born out of your immersion in a field that you have *mastered*, and from which you have identified, after deep reflection and thought, a unique research problem for your doctoral study.

In this chapter, I share how I navigated and negotiated this terrain and how I chose to respond to particular challenges that contributed to my own unease and resistance, but which pushed my boundaries in many positive ways. It is important for doctoral scholars to insert themselves into their research in meaningful ways, and claim the doctoral space for themselves.

DOCTORAL TRADITIONS AND CONVENTIONS

In embarking on your doctoral study, you have to be aware that the doctoral process has power to shape and mould you in different ways, as it should. You step into an academic space of "doctoral natives" who have paved the way by creating strong traditions and conventions of doctoral writing and dissemination, which have come to be accepted as the unquestioned model for this kind of research (Denzin 2001; Hanrahan, Cooper & Burroughs-Lange 1999). Your status as "doctoral immigrant" is highly dependent on your ability to charter your own course in already well-established waters. The challenge is that the standard chapters, such as the introduction, literature review, findings, discussion and conclusion, tolerate few variations on the traditional theme. Even in this digital age, the dissemination of research findings is confined mainly to conventional paper-based versions, and research excellence is measured through monographs or academic journals (Carrigan 2013).

Such boundedness to conventions and traditions begs the question: whose conventions, whose traditions, and to what end? There seems to be little space for emerging researchers with alternative research methodologies to illustrate their findings in creative, unique and mysterious ways that are considered legitimate scholarly research. You might find, like I did, that the presentation of the PhD thesis using the traditional, canonical, westernised format can be limiting and limited in allowing you to express yourself creatively, as it does not capture the emotional labour (Zembylas 2007, 2012; Ahmed 2004) involved in the project. Your final PhD product, like mine, might not be a fair representation of the sensory, emotional and kinaesthetic aspects involved (Jones 2006); nor will it necessarily enable the cultural expression that allows the text and audience to come together easily and inform one another (Denzin 2001).

You might find that the traditional scientific and social science doctoral model gives an "over-simplified picture of how learning happens and what knowledge is, since it presents learning as a more or a less linear, impersonal and individualistic process" (Hanrahan et al 1999:401). The actual process is far from the rational, deliberate and clinical one it appears to be. It is a highly creative project, which involves false starts, readjustments, redefinition and uncertainty (Scrivener 2000). Because the traditional doctorate is embedded in a problem-solving rather than in a creative production approach (Berridge 2008), it cannot fully capture the scope of approaches arising from different views of the world which may embody alternative understandings of how knowledge is created (Haberman 2009). The conventions of doctoral theses are also "detached from the personal, cultural and historical context of the researcher" (Hanrahan et al 1999:401) and the nature of "scholarship" is not receptive and representative of scholars who are not of western tradition. As a doctoral scholar writing in the "Global South", I have found the traditional thesis to have limited scope for grey areas or creative space for expression through the use of colour and shape, for example. There is little room for speculation, hearsay, gut feel, intuition, mystery or transcendental wisdom that may be borne by bearers who are natural researchers through their deep experiences of life.

You also might find that the accepted conventions of academic doctoral research do not always accommodate the scholar's cultural repertoire or style of writing (Canagarajah 2006). The limitations and boundaries of the printed page may offer little space for exits and entrances characteristic of creative writers in any discipline (Berridge 2008). Despite these conventions being upheld, there is evidence of shifts in reporting academic work. Texts that mark cultural shifts (such as those used in social justice research) have succeeded in challenging assumptions and practices regarding writing within academia (Richardson 1994). These shifts include alternative methods such as narratives, autobiography, auto-ethnography, and photo-elicitation to generate deep and rich accounts of research participants' views and insights by *showing*, rather than only *telling* (Phelan 1998:13). If you are interested in adopting alternative approaches, you may contribute to transforming doctoral study – provided that your work still upholds the benchmarks of scientific rigour.

DOCTORAL OR DOCTORED?

Most self-help manuals on the doctoral journey (Sternberg 1981; Rose & McClafferty 2001; Kamler & Thomson 2008; Oliver 2004; Hochschild 2003) claim that the scholar's greatest achievement is adding an original contribution to the existing body of knowledge, but I would argue that this is a vital by-product of an even greater accomplishment. A more tacit outcome is the development in the scholar, of a particular way of interacting with knowledge and with the world. If you are consciously involved in the process of being and becoming the doctoral scholar, your own traditions, practices and ways of seeing the world will alter and transform you in ways that are irreducible to the outcomes achieved in the thesis. If more of us do this, the greater the potential is for the boundaries to be extended and for more creative expression and dissemination to be accepted as part of an academic discourse in doctoral research.

As a prospective doctoral scholar, you need to be aware that the liberating process of coming into being as a PhD scholar and writer may be denied to you if you stick too rigidly to prescribed traditions and conventions. There are many ways in which traditions and conventions, if left unchallenged, dominate to the extent that you do not recognise yourself anymore. In the current global and international climate, we need to critique the normative way that research in the social as well as in the natural sciences functions, as if neutral and absent of ideology (Richardson 1994). More significantly, if you are uncritical of instead of claiming your space as doctoral scholar, you may become "doctored" in the process. If you do not want to be doctored into submission, which can leave you feeling like a passive impostor in your own work, find a way to insert your own expression and voice that pushes the doctoral envelope further. I therefore urge you to think about what *your* needs are and consider how *you* could best present your work in ways that are creative, unique and meaningful to your study.

THE HEAD, HEART, HAND OF DOCTORAL STUDY

One of the ways to shift paradigms is by experimenting with different ways of "knowing, acting and being" (Dall'Alba & Barnacle 2007:10), and by troubling the knowledge that has come to be accepted as the truth (Dall'Alba 2009). As a doctoral student, I was aware that emotional and affective spaces (Zembylas 2007) regarding my self-esteem and confidence to write well had opened up. Using the concepts of knowing, being and doing (Martin & Mirraboopa 2003), discussed below, I was able to conceptualise the doctoral process as a holistic and integrated one. I did not have to deny or ignore the emotionality, and this awareness encouraged me to see that the head (knowing), heart (being), and hand (doing) each had a role to play and that I could embrace all three domains. It is in this meta-reflexive space that you can develop a strong scholarly voice and sense of purpose as a person, researcher and academic, and come to know yourself as a doctoral graduate in the making.

KNOWING THE DOCTORAL SCHOLAR

Knowing yourself is critical before you start your studies as this will affect your purpose, motivation and sustained interest in the PhD. There are various ways in which our lives intersect with academic knowledge at the crossroads of undertaking a PhD. I started looking at the possibility of doing a doctorate to offset my own existential crisis as an academic in higher education who was plagued by questions: What was the point of it all? What would be the outcome? Like many others, I chose to do a PhD so that I could make a difference, but I must admit that I partly succumbed to the pressure to enter the doctoral marathon with the purpose of obtaining a better academic position in higher education. I was aware that, if I wanted to make a difference in academia, I needed to learn to play by the rules before I could break them. A doctorate provided me with such credibility. If your reasons are similar to mine, I would suggest that your key challenge at the outset is to figure out how to channel your ideas, values and beliefs into an academic project that will not only contribute meaningfully to your chosen field of study, but that will also sustain your own interests and passion. If your reasons are purely for certification and credentialisation, you might find it difficult to reconcile who you are, what you know and what you believe with what is expected of you as the doctoral scholar. In a country like South Africa – which is riddled with the master narratives of class, gender, race, ability, ethnicity and language (Mangcu 2015; Mbembe 2015) – I have found that the tension between *knowing* and *being* becomes pronounced and plays itself out in the doctoral space[1]. As such, the doctorate becomes a site for ongoing struggle. With a good sense of self as you embark on a PhD, you will keep grounded and focussed on the key research questions in ways that are meaningful to you.

BEING THE DOCTORAL SCHOLAR

As doctoral scholars, we come into our studies with a wealth of experiences, conditioning and positions that strongly shape who we are and who we become. This is especially true in the social sciences, where such influences are crucial to how

---

1   This tension between knowing and being is also emphasised by other authors in this book – see for example the contributions of Andre van der Bijl (Chapter 7), Langutani Masehela (Chapter 12) and Catherine Robertson (Chapter 13).

researchers shape their studies to raise awareness of social issues. My positionality as doctoral scholar and researcher was set against this backdrop.

It was fortuitous therefore that, at the beginning of 2011, I was accepted to be part of the Social Inclusion Doctoral Project at Rhodes University, the first of its kind, funded through a grant from the National Research Foundation. I had found the perfect medium to channel my efforts through a cohort approach, which drew on a collaborative pedagogy and socio-cultural theories of learning. The idea of co-creating and co-producing knowledge in a shared, supportive and scaffolded environment, rather than as an individualistic and solitary learning activity, resonated with me and spoke to my personal objectives of studying in a way that was meaningful, purposeful, valuable, critical and transformational. If you too thrive in collaborative learning contexts, try to find a community of post-graduate scholars at your university or elsewhere with whom you can connect and share ideas, and from whom you can learn.

Apart from the collaborative support of peers and others, the doctoral journey cannot be undertaken without a knowledgeable guide, in the form of a supervisor. The role of the supervisor is crucial and critical to the direction, detours and new paths that the scholar takes. I have been fortunate to have had two supervisors who have provided me with a safe space to discuss, debate, share, extend and shape the research project and doctoral journey in meaningful ways. As experts and authorities in the higher education field, they gave me excellent counsel. Through the many occasions of despair, they were able to guide me even when I could not find my way. Through such a positive supervision experience, I am in awe of what potential there is for other novices like me to be mentored and supported in such meaningful ways, by similar supervisors who had just the right balance between guiding, steering, and leading, without compromising the scholar, and who provided the conducive energy and influences for the exercise of agency of the scholar[2].

Being a doctoral scholar means that the way in which you argue, justify, defend, conceptualise and theorise your study also says something about you as a responsible scholar in the making. Your research design and methods are equally under scrutiny and many of your choices have to be rigorously defended in your thesis. This is where the process of *coming into being* as a doctoral graduate is important. To

---

[2] I am drawing on Margaret Archer's (1995; 2003) notion of agency which refers to the social explanatory theory used to account for human action, agential choices and causal relations. "Agency" points to the capacity of people to act on their social worlds in a voluntary way, based on their personal and psychological constitutions. The double-loop of people acting on themselves while being acted on is salutary to the existence and acknowledgement of the human agent as having independent powers and properties (Archer 2003). See Chapter 12 in this book that also draws on this particular notion.

pay homage to this process, I included a pre-introductory chapter in my doctoral thesis titled "Chapter Zero", appropriately named to invoke the notion that Chapter One, or the background and context chapter (as it is conventionally known), does not simply emerge by itself from nowhere. Through the concept of Zero, I revoked the notion that "nothing comes from nothing" (a quote from Shakespeare's *King Lear*, echoing the proposition of Parmenides, a pre-Socratic Greek philosopher) as I believe that there is always *something* to be developed, shaped and nurtured from ground zero into something greater. This is something you might consider doing if you too want to remind the reader that a great deal of preparation, planning and designing, as well as heart and soul, led you to the thesis. You might decide to include a reflective chapter or addendum such as this to offer a narrative on your own doctoral journey and the assertion of your doctoral Self. Such a contribution encourages examiners, scholars and researchers to acknowledge that real people do research, and that subjectivity is in the nature of being real (Sayer 1992). It does not have to detract from the rigour of the investigation. To this end my Chapter Zero (Behari-Leak 2015) had a very personal touch, and included pages in colour, with watermarked images, photographs of key people and influences, and graphics and symbolic representations that captured mood and intent. In this way, I inserted and asserted the doctoral scholar as a knowing, thinking, feeling and valuing human being.

DOING: STEPPING INTO THE SPACE AS DOCTORAL SCHOLAR

Doctoral agency is crucial to the depth and quality of your thesis. What you do is as important as what you choose not to do. My supervisors made me aware that stepping into the doctoral space was the most difficult hurdle to overcome. You need to be aware that you are stepping into this space with specific identities. I, for example, was aware that I was stepping into that space as a raced, gendered, languaged and classed individual, and this awareness helped me to locate and position myself alongside my study, and move from understanding who I was to what I could do (Archer 1995). This is where the shifts began to happen for me, and may well happen for you, for as your knowledge and understanding shift, so too do your identity and agency; not just as a cognitive exercise but as real shifts in your thinking, feeling and actions as well as your valuing, attitudes and discourse.

When these shifts happen, you cannot become invisible and silent (Maton 2001). Your voice is important and the doctoral experience is an embodied one, one that you should claim fully. This does not mean that the tension between the traditions and conventions of the doctorate and your location in the process will be eradicated, but remember it is through the activities of agents who hold ideas and who act within social contexts on and within social structures that social change may be effected (Archer 1995). You need to hold onto your personal project: What are my commitments and interests and what will my study achieve? This sense of identity and agency is what will shape the choices and decisions you make and will sustain you throughout the process.

LOCATING THE DOCTORAL SCHOLAR IN AN EMERGING PARADIGM

Once you have accepted that you have a right to be here, your next quest is to find a research methodology and framework that allow you the freedom to be creative while you are attending to the doctoral project's central concerns and questions. In my case, I was not convinced that the conventional modes of inquiry usually associated with research in the humanities, namely interviews, observations, document analysis and discussions (Alvesson 2003), would contribute to my study in dynamic ways. I had found that when the data "out there" becomes the property of the researcher "in here", it renders the voices and identities of the contributors silenced after their role has been fulfilled (Denzin 2001).

If you are also exploring research of a social science nature that involves other people, you might want to consider how you engage with your research participants. In my study, I wanted to *generate*, and not merely *collect* data (Behari-Leak 2015), in order to reflect a mutually beneficial relationship between "subject" and "agent". An emerging paradigm known as the "Third Space"[3] (Bhabha 1996) provided the framework for me to conceptualise the possibility of this perspective. As an alternative way of understanding research and its purpose, you might also be interested in locating your research in this hybrid space to look critically at the taken-for-granted assumptions of the researcher and researched[4].

The research methods that I chose included participatory learning and action techniques (Chambers 2006), which used drawings, free writing, problem trees, rivers of life and community maps to engage my research participants in the research process. Through these methods I was able to generate rich data for the purposes of my study, which the

---

[3] A new way of working with research participants and research data signals the move away from externally imposed denial and detachment of the subject who is doing the research from the object of study, to a reclaiming of the role and involvement of the self, particularly where the self is personally involved (Denzin 2004). This "Third Space" provides the framework for understanding research as a "hybrid space" where the researcher and the researched share integrity of process in a mutually beneficial exchange (Denzin 2004).

[4] See Chapter 6 by Soraya Abdulatief that addresses this issue in more depth.

traditional interview as a research method might not have been able to do. The process took the form of a photo voice story (Wang & Burris 1997), through which participants shared their experiences using photographs they had taken in response to my research questions and prompts. These stories were shared in a story circle, recorded and later transcribed for analysis. I strongly suggest that you explore and find the set of research methods that speaks to what you are trying to achieve, rather than settling for tried and tested methods, just because many have followed that route before.

CONCLUSION

The doctoral journey encompasses both cognitive and affective elements that require a doctoral scholar to engage, not only with the theoretical and research framework, but also in the doctoral experience itself and in the process of stepping into the doctoral space. For me, like many other South African scholars, this meant exercising my doctoral agency by facing my fears, accepting my limitations, playing to my strengths, setting achievable goals and intentions, and making decisions to act on my educated guesses and hunches. In being critically reflexive, I was able to find synergies between my own interests, the research purpose and thesis outcomes.

As principal author, your doctoral voice and positionality need not be minimised. Explicit acknowledgement of who you are as the scholar and how you have conceived of the project makes it possible for readers to resonate with more than the research findings. Achieving this balance requires a healthy and robust supervision relationship, as well as collaboration with others on a similar path. In the South African context, this collegial social learning and socio-cultural dimension should not be underestimated, especially as we become more connected and multimodal in the digital age. In considering different ways of "doing your PhD", you may contribute to an expansion and extension of the traditional PhD canon so that cultural diversity can be acknowledged and appreciated as legitimate ways of doing research. The more scholars are able to take their supervisors, examiners and readers on this journey, the broader research horizons become.

REFERENCES

Ahmed, S. (2004). *The cultural politics of emotion*. New York, NY: Routledge.

Alvesson, M. (2003). Methodology for close up studies: Struggling with closeness and closure. *Higher Education,* 46(2):167-193. http://dx.doi.org/10.1023/A:1024716513774

Archer, M. S. (1995). *Realist social theory: The morphogenetic approach*. Cambridge, UK: Cambridge University Press. http://dx.doi.org/10.1017/CBO9780511557675

Behari-Leak, K. (2015). *Conditions that enable or constrain the exercise of agency among new academics in higher education, conducive to the social inclusion of students*. (Unpublished doctoral thesis). Rhodes University, South Africa.

Berridge, Sally (2008). What does it take? Auto/biography as performative PhD thesis. *Forum: Qualitative Social Research,* 9(2), Art. 456. Available online at http://www.qualitative-research.net/index.php/fqs/article/view/379/825

Bhabha, H. K. (1996). Culture's in between. In S. Hall, & P. du Gay (Eds.). *Questions of cultural identity* (pp. 53-60). London, UK: Sage.

Canagarajah, S. (2006). Toward a writing pedagogy of shuttling between languages: Learning from multilingual writers. *College English,* 68:589-604. http://dx.doi.org/10.2307/25472177

Carrigan, M. (2013). *The shifting language of research 'participation'*. Available online at http://sociologicalimagination.org/archives/author/markcarriganauthor

Chambers, R. (2006). *Notes for participants in PRA-PLA familiarisation workshops in 2006*. Sussex, UK: Institute of Development Studies.

Dall'Alba, G. (2009). Learning professional ways of being: Ambiguities of becoming. *Educational Philosophy and Theory,* 41(1):34-45. http://dx.doi.org/10.1111/j.1469-5812.2008.00475.x

Dall'Alba, G. & Barnacle, R. (2007). An ontological turn for higher education. *Studies in Higher Education,* 32(6):679-691. http://dx.doi.org/10.1080/03075070701685130

Denzin, N. (2001). The reflexive interview and a performative social science. *Qualitative Research,* 1(1):23-46. http://dx.doi.org/10.1177/146879410100100102

Denzin, N. K. (2004). The war on culture, the war on truth. *Cultural Studies – Critical Methodologies,* 4(2):137-142. http://dx.doi.org/10.1177/1532708603256627

Haberman, M. (2009). *Performative writing in performance studies: Filling in missing spaces*. (Unpublished MA thesis). University of Maine, Orono, ME. Available online at http://digitalcommons.library.umaine.edu/etd/1029

Hanrahan, M., Cooper, T., & Burroughs-Lange, S. (1999). The place of personal writing in a PhD thesis: Epistemological and methodological considerations. *International Journal of Qualitative Studies in Education,* 12(4):401-416.

Hochschild, A. (2003). *The commercialization of intimate life: Notes from home and work*. Berkeley, California: University of California Press.   PMid:12753182

Jones, K. (2006). A biographic researcher in pursuit of an aesthetic: The use of arts-based (re)presentations in "performative" dissemination of life stories. *Qualitative Sociology Review,* II(1):66-85.

Kamler, B. & Thomson, P. (2008). The failure of dissertation advice books: Toward alternative pedagogies for doctoral writing. *Educational Researcher*, 37(8):507-514.

Mangcu, X. (2015, July 31). *Xolela Mangcu on biko and race in 'post-apartheid South Africa'*. The Mail and Guardian. Available online at http://mg.co.za/article/2015-07-30-xolela-mangcu-on-race-in-post-apartheid-south-africa

Martin, K. & Mirraboopa, B. (2003). Ways of knowing, being and doing: A theoretical framework and methods for indigenous and indigenist re-search, *Journal of Australian Studies*, 27(76):203-214. http://dx.doi.org/10.1080/14443050309387838

Maton, K. (2001). The critical and real need of educational research for critical realism. *Journal of Critical Realism*, 4(1):56-59.

Mbembe, A. (2015) Decolonizing knowledge and the question of the archive. Public lecture. Available online at https://africaisacountry.atavist.com/decolonizing-knowledge-and-the-question-of-the-archive

Oliver, P. (2004). *Writing your thesis*. Thousand Oaks, CA: Sage.

Phelan, P. (1998). *Introduction: The ends of performance*. New York, USA: University Press.

Richardson, L. (1994). Writing a method of inquiry. In N. K. Denzin, & Y. S. Lincoln (Eds.), *Handbook of qualitative research* (pp. 516-529). Thousand Oaks, CA: Sage.

Rose, M., & McClafferty, K. (2001). A call for the teaching of writing in graduate education. *Educational Researcher*, 30(2):27-33. http://dx.doi.org/10.3102/0013189X030002027

Sayer, R. A. (1992). *Method in social science: A realist approach* (2nd ed.). London, UK: Routledge.

Scrivener, S. (2000). "Reflection in and on practice in creative-doctoral projects in art and design." *Working Papers in Art and Design 1*, 1-16. Available online at http://www.herts.ac.uk/artdes/research/papers/wpades/vol1/scrivener2.html

Shakespeare, W. (n.d.). *King Lear*. Act 1.1 and Act 4.4

Sternberg, D. (1981). *How to complete and survive a doctoral dissertation*. New York, USA: St. Martin's.

Wang, C., & Burris, M. A. (1997). Photovoice: Concept, methodology, and use for participatory needs assessment. *Health Education & Behavior*, 24(3):369-387. http://dx.doi.org/10.1177/109019819702400309 PMid:9158980

Zembylas, M. (2007). Theory and methodology in researching emotions in education. *International Journal of Research and Method in Education*, 30(1):57-72.

Zembylas, M. (2012). *Reinstating or disrupting the dichotomy of reason/emotion in higher education? A historicized approach: The point of critique is not justification but a different way of feeling: Another sensibility*. Keynote to the Higher Education Close-up 6 Conference, Rhodes University, July 2012.

PART FIVE

POSTGRADUATE STUDY
AS A SOCIAL PRACTICE
IN SOUTH AFRICA

15
SO WHAT DO YOU THINK? THE ROLE OF DIALOGUE IN DOCTORAL LEARNING

Jacqueline Lück

INTRODUCTION

When I first articulated that I was embarking on a doctoral study, the inevitable question I got asked was, "So what are you doing?" Anxiety would grip me in response to this question. I found myself stymied and could not clearly explain what I wanted to do. Although frightening, such dialogues are essential, even if you feel that they are not fruitful since you may not yet have the ontological, epistemological or methodological lenses for your study. My first thought in these conversations would be that I wanted to solve all the problems in my field. My study was to be something quite revolutionary. I stammered and stuttered my way through a long rambling answer and could see from the quizzical look on the face of my interrogator that my answer was barely sufficient. You may feel the same way as you begin to formulate a focus area for your study. But continuing the dialogue with yourself and others will help you to eventually see your study focus more clearly.

A doctoral study can be shaped and reshaped through such dialogue with a number of significant others in your community of practice. You may have heard talk of a doctoral study as lonely (Harrison 2007, Brailsford 2010) and therefore, by implication, lack dialogue with others. The doctoral journey can be compared to popular conceptions of an only child in a family, as doctoral candidates are often thought of as solitary (no siblings at hand), maladjusted (abnormal focus on your studies), selfish (too much time spent away from significant others), spoilt (spending time on your passion), privileged (by virtue of doing a doctorate), and overly intellectual (preoccupied with a research project that requires extensive periods of solitary thinking).

This chapter attempts to debunk the myth of the lonely doctoral scholar by showing how community dialogues can assist in the development of a more adjusted, engaged and focussed scholar[1]. Dialogue within a community also resonates particularly with us as South Africans, as it speaks to the African concept of Ubuntu[2]. This concept is often illustrated through the Nguni proverb of *"umuntu ngumuntu ngabantu"* or *"a person is a person through other persons"* (Gade 2011:487). This means that we find value and meaning through our interconnectedness and interaction with others, which also holds true for your doctoral studies.

Bernstein (1983:162) notes that "[w]hat is most characteristic of our humanity is that we are dialogical or conversational human beings". For a doctoral study, this means a focus on communities of practice to mediate your understanding of your study. Engaging in ongoing iterative conversations with communities of practice in your field allows you to refine a doctoral focus. These conversations could include supervisors, colleagues or critical friends, higher degrees committee members, other scholars at your proposal presentation, practitioners at conferences, discussions with scholars who are using similar theoretical lenses or doing similar research, as well as online communities[3]. I will discuss each of these possible dialogic partners in turn and how they might facilitate your doctoral development before, during and after doctoral study. I recognise that these spaces could be daunting to enter when you are not yet eloquent in the field. However, there is value in such engagement as it may help with the focus that is often so elusive in the initial stages of a doctoral study, help you to conceptualise your study throughout your journey, and make the journey less lonely.

DIALOGIC SPACES AND COMMUNITIES OF PRACTICE (COP)

The doctoral journey can be framed within notions of dialogic spaces (Bakhtin 1990) and communities of practice (Lave & Wenger 1991). Language as used in dialogue involves a multiplicity of speakers where truth is negotiated (Bakhtin 1990), while critical dialogic engagement is that which provides enabling transformations (Bebbington, Brown, Frame & Thomson 2007). What you can draw from dialogics as a scholar is how human agency is understood and with what agency it provides you in understanding your own practice (in this case as a scholar-in-becoming). In this view, you collectively (re)produce and transform praxis (making the link between theory and practice) as the meanings which you put upon your situation can be changed as a result of dialogue (Bebbington *et al* 2007). For example, you may

---

[1] Also see the other chapters in this part of the book (Part 5), where different contributors reflect upon postgraduate study as a non-isolated, social practice.

[2] See the chapter by Langutani Masehela (Chapter 12) where the concept of Ubuntu is addressed in more detail.

[3] See Chapter 17 (by Wolvaardt *et al*) for a discussion on critical friends.

CHAPTER 15 • SO WHAT DO YOU THINK? THE ROLE OF DIALOGUE IN DOCTORAL LEARNING

initially have grand ideas of solving all the problems of a particular situation (as I did), but learn through dialogue that a narrow focus also can be meaningful.

Voice plays a significant role in your activities as scholar. Voice emerges in your dialogical conversations to take you further along by encouraging and shifting your thinking. We usually discover "who we are by addressing ourselves to others or the voices of others within us" (Murchison 1998:465). Our individual and collective scholarly voices mould our studies towards completion.

Often though, there are many voices giving input on what you are doing in your study and how you should be doing it. Burton (1997) says that these voices are the meanings competing for supremacy. This struggle over meaning is part of the dialogic process. As meanings are linked to power, it may influence who or what is deemed legitimate. Bebbington et al (2007) argue that there has to be recognition of the authenticity of others to whom you listen to and discuss, to seek underlying values and assumptions in multi-voiced exchanges. Through dialogue you can speak back to authoritative discourses and make your own contributions. Dialogic conversations encourage reflexivity, and reflection is what separates the novice from the expert (Daley 1999). Theorising dialogically helps to refine your focus and conceptual lenses through authentic conversation. There is always room for inquiry as dialogics is by its very nature ontological by seeking a point of view on what is considered as the so-called truth. As a developing scholar you have the capacity to resist, inquire, confront and make personal meaning for your own studies out of such conversations (White 2009). In order to do this, you have to take an additional step outside of the dialogue to make sense of the moment, based on what can be seen. Bakhtin (1990:ix, part 1) describes this as an "excess of seeing", where you step outside the dialogue to see the value it has for your doctorate and how you can speak to a particular point of view raised in the dialogue in your doctorate.

Related to dialogics is the notion of Communities of Practice (CoP) as concepualised by Lave and Wenger (1991), who developed a model of situated learning that sees learning as occurring within a community of practice. A CoP is defined as people engaging in "a process of collective learning within a shared domain of human endeavour" (Wenger 1999:1). He describes the shared domain as meaning everyone who is committed to the domain and share competence; the community as members engaged in joint activities and joint discussion, helping and sharing information and the practice as shared practitioners with a shared repertoire of resources. As such, CoP can be described as "a set of relations among persons, activity and world, over time and in relation with tangential and overlapping communities of practice" (Lave

& Wenger 1991:98). For your doctorate this means sharing ideas with individuals who have common concerns and passions.

According to Lave and Wenger (1991) people join such communities initially at the periphery. This learning by newcomers is called Legitimate Peripheral Participation. As you become more competent you move to the centre. When you embark on a doctoral study in a particular field, you may be doing so initially as an outsider. You do not yet know the discourse and ways of being in the field. You are thus not able to speak eloquently within and contribute substantively to the discourse at this stage. However, you need to draw on the idea of the value of the social participation first, as Hodkinson and Hodkinson (n.d.) argue that learning in a CoP is a social process where identity, knowing and membership are significant. This initial social participation leads you to eventual full participation in the socio-cultural practices of a community (Lave & Wenger 1991).

Those involved in CoPs often have vested interests, but as the nature of a dialogical relationship also involves self-reflective spaces, these encounters will allow you to assess the merits of what others (who often will have opposing views) are saying and how these views speak to your doctoral study. Fundamentally though, a CoP has the potential to open up dialogic spaces to engage about your doctorate and the voices that emanate from CoPs help to shape and reshape your doctorate. There are many instances of dialogues with your community of practice before, during and after a doctoral study that are valuable in shaping your study.

COMMUNITY DIALOGUE

Taylor (1994) talks of communities as not only whole communities, but layered communities, crisscrossing communities and partial communities. In doctoral studies, these communities include supervisors, colleagues, higher degrees committee members and doctoral scholars, scholars and practitioners at conferences and online communities and conferences who may consist of the same or different people at different times. The dialogic spaces that these different and ever-changing communities create could allow you to conceptualise and refine your study.

Dialogue with supervisors

The most significant space for dialogue is the one between you and your supervisor. You may have the opportunity to choose your own supervisor or you may be allocated a supervisor. No matter how this relationship came to be, its functioning is fundamental to the success of your study. Open and ongoing dialogue increases the chances of a successful doctoral journey.

CHAPTER 15 • SO WHAT DO YOU THINK? THE ROLE OF DIALOGUE IN DOCTORAL LEARNING

Being the legitimate peripheral learner (Lave & Wenger 1991) may impede your communication with your supervisor. Begin with the move to full participation by opening the dialogue with your supervisor through a discussion of your initial thoughts; what it is you are proposing to do. This could take the form of the following statement, "*I am interested in looking at ...* (insert your topic of interest), *because ...* (insert your rationale for wanting to do so)." As focus areas are often broad in the beginning, the response from your supervisor could go along the lines of, "*There are a few focus areas to be found within what you say. At the moment, there are too many different issues battling each other to be in the foreground.*"

Furthermore, your supervisor may outline to you what the different (perhaps competing) focus areas are in your study. Your area may need narrowing down and ongoing discussions would assist here. Your dialogue could then move to a dialogue where you critically reflect on your focus based on the input obtained from your supervisor, "*I have had a look at your synthesis of my focus. I have given it some thought and have decided to go with the following focus ...*"

Ongoing dialogue thus continues to take you into new spaces where you are left with more new questions which you further refine with your supervisor in the initial stages of your study. Once you have formulated what it is you want to focus on, planning a regular dialogue (for example once a week or month, depending on your circumstances) keeps the momentum going. The dialogue occurs around your writing as it progresses. Beware of not working too long on honing a section or chapter before sending to your supervisor(s). You may want it to be perfect before you send it off for comment but the dialogue will falter if regular writing is not discussed frequently. A long lull in writing and communication sets up more and more barriers which become difficult to overcome.

A doctorate is often tied to one's sense of identity entailing the learning of "doctorateness" and the negotiation of a new identity (Harrison 2007:9), and receiving feedback becomes a further obstacle to progress. Seeing feedback as your supervisor shining a clearer light on your ideas may be a good way of dealing with supervisory critique. The space should not be a combative one that mitigates against the growth and enrichment of the process. Areas of conflict should be addressed in positive ways and not allowed to simmer. The dialogue that forms part of feedback is one of mutual respect though the supervisor is in the position of having more authority on the field and study itself – at least initially. Receiving feedback does not mean that you cannot assert your own ideas.

The dialogue continues and intensifies as you approach the final stages of submission. Here it is crucial for you and your supervisor to collectively map out how often you will be conversing and what both parties expect from these conversations. You do not want to be to part of a one-way conversation where there are no responses, especially since doctoral study is seen as involving a process of becoming (Barnacle 2005) and thus a move to a critical, independent and responsible scholar (Lin & Cranton 2005).

Dialogues with colleagues and critical friends

A different dialogic space is that of colleagues who could give you rich feedback on your study. Perhaps you are in an educational institution where you could present your research project at a research seminar or departmental meeting. This space could alert you to areas you may not have considered or critiques on the theory you are using. Colleagues who have gone on this journey before you may have good advice about pitfalls and possibilities. Even if you are not in an educational institution, colleagues are still of value and you may seek opportunities such as a formal staff meeting or informal chats to present your project. This space helps you focus on the rationale of your study, especially if it is related to the field you are working in. If you are studying full time and have no colleagues with whom to discuss your study, critical friends can fill this space. Even if they are not studying or have not studied, critical friends can help you by asking questions. They would be holding a mirror for you to see your study's reflections and this assists in gaining more clarity. In the initial stages of your study, such questions help you to see what your doctoral study is about and who it is aimed at.

Dialogue at proposal presentation

Institutions in South Africa often require of doctoral candidates to do a formal presentation (some call it a defence) of their doctorate. Other scholars, professors from the university's higher degrees committee, as well as internal and external examiners could be present. The audience would also usually have read the proposal beforehand. At this session, you usually prepare a presentation outlining the rationale for your study and argue as to why it warrants a study of this nature. You would also provide your ontological, epistemological, methodological and axiological positions as it pertains to the research design (Frick 2011).

Questions from the audience constitute the real dialogue and therein lies the value of this space. At a postgraduate seminar I attended, a member of the audience asked a doctoral candidate, "What troubles you?" This question was in reference to what the candidate wanted to do. The audience member indicated that he was not getting a sense of what the focus area of the study was. The candidate then clarified in more detail what her focus area was. This may resonate with you because you too may have trouble conceptualising your research in the beginning stages of your study. If you are given feedback on the areas you presented and especially those you may have to engage with more fully, it could greatly benefit your study in the long term. You also respond to questions and both the questions and your reflections upon them allow you to give and gain more clarity on the various aspects of your study.

Dialogue at conferences

Conferences are further important dialogic spaces with a community of practice. You may be wary of presenting your study at a conference until after graduation, but these spaces can also help you move forward during your doctoral journey.

My supervisor encouraged me and others to present our proposals at conferences as work in progress. The studies of those of us who took up the challenge emerged stronger as a result. Decide on conferences that speak to your field of study as these are the audiences with whom you want to engage. You may only have your rationale, theory and methodology to talk about at this stage. But that is enough. The feedback you will get will encourage further dialogics with your supervisor in order to address any concerns that arose, or to further refine a particular area of your study.

You could also present on your initial data findings at a conference. You may not have analysed all your data, but only a section of it. You could speak to it as a work in progress and discuss with conference participants the merits of the claims you are making. This could allow your conceptual and analytical lenses to become even sharper.

Post-doctoral conferences are also spaces that could continue to shape your work as you take the findings forward. The audience may of course tell you what you should or should not have done but the main idea is to open up spaces for your findings and recommendations. They should engage with the implications of your study and the contribution it has made to new knowledge. How your study advances your field will be significant conversations. You may also get ideas about how to take your study forward by applying new conceptual lenses.

It is also important to share your findings with practitioners in your field. There were solid reasons for embarking on your study and your recommendations need to be part of conversations in practice. Practitioners do not necessarily attend academic conferences, but it is necessary to find or create dialogic spaces where you can feed your work back into practice if you want it to have relevance beyond academia. Also remember that you have a responsibility to the practitioners and respondents (where relevant) to make your results known as widely as possible.

Dialogue with experts

You or your supervisor may know of experts in your field with whom you could have additional sessions. A theorist or scholar whose work you are using may be coming to present at a conference and a meeting could be arranged for you to have a conversation with him/her. If a face-to-face meeting is not possible, you could connect with such a person online. A leap in learning or the crossing of a conceptual threshold (Whisker, Kiley & Aisten 2006) could result from engaging with someone who is intimately connected to the theory.

Publishing articles prior to the examination of your doctorate can create another kind of dialogic space for engagement with experts. You get valuable feedback via peer review. Publishing articles are not only for people who are doing their doctorates by publication.

Your discussions about your work need to continue beyond your final submission and after completing your doctorate. You would not want your study to be gathering the proverbial dust on a shelf. Your institution would usually place your study on an online repository and you may have conversations initiated about it by scholars who access it. However, you can create further dialogic spaces to converse about your study. You can set up informal discussions and meetings with practitioners who are affected by your study's results to discuss how they could be taken forward. You need to discuss how you can enhance what is already being done.

Dialogue with other doctoral scholars

Discourses traditionally construct academics as having academic freedom and autonomy to conduct independent enquiry in research (McKenna & Boughey 2014). They argue that such autonomy needs questioning if it does not lead to excellence in both research and teaching. To respond to such obstacles and others, some institutions of higher learning are starting to use structured cohort models of supervision to alleviate these obstacles. These cohort models provide spaces for doctoral scholars in a similar field to engage in a collaborative and sustained manner. It develops collegiality and support for scholars. It mitigates against the isolated space of a doctoral study and allows for more systematic and rigorous study, especially for scholars who start off without a strong knowledge basis (McKenna 2014). The cohort space could be face to face or online. Here you can speak about an area you are grappling with or an experience of illumination. You are also afforded opportunities to dialogue with expert scholars or supervisors to whom you can present your work in progress. These dialogues could result in further joint projects such as conference presentations or articles[4].

Online spaces

Technologies allow us to make meaning of our realities through dialogue in virtual spaces. Some institutions create such online dialogic spaces for you to engage with your own and others' ideas. These spaces also can be repositories for literature you may want to access. They could also have proposals and completed doctoral studies of other scholars you may want to reference or consult. An online space such as a blog, website or facebook page may exist for scholars who are using similar theoretical frameworks. Examples of useful blogs are The Thesis Whisperer (http://thesiswhisperer.com/) started by Inger Mewburn and to which many people contribute, and the Doctoral Writing SIG (https://doctoral writing.wordpress.com/) managed by Claire Aitchison, Cally Guerin and Susan Carter. An example of a local South African blog is PhD in a Hundred Steps (https//phdinahundredsteps.wordpress.com/) with posts by Sherran Clarence[5]. Some sites even list the top blogs for doctoral study by discipline and theme and some are for light relief like PhD comics (http://phdcomics.com/comics.php). There are thus numerous online dialogical spaces to cater to your different needs.

CONCLUSION

The doctoral study does not need to be a lonely conversation that only you and your supervisor are privileged to be part of. It makes it all the more worthwhile if it is informed by significant others. Seek the voices of others to enrich your own voice so that what you envision becomes a rich process. Think about your doctoral study as one that involves a community of practice with dialogic spaces. The value of a community of practice lies in the alleviating of the pains of the substantial doctoral task. Your elusive voice emerges stronger as your theoretical, epistemological or methodological lenses become more and more nuanced. Significantly, you emerge more adjusted through your engagement with significant others. This chapter has illustrated the value of dialogics within a CoP to make sense of and enrich the doctoral experience.

---

4   See Chapter 16 by Puleng Motshoane for a discussion on cohort models.

5   Sherran Clarence also contributed to this book (see Chapter 11), where she used extracts from this blog to substantiate her argument on crossing thresholds.

REFERENCES

Bakhtin, M. M. (1990). *Art & answerability: Early philosophical essays*. (1st Ed). Austin, USA: University of Texas Press.

Barnacle, R. (2005). Research education ontologies: Exploring doctoral becoming. *Higher Education Research and Development*, 24(2):179-188. http://dx.doi.org/10.1080/07294360500062995

Bebbington, J., Brown, J., Frame, B. & Thomson, I. (2007). Theorizing engagement: The potential of a critical dialogic approach. *Accounting, Auditing and Accountability*, 20(3):356-381. http://dx.doi.org/10.1108/09513570710748544

Bernstein, R. J. (1983). *Beyond objectivism and relativism*. Philadephia, USA: University of Philadephia Press.

Brailsford, I. (2010). Motives and aspirations for doctoral study: Career, personal, and interpersonal factors in the decision to embark on a history PhD. *International Journal of Doctoral Studies*, 5:14-27.

Burton, M. (1997). Determinacy, indeterminacy and rhetoric in a pluralist world. *Melbourne Law Review*, 21:544-583.

Daley, B. J. (1999). Novice to expert: An exploration of how professionals learn. *Adult Education Quarterly*, 49(4):133-147. http://dx.doi.org/10.1177/074171369904900401

Frick, B. L. (2011). Facilitating creativity in doctoral education: A resource for supervisors. In A. Lee & V. Mallan (Eds.). Connecting the Local, Regional and Global in Doctoral Education (pp. 123-137). Serdang, Malaysia: Universiti Putra Malaysia Press.

Gade, C. B. N. (2012). What is Ubuntu? Different Interpretations among South Africans of African Descent. *South African Journal of Philosophy*, 31(3):484-503. http://dx.doi.org/10.1080/02580136.2012.10751789

Harrison, L. (2007). Enhancing higher education, theory and scholarship. Proceedings of the 30th HERDSA Annual Conference on Enhancing Higher Education, Theory and Scholarship, Adelaide, Australia.

Hodkinson, P., & Hodkinson, H. (n.d.). *Rethinking communities of practice: A case study of school teachers' workplace learning*. Retrieved from http://www.tlrp.org/project%20sites/IILW/pr5%20H-Tampere,Paper%20141.htm

Lave, J., & Wenger, E. (1991). *Situated learning: Legitimate peripheral participation*. Cambridge, UK: Cambridge University Press. http://dx.doi.org/10.1017/CBO9780511815355

Lin, L., & Cranton, P. (2005). From scholarship student to responsible scholar: A transformative process. *Teaching in Higher Education*, 10(4):447-459. http://dx.doi.org/10.1080/13562510500239026

McKenna, S. (2014). Higher education studies as a field of research. *The Independent Journal of Teaching and Learning*, 9:6-16.

McKenna, S., & Boughey, C. (2014). Argumentative and trustworthy scholars: The construction of academic staff at research-intensive universities, *Teaching in Higher Education*, 19(7):825-834. http://dx.doi.org/10.1080/13562517.2014.934351

Murchison, B. C. (1998). Speech and the self-realization value. *Harvard Civil Rights – Civil Liberties Law Review,* 33:443-503.

Taylor, C. (1994). The politics of recognition. In A. Gutmann (Ed.). *Multiculturalism examining the politics of recognition* (pp. 25-73). New Jersey, USA: Princeton University Press.

Wisker, G., Kiley, M., & Aisten, S. (2006). Making the learning leap: Research students crossing conceptual thresholds. In M. Kiley & G. Mullins (Eds.) *Quality in postgraduate research: Knowledge creation in testing times* (pp. 195-201). Canberra, Australia: CEDAM.

White, E. J. (2009). *Bakhtinian dialogism: A philosophical and methodological route to dialogue and difference?* Paper presented at Annual Conference of the Philosophy of Education Society of Australasia. Retrieved from http://www2.hawaii.edu/~pesaconf/zpdfs/16white.pdf.

Wenger, E. (1999). *Communities of practice: Learning, meaning, and identity.* Cambridge, UK: Cambridge University Press.

16 THE BENEFITS OF BEING PART OF A PROJECT TEAM: A POSTGRADUATE STUDENT PERSPECTIVE

Puleng Motshoane

INTRODUCTION

There are a number of policies, both nationally and internationally, that argue for increased postgraduate outputs. The Academy of Science of South Africa's (ASSAf) report on postgraduate education concluded that "there is a broad consensus in the science community in South Africa that not enough high-quality PhDs are being produced in relation to the developmental needs of the country" (ASSAf 2010:15). The National Development Plan (NDP 2011) suggests that the number of PhD graduates per year, which was 1 421 in 2010 and 1 872 in 2013, be increased to 5 000 by 2030 in order for South Africa to be competitive with other developing countries such as Brazil and Ireland. Like South Africa, these two countries have developed ten-year plans for doubling the number of academic staff who hold doctoral degrees in all fields (ASSAf 2010:99). The challenge in South Africa is how the outputs can be escalated as the students are mostly part-time students of mature age with full-time jobs.

The ASSAf Report (2010) furthermore indicates a need to develop a comprehensive understanding of the dynamics of postgraduate education in South Africa. Mouton (as cited in Dell 2010) claims that about 80% of South African doctoral students are part-time and generally take longer to complete their degrees than their European or American counterparts. The reality is that with reduced access to the university facilities and staff, distractions from work, and so many years in which to lose motivation and direction, most part-time students give up after a lot of time invested in the study and never obtain their PhDs. The age of the student at time of enrolment, coupled with professional and family commitments are among the reasons for doctoral candidates' attrition (ASSAf 2010).

In order to address this challenge, the Centre for Higher Education Research, Teaching and Learning (CHERTL) at Rhodes University is offering a structured postgraduate programme. The draws scholars from different parts of South Africa and Africa with the aim of escalating doctoral production and create a cohort structure within which such production can be supported. I form part of this initiative as a doctoral student investigating the differentiated nature of 22 public universities in South Africa[1]. This chapter elucidates my postgraduate experience so far, even though I am still on the journey to complete my own study. It foregrounds my own experiences as a postgraduate student studying both part-time and at a distance, and highlights the importance and benefits of being part of a project team and the networking opportunities it affords.

STARTING THE DOCTORAL JOURNEY AS A TEAM MEMBER

My doctoral journey had a somewhat difficult start. I did not have a clear topic when I joined the project, but being part of the programme helped me to structure my thoughts from the beginning. During the first year of my study, I aimed to study a topic that was part of a project already underway in my department, but unfortunately this did not crystallise. I had to start all over again. It took me two years to come up with a feasible proposal. Being part of a team that encouraged me, kept me going as I searched for a new research topic. The team encouraged me to read more and think of other possibilities for research. The academic conversations helped me to identify a possible research project. Discussions I had with other postgraduate students who were already on the scholarly journey also helped a lot as they often asked questions which I found difficult then, but appreciate today. The questions helped me to structure my thoughts and develop a clear focus. Eventually, I found that being excited about your study topic is the main ingredient to success, and working within a team helps to build and retain such interest. As a student, you need the support from your team members and networks throughout the journey.

WORKING IN A COHORT PROJECT TEAM

There are a number of benefits to working in a project team. In my case, we are seven postgraduate students studying an overarching question focussed on the differentiated nature of the higher education institutions in South Africa. The cohort programme is designed to draw on students and staff from multiple paradigmatic perspectives, with multiple orientations and methodological perspectives to educational research (Samuel & Vithal 2014). The individual studies focus on a

---

[1] The other three public institutions are excluded as they are fairly new and small. Mangosuthu University is not new but does not offer postgraduate studies.

number of different issues within the scope of the broad research question and we as students develop our own research questions within the broader project. The overall project aims to identify the structures and mechanisms from which events and experiences related to teaching and learning emerge in order to enable or constrain social inclusion in higher education. For instance, the topics range from supervision development, curriculum, policy studies, plagiarism to eLearning. This is just one example of what a project team of this nature might look like.

The project team is part of the bigger postgraduate programme, which is structured to support the students regardless of where they are in their candidacy. I have been in the team a year longer than the rest of the members and learned a lot in terms of higher education issues as I was fairly new in the higher education sector. The project team allowed us to undertake research into various aspects of differentiation within the South African higher education sector. Some scholars in the team are academics and some are non-academics from different higher education institutions in South Africa. Phillips and Pugh (2005) argue that it is unusual in the Humanities and Social Sciences for scholars to use a shared framework, which tends to be more common in the Natural Sciences. However, they also highlight that "there are [natural] scientists who give an individual service to their postgraduate students and social scientists who build up a team of students all working on related aspects of the same topic" (Phillips & Pugh 2005:4). This is where my project team is located. The peer support that is provided is highly valued.

Being part of a project team gives you a chance to present your initial thoughts and draft writing to your team members. Team members can provide valuable feedback that you would never have thought of as an individual. The support of more advanced scholars is also necessary as they can help steer the person or group in the right direction. A team offers you the space to explain a concept and your understanding thereof. As scholarly readings are often difficult to understand, it helped me to hear and comprehend how others articulate concepts related to my study focus, especially the theory part as it is the golden thread for the entire study. I also found myself in a position to explain the theoretical concept to the team and indicate how they could implement it in their own studies, whereas the other team members could eventually provide me with their insights on the concepts in return. Such discussions helped me to make sense of complex concepts within my own study. Team members who are ahead of you in the process and managed to cross conceptual thresholds (Wisker 2015) in their own studies are invaluable resources for advancing your own learning[2].

---

2   Also see the chapter by Sherran Clarence (Chapter 11) that focusses specifically on threshold concepts.

DIFFERENT FORMS OF SUPPORT

Team members may support each other in different ways. Modern technology allows us to communicate with people without the constraints of time and distance. We use online seminar sessions once every six weeks or sooner, depending on the needs and commitments of the individuals within the team. You can organise online sessions in which you present your progress and frustrations to each other, and someone who just completed their studies (in my case, the main supervisor) would give the necessary guidance and support. It is during these online seminar sessions that concepts are clarified through presentations from team members. Our sessions started with small assignments that addressed the common issues, like the differentiation of South African higher education institutions. Everyone in our team comes from different parts of South Africa, which bring different experiences to the team as a whole. It is also possible to create a mobile group which would enable you to pose questions whenever you get stuck or confused, or provide moral support when needed. Posing questions to the group is also helpful if you are behind schedule on your reading and need to catch up with the rest of the team.

Though online seminar opportunities are undoubtedly valuable, the significance of face-to-face contact should not be underestimated. Our team only gets the opportunity to meet face-to-face during postgraduate weeks when we come together with other students who are part of the bigger cohort project. Such meetings create safe spaces within which you can bounce your ideas off each other and get constructive feedback. Such feedback does not mean that you will always get the right answers to the questions you have posed, as you are all still learning. It also does not mean that the feedback you receive will be correct in every respect. But using your team as a sounding board may give you input on further readings or on key issues you did not understand before and that might add value to your study. Team work is reiterative as you return to follow-up meetings to discuss your understandings and get further clarification while giving feedback to others.

The students in a team might be either at a Master's or a doctoral level, but the ensuing discussions and feedback may be useful to both study levels. I once attended such a meeting as I considered the supervisor as a potential study leader. What I learned from the meeting was the importance of sharing your work in progress in an informal way. Such informal discussions assist students in understanding particular methodologies or epistemological opinions that they would like to follow (Samuel & Vithal 2011).

NETWORKING BEYOND THE FORMAL STUDY COHORT: THE VALUE OF CLOSED NETWORKS

Supervisors cannot necessarily provide students with all the support they need, hence the need for networks. Whereas the previous team I mentioned is focussed on a doctoral project, consisting of both male and female students, I also belong to a closed network that consists of women only. We are eight enthusiastic and determined women pursuing doctoral studies at various institutions. We are at different levels in terms of our postgraduate journeys. We have formed social learning spaces that allow collaboration and accomplishment of work related to our studies (as proposed by Brown & Lippincott 2003). We share readings and decide on a reading for discussion at each meeting. We meet at six- or eight-week intervals (depending on our availability), and present our work in progress to each other. During these meetings we engage in discussions that inform major concepts in your studies. It is during such meetings that the group creativity is unleashed and new ideas are generated. This group is influential in my learning and progress as they understand the journey and the challenges I am facing. This network helped me in knowledge construction beyond which I was capable of on my own. I struggled to make sense of theory and I had to seek the support from my team members. They have helped me to understand theory as I listened to how they applied theory in their own studies. Each meeting has its own aha moments whereby imperative concepts are clarified. Meetings like these helped me to cross conceptual thresholds throughout my postgraduate journey. Difficult concepts and challenges can be discussed to clear the ground for a successful study. Student and supervisor relationships are discussed, as well as sharing the feedback that you receive. You may find that within the group only one person is a good writer, as is the case in our team. Sharing the feedback helps us learn from each other's mistakes and avoid repeating the same mistakes in the future.

Although each person's study is different, the nature of postgraduate study is the same one way or the other. During closed network meetings, team members share their challenges and what they have been battling with since the last meeting. Such meetings help those who have been stuck, as the sharing and support give them the courage and the momentum to pick up from where they got stuck. A network increases the chances of staying on track as you always know that someone else has the same challenges you have. You can even agree on teaming up with another network member to meet in-between to discuss your progress or difficulties. In addition, the group provides me with a network of people who will be there when I need someone who better understands the journey and who will also understand what I am going through. This helps to release stress and discuss study-related matters your family and community support systems might not understand.

The focus of the closed network group is to constructively critique each other's work and offer constructive feedback, even though this might be difficult initially. It is therefore important that networks operate in a fluid manner, so that there are others who can acquaint you with this process. Such networks need to offer a safe space, unlike some formal groupings where you may feel silenced by those who are already ahead of you on their scholarly journey. The hallmark of constructive feedback is that it comes with uncomfortable questions that you might not welcome at first, but that is necessary to improve your study in general and your writing in particular. Feedback is not meant to be positive at all times and that is where we draw support from each other to better understand the feedback in a way that is not disheartening. Closed networks helped me refocus when my study got confusing or outside its intended scope. At some point I was not sure whether I was looking at supervision "development" or "support" and the discussion with my network helped as we unpacked the concepts, and decided that "development" was the best term to use. As such, the closed network has helped to strengthen my confidence and reminded me to not be too hard on myself.

The success of closed networks depends on someone from the group taking the lead in organising the structure of the meetings. Such a network can help you accelerate your progress as you are held accountable to each other. It helps to identify a knowledgeable other to help you along. In turn, network members build their own (informal) supervision profile through the support and guidance they provide to the other members. You might also find it easier to join other networks through getting to know the members of an established network.

THE BENEFITS OF NETWORKING BEYOND YOUR ESTABLISHED NETWORKS

Not everyone has the opportunity to belong to a project team, but students can form collaborative groups and build networks themselves. Networking, in addition to being part of a project team, can be really useful. The isolation of studying both part-time and at a distance can be both depressing and discouraging. The feeling of isolation can be attributed to confusion about the programme or the requirements of the programme which quickly grow into a feeling of being overwhelmed and left behind (Ali & Kohun 2006). My experience is that a lack of support can have a negative influence on academic progress. Building a supportive scholarly network might help to counteract isolation. However, building networks is your individual responsibility and it will not happen by itself.

You can form network groups by meeting other postgraduate students in institutional workshops, seminars or conferences. Postgraduate centres at universities often offer a range of workshops or seminars to help students navigate the postgraduate journey. Such opportunities are useful as you meet other postgraduate students registered within the same institution. The feeling of isolation occurs at different stages in the doctoral programme (Ali & Kohun 2006), and these networks will be helpful during such times. I build networks whenever an opportunity avails itself. I then exchange contact details and follow up immediately before my new contacts forget who I am. One of my network contacts recently got feedback from the external examiner, which she shared with me without me asking for it. She knew that it would benefit me later on, and I am grateful for her generosity of spirit and insight.

Scholarly conferences where you present your study ideas are especially good networking opportunities. The feedback you get may help you to narrow your study focus, choose the most appropriate theoretical or analytical frameworks, or interpret your data. This does not imply that you should incorporate every piece of feedback that you receive, but getting as much feedback as possible may help to refine your study. Feedback helped me identify the gaps that I could not recognise when working in isolation or only with my supervisor.

I met people at conferences who have been through the postgraduate journey and they were very helpful. They were willing to provide advice based on their experiences. However, choose conferences that are related to your study topic. I was fortunate enough to find a conference that is related to my study. When I got there, I was the only student on the programme and had to present my work to mostly established scholars. The conference participants were my whole list of references that I had at that time. I was nervous and delighted at the same time to see them all there – I could put the faces to the names, engage with them and was able to network with most of them. I found that these scholars were eager to answer my questions and willing to converse with me as a student. However, you need to be careful of scholars who cannot see beyond their own research agendas, especially if your study is still in its initial stages. Knowing your study well will help you answer their questions without derailing your focus[3].

---

3 Also see the chapter by Soraya Abdulatief (Chapter 6) where she, as a first-generation student, expolores how she had to learn how to ask and answer questions in a scholarly conversation.

FINAL THOUGHTS

In this chapter I explored the value of postgraduate cohorts and networks as a means to facilitate postgraduate learning and development. The cohort team project model of doctoral education was explored, whereby students share a common research question with each student having a different focus. Networks offer more informal ways of supporting the postgraduate endeavour. The chapter also highlighted the benefits of networking beyond your team or closed networks with the hope of avoiding the feeling of isolation that comes at different stages during the postgraduate journey. Support can thus take on different forms and can be structured in both formal and informal ways. Finding the kind of support suitable to individual needs may help in surviving and succeeding at the postgraduate level. Constructive and positive feedback from a cohort team or network can be a motivator for postgraduate students, if it is offered in a collaborative and positive spirit.

REFERENCES

Academy of Science of South Africa. (2010). *The PhD study: Consensus Report*. Pretoria, South Africa: ASSAf.

Ali, A. & Kohun, F. (2006). Dealing with Isolation Feelings in IS Doctoral Programs. *International Journal of Doctoral Studies*, 1(1):21-33.

Brown, M. K., & Lippincott, J. K. (2003). Learning spaces: More than meets the eye. *Educause Quarterly*, 26(1):14-17.

Dell, S. (2010). South Africa: Decline in PhD numbers a major problem. *University World News*, 60(22):1-2.

Denholm, C., & Evans, T. (2012). *Doctorates downunder: Keys to successful doctoral study in Australia and Aotearoa New Zealand*. Australia: ACER Press

Republic of South Africa. (2011). *National development plan: Vision for 2030*. Pretoria, South Africa: Publishing Media Club.

Phillips, E. M., & Pugh, D. S. (2005). *How to get a PhD*. (5th Ed) Buckingham, UK: Open University Press.

Samuel, M. & Vithal, R. (2011). Emergent frameworks of research teaching and learning in a cohort-based doctoral programme. *Perspectives in Education*, 29(3):76-87.

Wisker, G. (2015). Developing doctoral authors: Engaging with theoretical perspectives through the literature review. *Innovations in Education and Teaching International*, 52(1):64-74. http://dx.doi.org/10.1080/14703297.2014.981841

17 SHARING THE QUEST OF DOCTORAL SUCCESS: CREATING A CIRCLE OF CRITICAL FRIENDS

Liz Wolvaardt, Hannelie Untiedt,
Mariana Pietersen & Karien Mostert-Wentzel

INTRODUCTION

Loneliness and isolation are constant companions on the doctoral journey. One strategy to overcome doctoral isolation is to create a circle of critical friends. A critical friend is defined as someone who, as a friend, is supportive and available to listen and, as a critic, offers thoughtful responses and raises points that the researcher has not considered (Whitehead & McNiff 2006). Rallis and Rossman (2000) suggest that this critical friend is external to the project. This friend serves as a sounding board and an evaluator, but the interaction takes place in conversations that produce learning. Critical friends can help you fill a void in your skill set (Kember et al 1997) and help to validate whether your data (and conclusions) are accurate (Gerardi, as cited in Foulger 2010). The benefits of critical friends are well documented in the literature on teacher education and action research, but not to the same extent in the context of postgraduate study.

In the South African context, an apprenticeship model (one-on-one supervision) rather than a cohort (group) approach is most commonly used in doctoral supervision (ASSAf 2010). This apprenticeship model may leave students feeling isolated. This model becomes especially problematic when the shortage of experienced doctoral supervisors and underprepared students is taken into consideration. The use of a circle of critical friends is one way to combat these potential challenges in the postgraduate experience.

This chapter describes our experiences as four doctoral students in participating in a circle of critical friends. Through our experiences we describe the roles participants need to take on, and what benefits and challenges such a group may offer. This chapter also outlines a strategy to set up and manage a circle of critical friends. Finally, we argue that our participation in such a group ensured that we did not only survive, but thrived on our respective doctoral journeys.

SETTING UP A CIRCLE OF CRITICAL FRIENDS

Our circle was a group of four female doctoral students who worked full-time at the same university. Benefits of an all-female group are described by Grant and Knowles (2000). All of us started our doctoral studies after reaching the age of 40 years and our circle was created based on a need to create a support structure. We had elements of a planned and emergent group (Cartwright & Zander 1960). The group was planned in the sense that two of us started talking about the possibility of establishing a support group. We knew the two other members independently and then invited them to become part of the study partnership, and so our circle became emergent and self-organising in the sense that the final formation of the group happened spontaneously (Cartwright & Zander 1968; Arrow, McGrath & Berdahl 2000). You can also think of a circle as a goal-focussed task group as you will all be united in pursuing an individualised, but common goal of graduation (Lickel et al 2000).

Although we had a shared need for support and a shared goal to graduate, we are quite diverse in terms of the disciplines, professional profiles and our doctoral topics, and we were at different phases of the research process. When setting up such a circle, it is important to ensure that members have some things in common. The commonalities we shared included a positive world and life view, limited time and energy available for studies, and using qualitative data in our respective studies. We also had the advantage of similarities in values, beliefs, social class and interests. When setting up a group, think of the similarity principle described by Newcomb (1961) – that people initially get to know those closest to them and later get attracted to those who are similar to them. In retrospect, the small size of our circle was beneficial in terms of being able to focus on the goal and tasks at hand, allowing us to complete tasks, use information effectively, and ensure that each of us had our fair share of attention. The size of a group influences its nature in many ways (Forsyth 2006) and is an important factor when creating a group as numbers of relationships increase as the membership grows.

Working and studying at the same institution made it easier to meet – a key element in maintaining momentum. Three of us work on the same campus, while the fourth member works a few kilometres away. Being located in the same building meant that we would regularly see one another in the corridors resulting in spontaneous, informal conversations. The regular face-to-face meetings varied in frequency from once a week to once every three to four months. The schedule of the meetings was dictated by our needs and the specific stage of our research. Grant (2006) emphasises the value of repeated experiences while also becoming aware of your own progress. Any group member had the authority to call a meeting. We never set out to create a set of norms, but when we look back we recognised that we established our norms informally during the start-up phase of the group. Adherence to the group norms is usually a requirement of any group for continued membership, and the norms we created (without saying them out loud) was an unbiased approach towards each other's work, professional context, personal situation, organisational climate, and organisational politics.

The values that underpinned our relationships relate to both critical readership (the cognitive domain), as well as critical friendship (the affective domain). The lessons learned from our rational way of knowing (critical readership) was complemented by our intuitive and affective ways of knowing (critical friendship). We identified professional integrity, accountability and taking ownership of our own studies as the key values that underpinned our critical readership. Not only did everyone take ownership of her own doctoral journey and successful outcome, but we also took ownership of each other's survival and success. Joint identification with the values that underpin a critical friendship is essential to group sustainability. Trust, personal integrity, empathy, flexibility, mindfulness, courage, purpose, focus, being receptive, compassion, patience, respect, resilience, avoiding harm, interdependence and balance were all important values to us. The result of this values-based approach to critical readership and critical friendship is that you can all claim improved self-knowledge and improved reflective practice. A critical stance and the giving and receiving of criticism were facilitated by this values-based approach. When setting up a circle, it is useful to include some discussion on what is important to all members (values) and how co-operation will take place (norms) in creating a safe space to develop relationships that are close but not competitive.

We did not set out to assign roles and indeed there was never any discussion of roles. Upon reflection, we could easily identify taking on the roles of coffee maker, mirror, resource provider, writing consultant, and deadline enforcer as described by Kember et al (1997), though these roles were not assigned formally. As we formed the circle based on existing collegial relationships there was never any need for someone to take on the role of building rapport. The awareness of how to function in the role of critical friend became clear to us during the process as we had the benefit of being both recipients within and contributors to the process. We assumed different roles at any given time. Our academic roles were idea generators, organisers and critical readers. Our personal roles included being motivators, showing or keeping the big picture in mind, managing expectations and keeping aspirations around the project realistic. Our academic and personal roles combined in our efforts to bring structure to some of the bewildering doctoral processes and to the expected format of our respective theses. These roles were not fixed or formal in our circle of friends, but we found ourselves taking on these roles naturally as the situation unfolded and often changed – and exchanged – in a single session. You need time and energy to fully understand the research that other critical friends are doing so that feedback is possible, but this is a worthwhile investment. By using a values-based approach, we quickly learned that it is possible to successfully merge the tension that exists between providing support while at the same time critiquing the work of friends (Grant 2006; Gibbs & Angelides 2008).

As critical friends we brought alternative perspectives to our common and individual experiences and, in so doing, we are convinced that we provided ourselves substantive protection against isolation and despondence. Sagor captures our experience well with the description of the critical friend as "one who does not have a stake in the problem, but is committed because of a complementary personal agenda" (as cited in Foulger 2010:148). Our complementary personal agendas were going through the same journey, willingness to share experiences to reduce the uncertainty and anxiety of the person in the group who (at that moment) was overwhelmed in their project. And – most importantly – had a stake not in the problem, but in the person.

WHAT TO ADDRESS DURING MEETINGS

One of the key characteristics of our collaboration was that the meetings provided a safe space for sharing successes, challenges and failures. We did not use a pre-set protocol to guide our meetings. Instead, one of us presented our individual project's progress at each meeting. We followed this brief update with key questions and provided feedback on any issue that the presenter might have had. We asked the presenter questions such as, "where are you now?", "what is your next step?", "what are the barriers you see or experience?", and "what can be done to overcome these barriers?". By using these questions as a framework, we ensured that the meetings were energy-giving and life-affirming events (Whitehead 2012). The update ended with identification of barriers and next steps. This process took approximately 30 minutes and each of the other members had approximately 10 to 15 minutes to update the circle on their projects using the same technique of identifying barriers and next steps. In this way the focus rotated between members, but ensured that overall momentum was maintained.

Resources that were tried and tested – or with which one of us had a personal experience – were discussed and shared. We shared literature sources, as well as learning opportunities, such as software training opportunities and research support sessions. Any questions regarding the use of software or reliable professional services (such as transcribers, statisticians, printers and language editors) were answered from within the group. Experiences of doubts and anxiety in different phases of the study are common and will peak when the reports needed to be finalised. We learned to view the doubts and anxieties as normal and transient. Anxiety was lessened by ending group meetings in a positive spirit.

BENEFITS AND CHALLENGES OF PARTICIPATING IN A CIRCLE OF CRITICAL FRIENDS

In hindsight, the extent of the academic and personal benefits of belonging to the circle astounded all of us. Some of us believe that we would not have successfully completed our studies without the circle, while for others it provided an essential life-line on the doctoral journey. All of us experienced one or more critical points (so-called crossroads) in our doctoral studies and the support of the group meant the difference between dropping out and pushing on. Family members and work colleagues seldom appreciate the burden of doctoral studies, but as fellow travellers the circle can provide a safe space to be honest about your doubts, fears, academic (cognitive) challenges and emotional (affective) challenges. We found two kinds of academic benefits of being a member of a circle of critical friends. The first benefit was on the cognitive level where we created new knowledge and developed professionally, and the second benefit was on an affective level where we gained knowledge of ourselves.

As we have diverse academic backgrounds and were engaged in diverse doctoral studies, the new knowledge that was created was the development of scholarship and professional growth. Foulger (2010:149) summarises this as "professional insights, stronger proof in the powers of our work, and an understanding of how co-mingling of thoughts and ideas can create a synergy not obtainable independently." The process of collaboration, asking questions and identification of the next steps during our meetings helped us to make our progress more explicit. Explaining to the group what we had done since the previous meeting helped us appreciate how much we had accomplished. Often many small administrative tasks needed to be done for the research to continue ethically and successfully. By listing what was completed, we realised that progress was made and this helped each of us to stay motivated and energised. Even when not much progress was made since the last meeting, the reasons for the lack of progress was explored (by using the key questions) so that each of us left the meeting with a strategy of what needed to be done to regain momentum.

This reporting on the progress since the previous meeting required of us to be self-critical in a reflective thinking process. We were interdependent on one another to provide feedback on a piece of writing, the structure of chapters, coherence, and overall clarity and sense making. This critical feedback was invaluable to us as either a first round, before sending drafts to the supervisor, or sometimes in the final round of writing. As critical friends we offered views on each study that were neutral, objective and provided valuable critique and reflective questions that needed a response. This unpolluted view improved the clarity of the written report. Formulating our thoughts aloud in the circle helped each member to understand their individual studies better. Speaking aloud in the group helped us to identify and address obstacles early in the research and kept the focus of the study clear. It should, however, be noted that the notion of talking as thinking is quite a western concept, and students from other cultures may find it strange (Lyubomirsky et al 2006)[1].

Our specific combination of members at different stages of the doctoral journey allowed us an opportunity to deepen our knowledge of ourselves, which offered possibilities for personal growth. For example, an absent-minded unstructured member got tips in time management and managing her study by observing the more organised members. Others found the circle a useful place for advice on how to build and maintain a healthy supervisory relationship, and deal with feedback from supervisors and examiners. Being involved in the circle undeniably stimulated our self-reflection and self-understanding (Gibbs & Angelides 2008; Wachob 2011), and confidence in our strengths and abilities.

Doing a doctoral study is a form of adversity with the potential of disturbing one's well-being. Indeed, you can expect to experience some form of burnout and anxiety at some point due to the fatigue of working long hours. In our case we all kept going as we knew that the others had survived the same phase and were able to safely progress to the next phase. A credo of "courage, patience and resilience" prevailed. When we were doubtful of our ability to continue, we would remind ourselves that we knew some

---

1 In this regard, see the chapters by Zondi Mkhabela and Liezel Frick (Chapter 2) on negotiating differences in epistemic positions, Langutani Masehela (Chapter 12) on agency and Ubuntu as complementary notions, and Catherine Robertson (Chapter 13) on identity in academic writing.

people who had completed and obtained doctoral degrees against all expectations. So clearly you not only need the cognitive ability to complete your doctorate, but also survival strategies and resilience[2]. An important part of surviving your doctoral studies is that you experience well-being, as conceptualised by Charney (2004). Well-being is the dynamic state that refers to persons' ability to develop their potential, work productively and creatively, build strong positive relationships, and contribute to their communities. We found that participating in our circle of critical friends had the inherent attributes that lead to our individual and joint well-being. In pursuing our studies as part of this circle, we often found ourselves in a state of flow, of being really engaged with something challenging, but doable. Because we selected worthwhile topics, our journeys were meaningful and mastery was developed in the progressive achievements of milestones.

Despite the overwhelming positive benefits of participating in a circle of critical friends, we experienced several challenges. Primary amongst these challenges were the emotional responses to the experience of pursuing doctoral studies, especially at the onset of the process. Common emotions were feelings of vulnerability, apprehension, and lack of self-confidence. Later in the process feelings of obligation and responsibility weighed on individuals when requests for assistance were in conflict with their own activities. In addition, one member became aware of a sense of dependency and felt unable to continue with changes without the circle's critical feedback. We therefore needed to also develop survival strategies.

SURVIVAL STRATEGIES

Resilience refers to "positive adaptation or the ability to maintain or regain mental health, despite experiencing adversity" (Herrman 2011:258). The strategies that helped us to prosper and arrive safely at the graduation line focussed on the self, our relationships and our actions. Despite our interdependence in the circle, each of us primarily relied on herself. Our self-sufficiency was developed through the sharing of authentic experiences. Group members in different stages of their studies experienced different obstacles and the sharing of these authentic experiences helped others when we reached that point in the journey. We realised from the start that because many hours of hard work would be required, we would need balance for the sake of our health and family relationships. Enjoying a meal together – in our case with a glass of wine – to celebrate the achievement of milestones contributed to our sense of balance. We reminded each other to take a break for a day or two when necessary

---

2 See Bella Vilakazi's chapter (Chapter 5) that focusses on becoming resilient through compassion and imagination.

in order to strive for some kind of work-life balance. The fundamentals for a happy successful life outside of the doctorate are vital. Good nutrition, exercise, enough sleep and spending time with friends and family will always be under pressure. When alone, we built in little rewards for ourselves, such as a special cup of tea or a quick walk in the garden. By keeping your focus sharp on your own or in the group, you may achieve better productivity and creativity.

The nurturing relationships within our supportive group were a protective factor that helped us to thrive beyond survival (as explained by Herrman 2011). The primary factor in resilience is "having caring and supportive relationships within and outside the family. Relationships that create trust, provide role models and offer encouragement and reassurance help bolster a person's resilience" (American Psychological Association 2015, "Resilience factors and strategies", para. 1). Our circle was central in reducing feelings of isolation. Even when working alone, we had a sense of support in absentia because we knew that the others both understood and cared. Grant and Knowles (2000) describe this benefit as imagining yourself in the company of others. The emotional support of belonging to a circle is a key survival tactic when you experience personal challenges. This nurturing relationship within the group was invaluable to us and as an all-female group, as we were comfortable to share our vulnerability and even tears with each other. One member spent one session just crying. Another member shared how she cried all the way from a supervisor's meeting until she reached home. After a follow-up meeting, she stopped crying at the first traffic light (a sign of progress for us). The work of Grant (2010) is of interest regarding this fragility and her work is useful to reframe the student-supervisor relationship. With support, negative emotions dissolved fairly quickly and we all left the meeting ready to continue. A key group strategy was to never allow our group members to indulge in self-pity or become fixated on the negative, but rather focus on taking action.

Taking decisive actions to achieve our goals was the final survival strategy. By ending each session with everyone identifying their next step, the overall goal – of obtaining the degree – remained alive. Our chances of reaching our goals improved when the intention was shared with others (as also explained by Fishbein 2008). In our circle the capacity to make realistic plans and take steps to carry them out was strengthened through joint problem solving. This problem solving was extended beyond academic dilemmas to include any problems that posed an obstacle to progress. For example, one member moved home and felt overwhelmed by her unorganised home environment. The whole group gathered on a Saturday afternoon and helped to arrange the furniture, paintings and other items to create a better study environment.

CONCLUSION

This chapter described our authentic experiences of acting as soundboards in a circle of critical friends in our doctoral studies. We shared the organic nature of how we set this circle up, how we supplemented our skills set, what we did at the meetings, what roles we fulfilled, and the academic and emotional benefits we gained in the process. This chapter also described the practical survival strategies of self-reliance, nurturing relationships and decisive actions that built resilience. Participation in the circle ensured that we did not only survive, but also thrived in our doctoral journeys.

Ours was a shared journey as we did not only take full ownership of our individual studies, but we also shared accountability and ownership for the successful completion of the other members' studies. Each individual journey had its obstacles and challenges, but by having critical friends who were not involved in the study itself, and who were able to think objectively and assisted in generating ideas in how to overcome obstacles, we were able to prevent the stalling of progress in our studies.

Our success in this circle was therefore not only graduation, but the life-affirming and energy-giving interactions (Whitehead 2012) that characterised our relationships. This chapter has contributed the notion of thriving as an outcome to participating in a circle of critical friends. By participating in a circle, we achieved the primary overarching goal of success of graduation by using the strategy of interdependent (rather than independent) ways. But graduation was not the only benefit. We experienced the uncommon benefit of PERMA (Positive emotions, Engagement, Relationships, Meaning/purpose, and Achievement/mastery), which is critical for true well-being (Seligman 2010:231). After all, not only is there life after a doctorate, but there is also life during the doctorate.

REFERENCES

Academy of Science of South Africa. (2010). *The PhD study: Consensus Report.* Pretoria, South Africa: ASSAf.

American Psychological Association. (2015). *The road to resilience.* Available online at http://www.apa.org/helpcenter/road-resilience.aspx

Arrow, H., McGrath, J. E., & Berdahl, J. L. (2000). *Small groups as complex systems: Formation, coordination, development, and adaptation.* Thousand Oaks, USA: Sage.

Cartwright, D., & Zander, A. (Eds.) (1968). *Group Dynamics: Research and theory* (3rd ed.). New York, NY: Harper & Row.

Charney, D. S. (2004). Psychobiological mechanisms of resilience and vulnerability. Reviews and Overviews. *American Journal of Psychiatry,* 161:195-216. http://dx.doi.org/10.1176/appi.ajp.161.2.195   PMid:14754765

Fishbein, M. (2008). A reasoned action approach to health promotion. *Medical Decision Making,* 28(6):834-844. http://dx.doi.org/10.1177/0272989X08326092 PMid:19015289 PMCid:PMC2603050

Forsyth, D. R. (2006). *Group Dynamics* (4th ed.). Belmont, USA: Thomson Wadsworth.

Foulger, T. S. (2010). External conversations: An unexpected discovery about the critical friend in action research inquiries. *Action Research,* 8(2):135-152. http://dx.doi.org/10.1177/1476750309351354

Gibbs, P., & Angelides, P. (2008). Understanding friendship between critical friends. *Improving Schools,* 11(3):213-225. http://dx.doi.org/10.1177/1365480208097002

Grant, B. M. (2006). Writing in the company of other women: Exceeding the boundaries. *Studies in Higher Education,* 31(4):483-495. http://dx.doi.org/10.1080/03075070600800624

Grant, B. M. (2010). Improvising together: The play of dialogue in humanities supervision. *Arts and Humanities in Higher Education,* 9(3):271-288. http://dx.doi.org/10.1177/1474022210379376

Grant, B., & Knowles, S. (2000). Flights of imagination: Academic women be (com) ing writers. *International Journal for Academic Development,* 5(1):6-19. http://dx.doi.org/10.1080/136014400410060

Herrman, H., Stewart, D. E., Diaz-Granados, D. E., Berger, E. L., Jackson B., & Yuen, T. (2011). What is resilience? *The Canadian Journal of Psychiatry,* 56(5):258-265.

Kember, D., Ha, T., Lam, B., Lee, A., Sandra, N. G., Yan, L., & Yum, J. C. K. (1997). The diverse role of the critical friend in supporting educational action research projects. *Educational Action Research,* 5(3):463-481. http://dx.doi.org/10.1080/09650799700200036

Lickel, B., Hamilton, D. L., Wieczorkowska, G., Lewis, A., Sherman, S. J., & Uhles, A. N. (2000). Varieties of groups and the perception of group entitativity. *Journal of Personality and Social Psychology,* 78:223-246. http://dx.doi.org/10.1037/0022-3514.78.2.223 PMid:10707331

Lyubomirsky, S., Sousa, L., & Dickerhoof, R. (2006). The costs and benefits of writing, talking, and thinking about life's triumphs and defeats. *Journal of Personality and Social Psychology*, 90(4): 692-708. http://dx.doi.org/10.1037/0022-3514.90.4.692 PMid:16649864

Newcomb, T. M. (1961). *The acquaintance process.* New York, NY: Holt, Rinehart & Winston. http://dx.doi.org/10.1037/13156-000   PMCid:PMC3803867

Seligman, M. (2010). *Flourish: Positive psychology and positive interventions.* Available online at http://tannerlectures.utah.edu/_documents/a-to-z/s/Seligman_10.pdf

Whitehead, J. (2012). *To Know Is Not Enough, Or Is It?* A presentation at AERA 2012 in Vancouver in the Symposium, "To Know is Not Enough": Action Research as the Core of Educational Research. Available online at http://www.actionresearch.net/writings/aera12/jwaera12noffke200212.pdf

Whitehead, J., & McNiff, J. (2006). *Action Research Living Theory.* London, UK: Sage.

PART SIX

MAKING SENSE OF
POSTGRADUATE OUTCOMES
IN THE
SOUTH AFRICAN CONTEXT

18 DARING TO BE DIFFERENT: A POSTGRADUATE STUDENT PERSPECTIVE ON ORIGINALITY

Emmanuel Sibomana

INTRODUCTION

Research is key to postgraduate study and constitutes the main difference between an undergraduate and a postgraduate degree programme. Given the limited emphasis placed on research in undergraduate studies (Miller, Rycek, Balcetis, Barney, Beins, Burns, Smith, & Ware 2008) and a surface approach to learning adopted by some universities in developing countries (Hunma & Sibomana 2013; Sibomana 2010; Sibomana 2014), the journey to becoming a researcher may be a daunting experience for many postgraduate students. Postgraduate students may face uncertainties due to a lack of a research background because they are from an education system where research was not emphasised. They may therefore not be familiar with different aspects of research, including those related to the nature of the research process and discourses around requirements such as originality or contributions to knowledge. Such students may thus be uncertain of what awaits them and how to deal with the challenges of meeting these requirements, which may cause them to doubt their academic abilities. This chapter focusses specifically on what the requirement of originality may mean to a postgraduate research student (specifically at the doctoral level) and how to identify and explain what is original or amounts to "new knowledge" in research.

RESEARCH NEEDS TO BE ORIGINAL, BUT WHAT DOES THAT MEAN?

Studying towards a postgraduate degree in South Africa requires research literacy that many prospective postgraduate students may lack. On the one hand, students come into postgraduate study with different attitudes, expectations, hopes and fears, while on the other hand, the university environment has its own requirements for such students. There is not always a match between the individual and the institution, which may create tension (Hunma & Sibomana 2013). This tension is likely to increase when student researchers do not understand certain aspects or conditions that are key to the acceptance of their research projects. One such aspect that challenges postgraduate students is the originality of research. Especially doctoral research projects are expected to achieve a higher level of criticality, as well as originality. Originality – or the so-called contribution to knowledge – is a prerequisite for a PhD thesis to be accepted within the research community (Gelling & Rodriguez-Borrego 2014; Gill & Dolan 2015).

The contribution to knowledge can be a confusing concept and, according to Gill and Dolan (2015), a source of uncertainty and anxiety for PhD candidates. Some of the reasons for this situation include the lack of an agreed definition of knowledge (Snowden 2014), the complex and multifaceted nature of originality and its openness to interpretation (Gill & Dolan 2015; Phillips & Pugh 2010), and the uncertainty of how it could be developed and assessed within doctoral education (Brodin & Frick 2011), to mention but a few. These reasons lead to confusion about what can and cannot constitute originality in PhD research and how it can be demonstrated (Gill & Dolan 2015), which makes it difficult for students to understand what is expected of them in this regard (Frick 2011). Indeed, originality in doctoral research can be demonstrated in up to nine different ways (Phillips & Pugh 2010), which may put the student in a precarious position when he or she and the examiner(s) approach it from different perspectives. The matter is made worse by the lack of institutional guidelines on what constitutes originality in a PhD (Phillips & Pugh 2010).

These challenges, paired with students' previous academic experiences, make PhD candidates' interpretations of originality vary from what may be truly original and ground-breaking (Locke, Spirduso & Silverman 2007), to that which is way beyond the scope of a postgraduate study (such as Nobel Prize winning projects, according to Petre and Rugg 2004), to a whole new way of looking at the discipline or the topic (Phillips & Pugh 2010), to almost meaningless contributions (Gill & Burnard 2012) with various points on a continuum in-between. Some students misunderstand originality or do not understand it at all; others underestimate it, while others overestimate it.

When I started working on my PhD I was not sure what originality meant. I thought that I was expected to invent something totally new or come up with a new theory, which I did not have the necessary knowledge or skills to do. I wondered whether there could be anything "new under the sun" (to quote Ecclesiastes 1:9) and if there is not, whether the requirement for originality is realistic. Reading other PhD theses did not make a difference: I read them, but I could not identify the "contribution" they were making to knowledge (at least the way I understood it), because there was no explicit "contribution to knowledge" headings in any of these theses. And to me, there was nothing new in these theses because everything therein had been researched in some way. This made me realise that as much as it is difficult for a novice PhD student to explicate what is unique about one's research (Gill & Dolan 2015), it is also difficult to identify it in other people's work.

Despite these difficulties, the candidate's understanding of what originality means is the starting point for identifying what constitutes originality or new knowledge in one's own research and for being able to articulate it. When I approached my fellow PhD students I realised that they were also struggling with this issue. Some of them understood originality as the percentage of the PhD thesis that belongs to the candidate as opposed to what is obtained from available literature and other research findings. This notion of originality confuses the contribution to knowledge and the student's own voice or, in other words, the student's own ideas or points. These points and ideas may not necessarily be original or address an original subject. This understanding implies confusion between the concept of originality and that of plagiarism. Others understood new knowledge only in terms of the subject matter of the research or, in other words, "the what". This type of understanding confines originality to only one aspect of research: what is being studied. This can be seen in the quick and superficial answer which I gave to a friend of mine who asked me whether for his PhD he could work more extensively on the topic which he had worked on for his Master's research. I told him that he could not because the topic had already been researched. In giving this answer I did not think of what "more extensively" could mean for him; it could mean the same topic but differently, in a different context and/or with different participants, which could be avenues for originality. Other fellow PhD students thought that all research is original in that no one has ever come up with the same findings in the same context and with the same participants.

The various understandings of originality explained in the above paragraph have implications (which are generally negative) for students' ability to identify and/or determine what is unique about their research projects. In addition to making it more daunting for students to identify and explain how original their research is, a lack of clear understanding of this concept may result in some PhD research projects lacking originality, making it impossible for them to be accepted and the degrees to be awarded (Gelling & Rodriguez-Borrego 2014). For instance, understanding originality as something that has never happened before may bring the students to search for something that may never be found. Alternatively, pursuing a highly original theme may be risky and jeopardise the student's intellectual abilities because he or she may not be able to articulate it effectively (Gill & Dolan 2015). Thus, as a PhD student you need to understand that while a PhD is expected to contribute to knowledge, there is no obligation for it to "redefine a subject area or discipline" (Gill & Dolan 2015:14). Indeed, knowledge claims can be small and still have a role in the discourse (Petre & Rugg 2004). Thus, it may be better to have a small and focussed original contribution than a big but extravagant one that you cannot defend.

The understanding that originality is only about subject matter narrows the possibility of identifying originality in one's research. In fact, originality can be related to all the aspects of research: the subject matter, the research methods and techniques and the research context (Brodin & Frick 2011; Gill & Dolan 2015; Petre & Rugg 2004). Indeed, there may be nothing new about what you want to research but the way you want to approach it may be original. For instance,

> ... some students follow the prescriptions of other researchers to the letter and simply apply a previously published method to a new body of data. Other research students will devise a method for investigating a particular topic, and this method may not have been previously used, or may have been described but not applied in detail. Their contribution is to the knowledge about that methodology (The research supervisor's friend, 2011, para. 12).

In short, you can make a contribution to knowledge by proposing a framework for reviewing the considerable knowledge and literature that is available about a specific topic (The Tesearch Supervisor's Friend 2011). But if you are not aware of this possibility, you may abandon the project all together because, in your eyes, it is not original. Therefore, a student who understands and approaches originality in terms of subject matter is disadvantaged: while there are three perspectives from which originality can be thought about, the student has only one perspective. Thus, in the process of determining what is new about a given research project, you need to think about it in all its facets.

Another challenge that some PhD students may face as a result of their limited academic literacy practices, is to know what is new and what is not in their areas of interest (Gill & Dolan 2015). As a result, what appears new for them may already be old or known for others, which calls for a full awareness of the state of existing knowledge in their area (Holloway & Walker 2000) in order to be able to share with their supervisors and examiners an understanding of what constitutes originality (Gelling & Rodriguez-Borrego 2014). Understanding what constitutes originality requires the extensive, careful and critical reading of texts (books, articles, essays, research reports and theses, amongst others). This may provide a better understanding of the research area and the aspects of the research that may be challenging, including its uniqueness or originality. This is how, after reading several academic texts in the areas of distance education, language education and language teacher education, I came to understand that originality in research is not necessarily a creation of a new theory or a totally new discovery; it can also be researching these concepts from a new and/or different perspective, with the aim of shedding more light on it by answering *original* research questions or answering ordinary questions in an *original* way. In my case, the contribution to knowledge was to undertake the first critical pedagogic analysis of Rwandan distance education materials for language teacher education, to undertake a redesign of a section of these materials and finally to investigate the responses of teachers to the original and the redesigned materials.

ORIGINAL BUT BASED ON OTHER PEOPLE'S WORK

Every area has been researched in one way or another and to different extents. Therefore, chances of finding something totally new are limited. Thus, as much as research needs to be original, it has to be based on what other researchers have done. As Petre and Rugg (2004:14) argue, research is "a discourse among many researchers, each providing evidence and argument that contributes to knowledge and understanding, each critiquing the available evidence". One way of building on other researchers' work is to use their theories and concepts to frame your research or, in other words, to develop a theoretical or conceptual framework, which will help you to analyse your data. Understanding the meaning of a theoretical framework and its role in the research, and to identify one that suits your own research does not come easily. For me, this challenge was amplified by my limited academic literacy practices coupled with a surface approach (Biggs 1987) and a banking approach (Freire 2007) that had characterised my previous academic experiences. Postgraduate study was my first encounter with the concepts of theory and theoretical/conceptual framework. It goes without saying that I was not aware of the various theories/theorists in my area and how these theories and theorists could inform my research, let alone understanding how original my research was (supposed to be). This limited understanding increased my anxiety and my doubt about my readiness and ability to undertake a PhD study programme.

Using other people's ideas to inform your own research requires a thorough understanding of these ideas. Integration and synthesis are not easy to achieve, especially for novice PhD students. I read about some theories and concepts and they did not make much sense. I ended up wondering why the scholars wrote these texts the way they did. Matters became worse when these particular theories were crucial to my research and what I needed to make my research original. Eventually, I got to understand that if concepts and theories are difficult to grasp, it is not necessarily because you are less intelligent, but it may be because you did not have enough time and/or opportunities to be exposed to them. Even established researchers sometimes find it difficult to understand some other scholars' work, so do not get discouraged. Understand that you are one of those people these concepts and theories were developed for and that, eventually, you will be able to understand them through continued engagement with them. Getting worried about what lies ahead is part of the normal process of carrying out PhD research (Phillips & Pugh 2010) and, I suggest, it makes you work harder. Reading about and reflecting on these concepts and theories extensively and critically may be necessary. This process may take a long time and the necessary insight and understanding may be slow. Alternative approaches to understanding the concepts and theories, and/or varying the kind of materials you are reading may be called for. Some scholars' writing styles are more accessible than others and knowing which ones are more accessible may be helpful. Changing the approach that you are using to read texts and reading different scholars who wrote about the topic of interest may also be helpful.

Apart from helping you to find appropriate theories for your research, reading extensively and critically can help you to identify the gap(s) in your research area. This could pave the way to identifying originality for your research. But the problem is that you may not be able to access and/or read everything that is available on the topic or in the area. This may increase your anxiety about whether what you claim to be original, really is original. In this case, your supervisors' assistance can make a difference; they are (or should be) more familiar with the key theorists/theories and scholars in your area than you are, and their guidance could help you to focus your reading and save you from reading "unnecessary" or less relevant texts. They can also help you to identify the gap, or point out one for you. In this case, you may need to carefully consider taking their suggested gap because dealing with something that does not originate from your own thinking may be challenging. I had to take the risk of revising and refocussing the suggested gap and, eventually, defining a gap in the current knowledge area to which I could make a feasible and original contribution.

CONCLUSION

Originality or new knowledge is a *sine qua non* for a PhD thesis to be accepted. In spite of the importance of this element, many PhD students start their research without a clear understanding of what originality means and how it can be identified and explained in one's own research. This situation is due to several reasons including the complex nature of the concept of originality, lack of agreement on what constitutes knowledge, lack of institutional guidance on what originality is, and the lack of a single formula on how to identify and explain originality. This situation brings PhD students to interpret originality in a variety of ways and these interpretations may have implications for their ability to carry out original projects. Reading critically and extensively in the research area, thinking about all the aspects of one's own research in a critical way, and setting realistic research goals are some of the strategies which PhD students can use to address originality in research. Also, institutions and research supervisors should not just set requirements for originality; they should help, support and accompany postgraduate students in the process of achieving originality in their research.

REFERENCES

Biggs, J. B. (1987). *Student approaches to learning and studying*. Victoria, Australia: Brown Prior Anderson.

Brodin, E. M., & Frick, L. (2011). Conceptualizing and encouraging critical creativity in doctoral education. *International Journal for Researcher Development*, 2(2):133-151. http://dx.doi.org/10.1108/17597511111212727

Freire, P. (2000). *Pedagogy of the oppressed* (30th anniversary edition). New York, USA: Continuum International Publishing Group.

Frick, B. L. (2011). Supervisors' conceptualisations of creativity in education doctorates. *Pertanika Journal of Social Sciences and Humanities*, 19(2):495-507

Gelling, A., & Rodriguez-Borrego, M. A. (2014). Originality in doctoral research. *Nurse Researcher*, 21(6), 6-7. http://dx.doi.org/10.7748/nr.21.6.6.s2

Gill, P., & Burnard, P. (2012). Time to end the vagaries of PhD examining? *Nurse Education Today*, 32(5):477-478. http://dx.doi.org/10.1016/j.nedt.2012.01.014 PMid:22381380

Gill, P., & Dolan, G. (2015). Originality and the PhD: What is it and how can it be demonstrated? *Nurse Researcher*, 22(6):11-15. PMid:26168808 http://dx.doi.org/10.7748/nr.22.6.11.e1335

Heath, S. B. (1983). *Ways with words: Language, life and work in communities and classrooms*. Cambridge, UK: Cambridge University Press.

Holloway, I., & Walker, J. (2000). *Getting a PhD in health and social care*. Oxford, UK: Blackwell Science.

Hunma, A., & Sibomana, E. (2014). Academic writing and research at an afropolitan university: an international student perspective. In L. Thesen & L. Cooper (Eds), *Risk in academic writing: Postgraduate students, their teachers and the making of knowledge* (pp. 100-128). Tonawanda, NY: Multilingual Matters.

Locke, L. F., Spirduso W. W., & Silverman, S. J. (2007). *Proposals that work: A guide for planning dissertations and grant proposals* (5th ed.). Thousand Oaks CA: Sage Publications.

Miller, R. I., Rycek, R. F., Balcetis, E., Barney, S. T., Beins, B. C., Burns, S. R., Smith, R., & Ware, M. E. (Eds.) (2008). *Developing, promoting and sustaining the undergraduate research experience in psychology*. Syracuse, NY: Society for the Teaching of Psychology.

Petre, M., & Rugg, G. (2004). *The unwritten rules of PhD research*. Berkshire, UK: Open University Press.

Phillips, E. M., & Pugh, D. S. (2010). *How to get a PhD: A handbook for students and their supervisors*. Maidenhead, UK: Open University Press.

Sibomana, E. (2010). *Challenges faced by postgraduate French speaking students who are learning in English: A case study of Rwandan students in the School of Education at the University of the Witwatersrand* (Unpublished Master's research report), University of the Witwatersrand, South Africa.

Sibomana, E. (2014). *The role of distance education materials in addressing the professional development needs of high school English teachers in Rwanda* (Unpublished doctoral Thesis), University of the Witwatersrand, South Africa.

Snowden, A. (2014). Ethics and originality in the doctoral research in the UK. *Nurse Researcher*, 21(6):12-15. http://dx.doi.org/10.7748/nr.21.6.12.e1244 PMid:25059082

The Research Supervisor's Friend. (2011). *How can you tell when there has been a contribution to knowledge (in a doctoral research study)?* Available online at https://supervisorsfriend.wordpress.com/2011/05/17/how-can-you-tell-when-there-has-been-a-contribution-to-knowledge-in-a-doctoral-research-study/

19 THE VIVA VOCE: THE LIVING VOICE OF A DOCTORAL THESIS

Ndileleni P. Mudzielwana

INTRODUCTION

Studying for a doctorate may take years of intensive work and study. During the process of writing a doctoral thesis, the student needs to be given the appropriate support by supervisors until the final stage of defending the thesis. Having spent some years writing the thesis with the assistance of supervisors, the thesis will go through the process of examination by experts in the field. These are the people who will make contributions by giving comments that will strengthen the thesis. They may question aspects of the thesis or identify gaps that need to be attended to. Depending on institutional policy and processes, a thesis may have two or more external examiners who are considered experts in the field in which the study is conducted and who are appointed by the university. The primary purpose of a PhD assessment is to determine whether the candidate is competent as an independent researcher in the discipline (Department of Education 2007).

Some universities expect doctoral students to give a verbal response to examiners' reports by participating in an academic discussion with the examiners. This is commonly called a *viva voce* (Latin for "with the living voice"), in general called a *viva* for short, or oral defence. In this way, the thesis becomes alive through the living voice of the doctoral candidate. Wellington (2010:72) describes the *viva* as a "rite of passage, a process of legitimation, a major event for decision making, the end of an era, a stamp of approval, ... a chance to shine, closure, a climax and a platform". In South Africa, conducting an oral PhD examination is not a universal practice (Unisa 2015). At the University of KwaZulu-Natal, for instance, an oral examination is not a requirement, but may be required by the examination panel. Faculties may exercise the option of conducting a *viva*, or may include it as a standard part of the examination process (University of KwaZulu-Natal, n.d.). At the University of Johannesburg, an oral examination may be required by faculties, but such requirement must be approved by the relevant faculty board and Senate (University of Johannesburg 2015). At Unisa, doctoral candidates were subjected to an oral examination by internal and external examiners until the beginning of the 1990s, but this was largely discontinued due to financial and time constraints (Ehlers 1999). Thus, even though each South African university determines its own requirements and practices, the *viva* remains a common and accepted practice at many universities (as is the case at Stellenbosch University and the University of Pretoria).

This chapter focusses on how to prepare for this aspect of obtaining a doctorate. Take note that the procedure regarding doctoral assessment may differ from one institution to another, also in terms of the procedures regarding the *viva*. Despite its many possible manifestations, the PhD *viva voce*, as an oral examination of the doctoral thesis, constitutes the final "test" of the PhD endeavour. Potter (cited in Watts 2012:1) identified three critical functions of the *viva*, namely (a) to check that the thesis is really the candidate's own work by posing questions that are designed to test authenticity; (b) to test the ability of the student to defend his/her work as a researcher; and (c) to present an opportunity to the student to clarify aspects of the study and clear up any misunderstandings. Burnham (1994:31) states that the "examination is an opportunity to strike up a good working relationship on which one can later draw references and in particular for recommendations when approaching academic publishers". Adapting this positive view of the *viva* would be advantageous to oneself, as the event is evaluated with the rigour "that makes a doctorate worth having" (Carter 2012:281). The purpose of the *viva* is therefore to confirm the value of one's original contribution to a body of knowledge and to show the examiners that you did the work yourself. It also proves that you have done extensive reading in the field, have a sound knowledge of the field, and have become an expert on a particular topic. The final examination of the thesis defence is for quality assurance. At the University of Pretoria's Faculty of Education, the doctoral defence is a requirement for obtaining a PhD. Here, the *viva* voce focusses on three aspects:

- the intellectual component of the thesis – referring to whether you are able to demonstrate "sufficient intellectual depth, breadth and dexterity of knowledge and understanding to qualify as a doctor";

- the textual component of the thesis – referring to whether one understands "with sufficient nuance and insight the complexities underlying the theoretical and methodological substance of the thesis"; and
- the personal component of the thesis – referring to whether the candidate expresses a "disposition appropriate for a new scholar in the course of conducting the defence" (University of Pretoria 2014:35).

The *viva voce* can only be done when the examiners feel the doctoral work has met the requirements of the university. This implies that the assessment of the quality of the thesis is shared among examiners who were involved in the assessment process. When highlighting the purpose of defending the thesis, Delamont, Atkinson and Odette (1997:148) explain that "when the thesis is sound and the external examiner is the right person, the 'examination' becomes something altogether more open/democratic and less confrontational than that term normally conveys".

The *viva voce* can be an overwhelming prospect and it may seem daunting and scary. However, defending a thesis is a live process, and should not be seen as a direct confrontation. Many doctoral students enjoy this experience of discussing their PhD research with interested experts. It is an opportunity for me, the student, to share my research with the examiners who may become my peers and colleagues within the disciplinary community. An oral defence allows me to showcase my efforts and present my research findings in a supportive environment. Such exposure provides me with the opportunity to discuss the work with experts in the field, to improve the arguments in my thesis, and to consider where to publish the work (Twigg 2003). At some institutions, such as the University of Stellenbosch Business School (USB), an open invitation to attend the *viva* is directed to members of the public to attend the event (USB 2015). It can therefore also be a useful networking opportunity of sharing information with other academics.

Students sometimes fear that even if the thesis has been approved by the external examiners, they may fail during the *viva voce* – which brings considerable discomfort considering the many years of hard work that went into completing the thesis. Thorough preparation for the *viva voce* is therefore essential. This chapter outlines the general procedures of the *viva voce* and provides some insights that helped me prepare for my *viva voce*. The discussion is divided into three phases, namely before the defence (Phase 1), during the defence (Phase 2) and after the defence (Phase 3).

PHASE 1: BEFORE THE DEFENCE

One will need at least a week or two to prepare for the *viva voce*. I started off by familiarising myself with the *viva voce* policy and procedures of my institution. In general, a *viva voce* panel constitutes a non-examining chairperson, internal and external examiners, the supervisors, possibly one appointed staff member of a school or faculty, and the student. At some institutions, the student takes part in choosing this panel. Try to obtain this type of information to ensure that you are fully prepared and know what to expect. Your supervisor should be able to provide you with the necessary information on who constitutes a *viva voce* panel at your institution and the procedures that are commonly followed.

Even though the thesis is the student's own work, at this stage, it becomes public property. The community of academics – in this case the examiners – was interested to know about me and my work. During my preparation, I took into account what I considered as the original contribution my doctoral work makes, as this is usually what the examiners would like to discuss[1]. This means that I had to have a command of what was happening in my subject area so that I could evaluate the worth of what others were doing in relation to my work. I needed to have the astuteness to discover where I could make a useful contribution, show a mastery of appropriate techniques that are currently being used, and provide an awareness of their limitations. I also had to communicate my results effectively in the professional arena and have a global awareness of what was published, written and discovered in the relevant academic community.

Before my defence, I took some time to practise supporting my answers with the specifics of my thesis. Watts (2012) suggests a re-read of the thesis, because without a proper re-familiarisation with the content, students will unlikely be able to offer an adequate defence of their work. I needed to be clear as to why I did the study in the first place. This included clarity on the objectives of the study, the research question, and how the objectives were linked with the research question. I had to make sure that my presentation was focussed on critical issues that could convince listeners that the work is mine and that I could add value to the body of knowledge. I had to be aware that one of the primary aims of the *viva voce* is to determine whether the thesis is my own work. I had to show that I am indeed an independent researcher capable of making an original contribution.

---

1 See the previous chapter (Chapter 18), where Emmanuel Sibomana unpacks what originality means in the context of a PhD thesis.

I practised with a friend, summarising my thesis out loud, and spoke to colleagues who had recently had been through the *viva voce* process. It was important that I practised out loud, as I had to train my voice to be audible enough to be heard by all the panel members without difficulty. In most instances, a supervisor would help you prepare for your *viva voce*, sometimes by conducting a mock *viva* to ensure that you are well prepared[2]. In general, a mock *viva* enables students to experience typical *viva* conduct and allows them the opportunity to practise defending and debating their work (Hartley & Fox, cited in Watts 2012). The mock *viva* may help to identify unclear or weak areas, and allow one to rehearse confident explanations (Jack 2003).

In my preparation, it was critical to update myself on recent literature. This implied that I had to practise "dropping names" of scholars, including the dates and titles of key works, into my discussion that showed my detailed knowledge of the field. I identified the possible weaknesses of my thesis and considered how I would explain them. I understood that the panel would appreciate my grasp of the study limitations. I also identified the strengths of my chapters and selected chapters or sections that I wanted to highlight. I considered ways of working references to my own work into the discussion. I prepared a short summary and practised speaking it out loud. I identified three or four key themes and prepared a few pages of points on these themes. I furthermore reviewed my research methods and made sure I could justify the choice of my methods.

Trafford (2003:118) identified four general questions that examiners typically ask to conclude the *viva voce*, which I kept in mind during my preparation:

- What was your contribution to knowledge?
- How would I critique your research/how would I repeat this research?
- What have you learned from completing this research?
- How will you use your research findings/what do you plan to publish?

PHASE 2: DURING THE DEFENCE

The defence may be up to an hour long, depending on the institution and the procedures followed. Because I practised my presentation, I was well prepared and confident. Thereafter, I faced questions from experts in the field. Usually an examination panel first asks the student to tell them about him- or herself and how they came up with the research question. Wellington (2010) recommends that giving students this opportunity to demonstrate enthusiasm and passion for their topic at

---

2 See in Chapter 2 how Zondi Mkhabela recounts his experiences of this process.

the start of the *viva voce* helps build their confidence and settle their nerves, which acknowledges the inherently stressful nature of the process.

During my presentation, the examiners asked questions to determine whether the work was indeed my own, what my personal disposition towards scholarship was, and to get an idea of my intellectual depth. They were also interested in my understanding of the field of study, my scientific textual knowledge, and my understanding of the theoretical and methodological substance of the thesis. This was the opportunity to relax and showcase my work. No matter how nervous I was, I had to focus and listen carefully to the questions they posed. I took a moment to pause before I answered the questions. Examiners are not looking for quick responses, but rather for thoughtful and precise answers. "Examiners are impressed by thoughtful, reflective candidates who give consideration to constructive criticism and are able to modify their arguments accordingly" (Burnham 1994:33). I expected to be asked to address the more controversial aspects of my thesis. I kept in mind that I did not have to defend everything about my thesis. If I did not have an answer to a question, I refrained from answering it or making promises – I rather replied by saying that the question is interesting and that I would consider it in future[3]. The more you relax, the easier it becomes for you to think logically and present yourself competently. It was necessary to remember that my work had both strengths and weaknesses. In identifying both the strengths and weaknesses beforehand, I was ready to discuss both these aspects of my thesis. This helped me not to take criticism personally, but rather see the examiners' comments and questions as an opportunity for me to share and discuss my work with other academics. I also had to prepare to ask questions and enter into a dialogue with my examiners. I need not wait until they invited me to develop my answers. If they did not allow me to develop my answer or if they kept interrupting me, I could ask, "May I finish answering my previous question, please?"

The following should be taken note of during the *viva voce*:

- Be prepared to discuss your research in the context of other work done in your field. Impress the panel by referring to recent research in your field as it relates to your work.
- Be ready to admit if you do not know the answer to a question.
- Be prepared to express opinions of your own argument, which should be presented in a friendly but decisive manner.

---

3   Also see the chapter by Soraya Abdulatief (Chapter 6), where she describes how she learned to answer questions from a scholarly audience.

- If the panel gives you the opportunity to sum up your thesis, spend the time wisely; always act professionally.

PHASE 3: AFTER THE DEFENCE

The academic judgement of the examiners is the crucial factor in arriving at a decision. This is the phase in which the importance of examiners gathering sufficient, relevant oral evidence to enable them to judge the worth and authenticity of the thesis is central to this process, and therefore the role of the *viva* in the final decision should not be underestimated. It is not customary for the panel to discuss the results in your presence. You may be asked to leave the room for the examiners to consider their decision and recommendations at the end of the *viva voce*. Usually the candidate and supervisors are called back by the non-examining chair after consensus has been reached.

You have the right to appeal if you feel that you have been treated unfairly during your *viva voce*. Rudd (1985, cited in Murray 2009:155) identified several grounds for appeal, including unfair treatment during the *viva voce* due to "ideological differences between students and staff", supervisor error, failure by the supervisor to alert the student during the early stages of the work to significant weaknesses in the study, and personal hostility directed towards the student by an examiner. This, however, does not mean that any student who receives a negative result should automatically appeal – you should be guided by your institution's regulations in this regard.

I felt drained after undergoing this strenuous, yet rewarding exercise. I rewarded myself by celebrating with those who supported me. If you are required to make corrections based on the report written by the panel, it is advisable to start with this as soon as possible after your *viva voce*, while the content of your thesis and the discussions during the *viva voce* are still fresh in your mind (Jack 2003). Then, it is once again time to plan for the future. Smith (2014:162) gives the following advice:

> You should consider continuing to publish your work along with your supervisors after you graduate. ... It might be possible to publish your work as a book chapter, or in some cases, as an entire book. Research shouldn't stop at graduation. In many ways, your journey has only just begun. Be prepared to continue your learning journey, and to pass on your experience and advice to other students.

CONCLUSION

This chapter provides ideas that can be useful during the oral defence of a thesis. It is clear that writing a thesis can be challenging. Reaching the final stage of the doctoral journey, this chapter encourages students to make a success of the last phase of the study – the *viva voce*. Going through the process of a *viva voce* can be emotional and taxing. However, if you remain focussed and prepare well, you will find that you can survive and succeed this last hurdle positively and professionally.

REFERENCES

Burnham, P. (1994). Surviving the doctoral viva: Unravelling the mystery of the PhD oral. *Journal of Graduate Education*, 1:30-34.

Carter, S. (2012). English as an additional language (EAL) viva voce: The EAL doctoral oral examination experience. *Assessment and Evaluation in Higher Education*, 37(3):273-284. http://dx.doi.org/10.1080/02602938.2010.528555

Delamont, P., Atkinson, P., & Odette, P. (1997). *Supervising the PhD: A guide to success*. Buckingham, UK: Open University Press.

Department of Education. (2007, October 5). Higher Education Qualifications Framework. *Government Gazette No. 30353*. Available online at http://www.che.ac.za/documents/d000148/Higher Education Qualifications Framework Oct2007.pdf

Ehlers, V. J. (1999). *Distance education doctoral program for nurses as offered by the University of South Africa (Unisa)*. Conference paper presented at the International Network for Doctoral Education in Nursing (INDEN), Royal College of Medicine, London. Available online at file:///C:/Users/User/Downloads/776-2248-1-SM.pdf

Jack, B. (2003). The final hurdle: Preparing for the PhD viva examination. *Nurse Researcher*, 10(2):66-76. http://dx.doi.org/10.7748/nr.10.2.66.s7

Murray, R. (2009). *How to survive your viva* (2nd ed.). Open UP Study Skills series. Maidenhead, UK: Open University Press.

Smith, P. (2014). *The PhD viva: How to prepare for your oral examination*. Palgrave Research Skills series. New York, NY: Palgrave Macmillan.

Trafford, V. (2003). Questions in doctoral vivas: Views from the inside. *Quality Assurance in Education*, 11(2):114-122. http://dx.doi.org/10.1108/09684880310471542

Twigg, D. (2003). *Preparing for the PhD viva voce – a personal reflection*. Paper presented at the Warwick Business School Doctoral Programme, University of Warwick.

Unisa. (2015). *Mock viva voce (mock oral examination)*. Available online at http://www.unisa.ac.za/default.asp?Cmd=ViewContent&ContentID=97824

University of KwaZulu-Natal. (N.d.). *Recommended examination policies and procedures for PhD degrees*. Available online at http://research.ukzn.ac.za/Files/Recommended_Examination_Policies_for_Procedure_for_PhD_degrees_1.sflb.pdf

University of Johannesburg. (2015). *Academic regulations 2015*. Available online at http://www.uj.ac.za/EN/Faculties/Documents/University-of-Johannesburg-Academic-Regulations.pdf

University of Pretoria. (2014). *Guidelines and procedures for postgraduate students and supervisors*. University of Pretoria, Pretoria.

University of Stellenbosch Business School. (2015). *PhD in Business Management and Administration*. Available online at http://www.usb.ac.za/Brochures/PhDBusEnglish.pdf

Watts, J. H. (2012). Preparing doctoral candidates for the viva: Issues for students and supervisors. *Journal of Further and Higher Education*, 36(3):371-381. http://dx.doi.org/10.1080/0309877X.2011.632819

Wellington, J. (2010) Supporting students' preparation for the viva: Their preconceptions and implications for practice. *Teaching in Higher Education*, 15(1):1-84. http://dx.doi.org/10.1080/13562510903487867

PUBLISH OR PERISH? COMMUNICATING RESEARCH WITH THE PUBLIC

Collium Banda

INTRODUCTION

The saying, "publish or perish" left me agitated, wondering about my ultimate academic destiny at the beginning of my doctoral studies. Whether I would succeed or fail seemed to depend on whether I publish or not. At one point, I heard the saying so often it left me confused as to whether doing a postgraduate degree was about studying or publishing. I was fully aware that publishing is the pulse that keeps alive the ideas that I worked hard to formulate. I kept wondering about two related aspects: if I published, who would read my work? And, as scholarly publishing is a lengthy process, how long would it take before my ideas would circulate into the public domain? I observed one established academic who liked to publish in newspapers but was annoyed when the readers complained that they found his articles too difficult to understand. Looking at the comments of his frustrated readers, I wondered if academics really intended to communicate to anyone at all, or just to themselves.

That one could publish scholarly works and yet find no readers, or publish in newspapers and fail to be understandable to the ordinary reader highlighted to me that the idea of effective communication is often not captured by the saying, "publish or perish". Von Winterfeldt (2013:14055) bemoans that "scientific information is rarely accessible in a format useful for decision making". This statement emphasises that scientists publish in a way that does not communicate to the public, in this case, the decision makers. This inaccessibility of valuable information to its intended audience nullifies the great and costly effort invested into its construction. This chapter affirms that without publishing scholarly works in books, journals and monographs, academics can indeed perish. However, this chapter more importantly highlights that the saying should be underscored by the idea of effective communication to a broader audience. As I learned during my doctoral studies, academics should not only publish for fellow academics, but also for the public – in a manner that is accessible to them.

To highlight the significance of fulfilling the saying, "publish or perish" in a communicative way, I start this chapter with a reflection on my own experience of what prompted me to communicate and share my research with the public during my studies. I then argue that fulfilling the principle, "publish or perish" in a manner that accommodates the public, requires a sense of partnership and hospitality towards the public. The chapter describes aspects involved in sharing research during postgraduate studies and offers a brief discussion of the steps that postgraduate students can take to develop skills to share their research with the public. I also highlight the risks that come with sharing your research with the public. The chapter closes with a brief discussion on what postgraduate students stand to benefit by sharing their research with the public during the course of their studies[1].

A QUEST FOR RELEVANCE

My interest in learning and developing ways of communicating to the public was stirred by the question, "How can my postgraduate studies be relevant to my community that is riddled with poverty?" When I started planning my study, I was captivated by the African Renaissance and became interested in developing a skill that would contribute meaningfully to the re-awakening of Africa. I did not just want a PhD; I wanted to do something that would empower me to play a relevant and transformative role in my community. I remember agonising over a statement by a Zimbabwean theologian, Ezra Chitando (2010:199), "[t]he seed of poverty thrives on the rich soils of Africa". Chitando's statement fittingly contextualised South Africa, a country so rich and yet at the same time so utterly poor. Thinking through this, the question that kept haunting me was, "How could my doctoral studies be relevant and useful in this context of rich soils that cultivate poverty and death?"

According to Baram-Tsabari and Lewenstein (2013:57), "learning science means learning to talk science with its own semantic patterns and specific ways of making meaning". This statement is true about all fields of study. By specialising in a particular field, one ends up talking that field with its semantics and ways of making meaning, which are often beyond the grasp of the public. As Von Winterfeldt (2013:14055)

---

[1] Also read the chapter by Simangele Mayisela (Chapter 3), where the ethical responsibility of the postgraduate student to communicate with non-academic audiences – in this case, respondents – is highlighted.

shows, in some cases, "only a small group of scientific peers can understand" this produced body of knowledge. In a country such as South Africa which is in desperate need for solutions to unlock the logjam of poverty, and un(der)development of knowledge is irresponsible. In order for my new discoveries to be relevant to my community, I have to learn to communicate in terms that are accessible to the public.

What steps could I practically take to achieve this? A workshop organised by the division responsible for postgraduate skills development on communicating science to the public at my university helped me put my quest for relevance to my community into perspective. The workshop introduced the basic skills of public speaking and writing science articles in popular language. The workshop showed me that academics can be agents of change in their communities by translating their scientifically created knowledge into the language of ordinary people. This meant that I should add to my skills acquisition "the ability to use *nontechnical language and norms*" (Baram-Tsabari & Lewenstein 2013:58). Learning to think in nontechnical language and norms would enable me to participate in platforms such as newspapers, public media, community meetings and even symposiums. These platforms provide useful opportunities to share your research findings with the public. Thus, I learned that academics should not just publish; they should also communicate. I discovered that while I still needed to strive to publish in academic journals, I did not have to depend on academic publishing to engage with my community. I could employ other means of communication, such as popular media, seminars and community meetings to address the relevant issues.

COMMUNICATING SCIENCE AS PARTNERSHIP AND HOSPITABILITY

Sharing research with the public involves two processes encapsulated by the ideas of partnership and hospitability. Partnership refers to the idea of your responsibility in sharing knowledge with your community. The idea of partnership comes from an illustration narrated by one of the conveners of a workshop on communicating science to the public about a student who shared her research findings with her ruralised grandmother. With great pride, the grandmother passed on the knowledge to her village community. In this illustration emerged a sense of the granddaughter being a delegate sent by her community on a mission of discovery, from which she returned to her community to report back on her findings. Ultimately, for me, this image translates to a sense of accountability to my community and to the taxpayers who contribute to the reality of my university education. The grandmother's interest in her granddaughter's postgraduate studies must have challenged the granddaughter to think beyond publishing in academic journals only, and consider communicating with the public as well. This illustration reminds me of the Biblical parable in which a person lights a lamp and then hides it under a bowl instead of putting it on the table where it lights up the whole house (Matthew 5:15). Limiting her sense of community to the academic world would have been the same as hiding her light under a bowl.

The idea of hospitality emphasises the aspect of inviting your community into a knowledge space where fresh ideas and insights are shared. As Gathogo (2007:108-109) shows, hospitality is a strong component of the ethic of the Ubuntu concept: "I am because you are"[2]. Being privileged to embark on postgraduate studies, I need to share what I have learned with my community. As someone from a village, I have learned that village meetings, community gatherings, church gatherings and even workshops are useful avenues for sharing my science. South Africa has an oral culture where we like to tell and listen to stories. In communicating my research, I have utilised these mediums.

When I share my research with the public, I often think of the openness of my university to the public. It is a fit analogy of partnership and hospitality that the university campus is not a fenced-off space but open to the public. The public can walk through the campus and interact with the learned and the learning. The botanical gardens are also open to the public. These are significant imageries that highlight how research is shared with the public. All the main pathways in the main campus converge on top of the university's underground library. The layout of the campus essentially demonstrates that the university exists and conducts its teaching activities for the public. As an emergent academic, I feel it is my obligation to play a part in the interaction between the university and the community. Communicating with the public is not only a form of accountability to these silent partners, but also includes them in the process and benefits of postgraduate research. It is an expression of our responsibilities as academics.

SHARING RESEARCH DURING POSTGRADUATE STUDIES

The critical underlying question in sharing research with the public is: what should be shared? With adequate preparation you can share anything from your research at any level, even at the initial stages. You can share the concepts, aspects, findings and also the problem issues you encountered during your studies. You can share the skills and abilities that you acquired during your studies. Sharing of knowledge can be approached by answering questions such as, "what discoveries am I making?", "what skills am I learning and developing?" or "how do the new insights emerging in

---

2   Also see the chapter by Langutani Masehela (Chapter 12) in this book that focusses on Ubuntu.

my study affect my understanding of, for example, the problem of xenophobia in South Africa?" During the early stages of my research, as I was formulating my research proposal, I would talk to people about the questions, ideas and perspectives I was pondering and even important literature sources during my reading. The discussions contributed meaningfully to finding the focus of my research. During the research stages, as I began to grapple with particular concepts and perspectives while I got deeper into my research, it meant that I had much more substantive knowledge to share.

Since the sharing of research is an act of partnership and hospitability, it is conducted in the language of the audience. As a good partner and host you speak the language of your listeners (Baram-Tsabari & Lewenstein 2013:58). To be willing to communicate to the public requires confidence in the usefulness and meaningfulness of your research within the current South African context. I seize opportunities to share my research with the public because I am confident that, while I can make only a small and limited contribution, my work can contribute meaningfully and usefully towards the realisation of a better South Africa. As an emerging academic, I endeavour to be confident that I have something important to contribute, and that it can be communicated in terms that are understandable to the public. However, diligent care must be taken to avoid being overly simplistic and condescending. We all want people to communicate with us and not speak over our heads. We all want knowledgeable people to make sense to us. Rather than being technical, complex and merely seeking to impress people with my knowledge, I have found that I need to keep the discussion along the lines of what I am studying and what I am discovering in my research. The personal skills I am developing enable me to strike interesting conversations with members of the public.

My university has for some time been holding an annual competition for postgraduate students on communicating science. By participating in the competition, I discovered that all science can be shared with lay people. Knowledge that has taken a complex and lengthy process to develop can be shared within a time segment that is as short as six minutes. At first, it seemed ridiculous to me to allocate such a small amount of time to a meaningful communication of science knowledge. While preparing our presentations, we kept wondering if it was at all possible to communicate anything sensible in such a short amount of time. However, the important lesson that I learned was that one does not need a lot of time to communicate sensibly and effectively. When I told a friend about sharing one's research in six minutes with the public, he mockingly dismissed the whole affair. "It's not possible; I have too much data," he replied. Yet this six-minute thesis competition taught me that with good public speaking skills I can explain my research concisely, to a variety of people, using appropriate slides and visual aids. Participating in this process taught me to think in snippets and morsels that the public can easily digest.

Should the postgraduate student always initiate the process and be in charge of the communication process? A good host must also, at times, be a good guest. To find opportunities of sharing your research, it is necessary to look out for bona fide calls for papers and presentations even in popular spaces, and make a constructive and an informed contribution. I have attended community meetings and open forums as part of the ordinary crowd, and found that the slot allocated to questions and discussions provided me with an opportunity to share my research by asking questions, making comments and providing alternative perspectives. Such participation has led to opportunities of being invited as a speaker at future events, simply from asking questions and making constructive contributions during the presentations of others. I particularly cherish the discussions that take place during the coffee-breaks of such events, as they are valuable opportunities to meet and share my knowledge with the public and those outside my field of study.

Electronic and social media also make it easy and fast to distribute information. Most online newspapers have a comment section where you can respond and interact with other people about an article. From the perspective of your research, you can use the comment section to interact and discuss topical issues related to your field. By carefully choosing appropriate spaces of sharing your research with the public, you can provide a useful and meaningful alternative. When you really put your mind to it, the possibilities of sharing your research during the process of postgraduate studies are endless. Online forums such as *The Conversation* and *Scibraai* provide spaces to share your research as well as interact with seasoned researchers.

RISKS IN COMMUNICATING SCIENCE TO THE PUBLIC

Communicating science to the public, particular while still studying, has risks. Not many people may be willing to trust the insights of a student. Even as a postgraduate student you still have a limited audience and reception because people would rather trust a qualified expert than an apprentice. This risk means that a prerequisite quality in communicating your research with the public is to be prepared to be a "suspect". Respect and confidence from the public is often earned by demonstrating tenacity and maturity. Furthermore, communicating your research to the public exposes you to criticism and public scrutiny, which could be harsh at times. However, if you aspire to make your research relevant to your community, or if you wish to pursue a lifelong academic career, you must be prepared to face criticism positively.

As an emerging academic in a South African context it is important to realise that the basic African worldview of life is permeated with traditional cultures and religious beliefs that have "supplied the answers to many of the problems of this life" (Mbiti 2015:15). In the South African context, this dynamic shapes the "science-citizen relations" (Irwin 2014:161) in that the century-old, tried-and-tested cultural and religious values function as the framework of interpreting new science-tested solutions. Von Winterfeldt (2013:14055-14056) highlights that the bridge between scientific knowledge and decision making is affected by beliefs and values. Therefore, in communicating your new scientifically tested research findings you stand to challenge deeply valued assumptions and traditions that have been the pillar and security of the society. This means guarding against the communication strategy of the "first-order" approach that treats the public as an empty vessel and thus uses "top-down" (or "one-way") communication (Irwin 2014:162 208). Rather, the strategy must adopt lower-order approaches of communicating science that recognise the public as concerned stakeholders that can contribute towards finding solutions to the problems they face (Irwin 2014:203-209). This means that communicating science to the public is a political exercise due to the sensitivity and the threatening nature of new data. This "call[s] for engaging in a respectful dialogue with the public" (Baram-Tsabari & Lewenstein 2013:58).

Fortunately, academics often allay the public of their fears, resulting in an embrace that grants the researcher trust and at times unquestioned authority. Moreover, when research findings are trusted as an outcome of a rigorous and objective scientific process, it may result in unquestioned public confidence in you as a researcher. The mere fact that you communicate tested and authenticated findings, not mere opinions, earns you a position of authority and trust in the community. This demands that researchers use the trust and confidence given to them honourably and responsibly. Therefore, as Fischhoff point outs, effective science communication "inform[s] people about the benefits, risks, and other costs of their decisions, thereby allowing them to make sound choices" (2013:14033). Ethical integrity must be observed when communicating research with the public.

DEVELOPING THE SKILLS OF SHARING YOUR RESEARCH FINDINGS

It is true that communicating research is a specialised process. But, it is also true that communication is an art and skill that can be learned, developed and improved (Besley & Tanner 2011:255 257). The communication of scientific knowledge involves the sharing of proven or tested information, educated assumptions and factual data. Sharing, therefore, requires proper and thoughtful planning to make it effective.

To learn and develop the skill of communicating with the public, the university is the place to start. Look out for opportunities at your university to acquire communication skills. The department of postgraduate skills development at my university runs a number of courses and seminars including public speaking and writing. The writing laboratory also offers assistance with writing skills. The workshop on communicating science addresses topics such as how to plan and structure a presentation. You also learn how to plan and lay out slides, and how to effectively use pictures and illustrations.

Most student development departments offer many useful career-enhancing training at minimal or no cost.

CONCLUSION

Sharing your research with the public during your postgraduate studies can benefit both the student and the research project. In this chapter, I have challenged postgraduate students to respond to the saying, "publish or perish" and encouraged students to communicate with the public. By publishing scholarly works such as articles, reports, books and monographs, academics remain alive. To be relevant in the South African context, it is not enough to write only for other academics; ordinary people can also be empowered by the knowledge created at universities.

I find that communicating to a wide audience keeps me grounded in the issues that affect my community, and constantly challenges me to be relevant. In the light of the myriad of complex problems South Africa faces, postgraduate students need to remain connected to the community by providing solutions to these problems. Postgraduate studies can be a lonely journey and sharing your knowledge with the public unlocks opportunities for support and companionship. Sharing your research with the public during the course of your studies is also beneficial to your research as it places it in the context of the lived experiences of your community. This sharing is an act of partnership and hospitality towards the community that benefits not only the student but also the community.

Communication is a skill and an art that can be acquired and developed. By taking advantage of opportunities to learn how to effectively communicate with the public – such as skills development and public speaking programmes offered by many universities – postgraduate students can include the public in their research to the benefit of the community and the country.

REFERENCES

Baram-Tsabari, A., & Lewenstein, B. V. (2013). An instrument for assessing scientists' written skills in public communication of science. *Science Communication*, 35(1):56-85. http://dx.doi.org/10.1177/1075547012440634

Besley, J. C., & Tanner, A. H. (2011). What science communication scholars think about training scientists to communicate. *Science Communication*, 33(2):239-263. http://dx.doi.org/10.1177/1075547010386972

Chitando, E. (2010). Equipped and ready to serve? Transforming theology and religious studies in Africa. *Missionalia*, 38(2):197-210.

Fischhoff, B. (2013). The science of science communication. *Proceedings of the National Academy of Sciences*, 110(Supplement 3):14031-14032. http://dx.doi.org/10.1073/pnas.1312080110 P Mid:23942127   PMCid:PMC3752170

Gathogo, J. M. (2007). Revisiting African hospitality in post-colonial Africa. *Missionalia*, 35(2):108-130.

Irwin, A. (2014). Risk, science and public communication: Third thinking about scientific culture. In B. Trench & M. Bucchi (Eds.). *Routledge Handbook of Public Communication of Science and Technology: Second Edition* (pp. 160-172). New York, USA: Routledge.

Mbiti, J. S. (2015). *Introduction to African religion* (2nd ed). Long Grove, USA: Waveland.

Von Winterfeldt, D. (2013). Bridging the gap between science and decision making. *Proceedings of the National Academy of Sciences*, 110(Supplement 3):14055-14061. http://dx.doi.org/10.1073/pnas.1213532110 PMid:23940310   PMCid:PMC3752167

INDEX

A

Academic
  conferences 90, 96, 177
  life 157
  standards 28
  writing 146-149, 151, 152, 196
Access 1-4, 30, 42, 43, 46, 56, 90, 93-95, 103, 109, 110, 178, 179
Accessibility 90, 110
Accountability 57, 75, 193, 199, 225, 226
Activity
  systems 78-86
  theory 78-80
African 35, 102, 137-141, 143, 150, 151, 172, 224
African worldview 150, 229
Agency 137-143, 162-165, 172, 196
Apartheid 13, 15, 23, 25, 26, 65, 70, 73, 77, 78, 101
Application 53-56, 59, 60, 75, 79, 85, 115, 153
Apprenticeship model 140, 191
Argument 19, 26, 33, 82, 83, 133, 146, 150, 152, 179, 209, 215, 218
Assumptions 14, 15, 18, 19, 26, 64, 118, 158, 159, 164, 173, 229
Authentic voice 146
Authorial
  presence 151
  self 151, 153
Autobiographical self 146-148, 150, 151
Axiology 33

B

Balance 47, 48, 55, 70, 75, 84, 105, 115, 116, 119, 121, 162, 165, 193, 197, 198
Barriers 25, 28, 41, 43, 59, 101, 104, 151, 175, 194
Book famine 93
Boundary zone 78, 81, 82, 84, 86
Burnout 107, 108, 196
Bursaries 54, 58, 95, 103, 109

C

Circle of critical friends 191, 192, 195, 197, 199
Coach 110, 116, 123
Cohort 162, 178, 179, 184, 186, 187, 190, 191
Collective engagement 2
Collegial support 2
Colonialism 26
Colonised scholarship 28
Communicating science 225, 227-230
Communication 26, 30, 59, 71, 82, 143, 175, 223-225, 227-230
Communities of practice 78, 172, 173, 174
Community 15, 17, 42, 44, 70, 73, 75, 78-83, 104, 120, 121, 134, 137, 141, 143, 146, 147, 153, 157, 162, 164, 171-174, 177, 179, 183, 188, 206, 215, 216, 224-226, 228-230
Compassion 61-64, 66, 193, 197
Compassionate rigour 33-35
Conceptual framework 83, 129, 130, 153, 209
Conference 45, 71, 96, 97, 149, 177-179, 189
Confidentiality 45, 46, 47
Consciousness-raising groups 16
Context 14, 18, 20, 23-26, 28, 31, 34, 35, 39, 54, 56, 61, 62, 65, 70, 85, 101, 102, 111, 117, 123, 131, 137-140, 143, 146, 147, 149, 150, 153, 154, 159, 163, 165, 191, 193, 207, 208, 216, 218, 224, 227, 229, 230
Creativity 107, 187, 198
Critical
  citizenry 2
  discourse analysis 70, 79
  emotional reflexivity 18
  friends 172, 176, 191, 192, 194-197, 199
Cultural expectations 27
Culture 2, 24, 26-28, 101, 102, 110, 120, 121, 138, 140, 196, 226, 229
Curriculum reform 7

D

Data 20, 31, 45, 46, 78, 95, 97, 106, 111, 122, 129, 130-132, 145, 153, 164, 177, 189, 191, 192, 208, 209, 227, 229
Deliberative engagement 65
Democratic justice 61, 65, 66
Dialogue 14, 16, 17, 18, 21, 171-179, 218, 229
Disability 59, 90-92, 95-97
Disabled student 89-92, 94-97
Discoursal self 146, 148-151
Discourse 17, 29, 34, 41, 70, 71, 78, 79, 82-85, 103, 137, 139, 140, 146-149, 160, 163, 173, 174, 178, 205, 208, 209
  practice 79, 82
Discursive
  perspective 79
  power 78

233

practice 79, 82
Dissertation 31, 82-84, 91, 148, 149, 153, 154
Diversity 7, 8, 13, 70, 101, 165
Doctoral
    education 23, 24, 34, 146, 190, 206
    immigrant 158
    journey 24, 77, 78, 80, 83, 85, 90-92, 115, 117, 118, 157, 160, 162, 163, 165, 171, 172, 174, 177, 184, 191, 192, 193, 195, 196, 199, 220
    learning 64
    pedagogy 23, 29, 35
Doctorateness 33, 34, 133, 175

E

Emotional support 46, 117, 198
Employability 2
Employment 26, 77, 85, 102, 107
Empowerment 19, 101-103
Enrolment 183
Epistemic induction 29
Epistemological access 2, 239, 244
Epistemology 33
Equity 3, 7, 102, 103, 107
Ethical
    clearance 41, 42
    dilemmas 39, 40, 42, 47, 48
Ethical dilemmas 7
Ethnicity 25, 149, 161
Eurocentric discourse 151
Examination 31, 32, 83, 91, 92, 94, 133, 134, 157, 178, 213-215, 217
Experiential learning 150
Expert 31, 33-35, 39, 77, 80, 83, 84, 143, 162, 173, 178, 179, 213-215, 217, 228
Expertise 1, 3, 7, 25, 34, 65, 72, 73, 86

F

Family 7, 14, 18, 53, 58, 59, 69, 73, 75, 76, 85, 95, 101, 103-108, 111, 116, 117, 120, 121, 137, 139, 140-143, 171, 183, 188, 195, 197, 198
Feedback 15, 16, 19, 32, 57, 58, 62, 64, 73, 74, 107, 133, 152, 175-178, 185-190, 194, 196, 197
Female students 101-104, 107, 110, 187
Financial support 29, 54, 110
First generation student 69
Foreign students 57, 58
Four Human Domains model 116
Friends 7, 8, 13, 15, 16, 18, 21, 59, 73, 85, 93, 95, 105, 106, 108, 121, 172, 176, 191, 192, 194-199
Full-time student 54, 84
Funding 29, 41, 53, 54, 58, 59, 71, 75, 77, 85

G

Gender 3, 13, 15, 17, 18, 24, 26, 69, 72, 101-104, 109, 149, 161, 163
Gentleness 21
Global
    North 3
    South 159
Graduates 3, 79, 80, 82, 84-86, 108, 116, 152, 183
Graduation 25, 32, 33, 53, 74, 84, 104, 134, 157, 177, 192, 197, 199, 219
Group discussion 47

H

Health 102, 105, 107, 109, 116, 117, 197
History 15, 18, 25, 26, 70, 101, 117, 120, 147
Hospitality 224-227, 230

I

Identity 8, 29, 39, 40, 45, 46, 47, 70-72, 109, 117, 118, 127, 128, 132, 134, 135, 146-149, 151, 153, 154, 163, 164, 174, 175, 196
Identity production 29
Imagination 7, 61-66, 197
Imposter syndrome 92
Inclusion 2, 60, 85, 89, 90, 185
Inclusive education 89
Industry 1, 2
Inequality 20, 26, 101
Institutional policies 7
Intellectual project 29
Internationalism 151
International student 58, 59, 152
Intertextuality 149
Isolation 23, 35, 75, 105, 108, 149, 152, 188-191, 194, 198

J

Joint degree 56, 57

K

Kindness 33-35, 111
Knowledge
    economy 1
    perspective 151
    production 3, 27, 29, 85, 140, 141, 146
Knowledge (body of) 23, 56, 57, 79, 160, 214, 216, 225

L

Language 7, 13, 27, 28, 43, 45, 59, 69, 71, 75, 79, 117, 120, 121, 132, 146, 151, 161, 172, 209, 225, 227

INDEX

Learning 8, 15, 23, 34, 56, 62, 64, 65, 70-77, 82, 85, 89, 90, 97, 109-111, 117, 122, 134, 142, 145-147, 150, 152, 159, 162, 164, 165, 173-175, 178, 184-187, 190, 191, 195, 205, 219, 224-226
    Doctoral 8
Librarian 34, 94
Literature 7, 9, 21, 31, 53, 56, 58, 62, 103, 111, 179, 191, 195, 207, 208, 217, 227
Literature review 149, 153, 158

M

Masculine knowledge practice 150
Mature student 86, 147, 150
Mentoring 7, 78, 108, 110
Method 29, 165, 208
Methodology 33, 56, 57, 73, 129, 152, 153, 164, 177, 208
Mutual vulnerability 15, 17, 20

N

Narrative 7, 9, 19, 21, 23-25, 27, 29, 33, 35, 104, 147, 159, 161, 163
    reflexivity 24
    space 24
Network 105, 108-110, 187-190
Non-examining chair 216, 219
Nontechnical language 225

O

Online group 109
Ontology 33
Openness 14, 19, 20, 43, 46, 206, 226
Oppression 15, 19, 86
Oral
    defence 213, 215, 220
    examination 32, 213, 214
Originality 8, 205-211, 216

P

Partnership 192, 224-227, 230
Part-time student 54, 55, 143, 183
Patriarchal society 8
Pedagogy of discomfort 18
Plagiarism 149, 185, 207
Political discourse analysis 79, 82
Postgraduate
    Education 1, 2, 3, 4, 183
    Journey 7, 17, 53, 59-62, 66, 72, 104, 120, 142, 143, 145, 187, 189, 190
    Pedagogy 2
    Qualification 1, 2, 109

Postgraduate student 3, 7, 8, 9, 15, 17, 35, 55, 60, 61, 65, 66, 71, 74, 75, 95-97, 103-105, 109, 111, 127, 137, 138, 139, 141, 142, 148, 152, 184, 185, 189, 190, 205, 206, 211, 224, 227, 228, 230, 244
Power 14, 16, 21, 27, 42, 58, 78, 79, 82, 83, 84, 102, 116, 146, 149, 151, 158, 173
Pre-doctoral stage 7
Privilege 14, 15, 16, 19, 21, 26, 31
Proposal 8, 25, 27-29, 41, 53, 55-58, 63, 69, 71, 72, 80, 111, 142, 172, 176, 177, 179, 184, 227
Public good 2, 4
Publish 41, 74, 215, 217, 219, 223-225, 230
Publishing 47, 73, 74, 178, 223, 225, 230

Q

Quality 27, 31, 34, 35, 89, 103, 109, 115, 119, 133, 163, 183, 214, 215, 228
Quality of life 115

R

Race 7, 13-17, 19, 21, 26, 69, 72, 161
Rainbow nation 13, 15, 16, 21
Reasonable accommodations 89, 90-92, 97
Reciprocity 19, 20
Relationships 21, 23, 24, 26, 27, 29, 33, 35, 40, 43, 57, 58, 62, 63, 65, 72, 80, 83, 84, 90, 96, 101, 104-106, 109, 110, 115, 117, 119-122, 128, 131, 132, 138-141, 143, 148, 152, 164, 165, 174, 187, 192, 193, 196-199, 214
Relevance 82, 137, 177, 224, 225
Research
    Design 40, 95, 132, 162, 176
    Ethics 39, 40-42, 48
    Problem 40, 56, 142, 158
    Proposal 25, 56, 63, 227
    Skills 77, 83, 142, 143
Researcher identity 39, 127, 132
Resilience 63, 66, 104, 106, 109, 152, 193, 196-199
Resiliency 101, 104
Responsibility 8, 42-46, 55, 65, 75, 90, 97, 101, 103-107, 110, 111, 116, 117, 142, 143, 150, 151, 178, 188, 197, 224-226
Rigour 33-35, 158, 159, 163, 214
Risk 3, 19, 46, 48, 108, 141, 210, 228
Rural 26, 30, 39, 42, 55, 102, 103, 139, 141

S

Safe space 162, 188, 193, 194, 195
Scholarly
    Becoming 79

Scholarships 9, 28, 29, 35, 54, 58, 70, 71, 75, 159, 195, 218
Science communication 8, 229
Scientific knowledge 150, 229
Self as author 146, 151-153
Self-help books 152
Self-hood 146, 150
Self-reflection 2, 116, 118, 123, 196
Sharing of research 227
Social
    Context 117, 138, 139, 149, 164
    Inclusion 2, 162, 185
    Justice 2, 15, 20, 65, 159
    Networks 109, 142
    Practice 8, 14, 70, 75, 79, 109, 121, 139, 146, 172
Sounding board 16, 109, 186, 191
Stereotypes 15, 25, 26
Storytelling 15, 19
Structural inequalities 13, 16
Student-supervisor relationship 3, 7, 23-27, 29, 30, 33-35, 58, 63, 66, 86, 138, 140, 198
Student voices 7, 8
Study
    Group 75, 139, 142
    Schedule 143
Success 3, 7, 8, 39, 71, 82, 83, 86, 96, 101, 103, 104, 109-111, 116, 121, 174, 184, 188, 193, 199, 220
Supervision 3, 4, 23, 24, 28, 29, 33, 34, 56, 57, 61-66, 83, 90, 95, 139, 142, 162, 165, 178, 185, 188, 191
Supervisor 2-4, 7, 23-30, 32-35, 53, 55, 57, 58, 61-66, 72, 74, 75, 78, 83, 84, 86, 90, 92, 94-97, 110, 111, 121, 122, 132, 133, 138-143, 148, 152, 162, 174, 175, 177-179, 186, 187, 189, 196, 198, 208, 216, 217, 219
Support 2, 7, 14, 17, 20, 29, 34, 46, 53, 54, 58, 59, 63-65, 71, 75, 89-92, 94-97, 101, 102, 104-106, 108-110, 117, 121, 132, 152, 162, 178, 184-188, 190, 192, 194, 195, 198, 211, 213, 230

T

Team 8, 13, 34, 97, 184-188, 190
Theoretical framework 17, 31, 57, 72, 73, 75, 153, 179, 209
Theoryology 129, 132
Thesis 28, 45, 59, 74, 76, 106-109, 111, 127, 129, 132, 133, 148, 149, 151, 153, 154, 157-160, 162, 163, 165, 179, 206, 207, 210, 213-220, 227

Third Space 70-73, 75, 76, 164
Threshold 8, 108, 127-135, 142, 178, 179, 185, 187
Time management 111, 196
Traditions 25, 28, 104, 141, 147, 157-160, 163, 229
Transformation 3, 7, 8, 19, 21, 33, 70, 77, 79, 101, 110, 127, 128, 134
Transport 72, 90, 95, 97
Troubled knowledge 15
Trust 28, 29, 32-35, 47, 134, 193, 198, 228, 229

U

Ubuntu 8, 105, 137, 138, 140-143, 151, 172, 196, 226

V

Virtual study group 75
Visually impaired students 90, 93, 94
Viva voce 8, 213-220
Voice 8, 9, 18, 24, 29, 42, 58, 59, 62, 73, 74, 97, 118, 119, 129, 146-149, 151-153, 158, 160, 161, 163, 165, 173, 179, 207, 213, 217

W

Wellness 115, 116
White fragility 17
White Paper 3 77
Woman 8, 18, 20, 26, 103, 104, 106, 108, 109, 116
Women 16, 26, 101-105, 107-110, 112, 116, 187
Work experience 54
Work-life
    Articulation 103
    Balance 8, 116, 198
Worldview 150, 229
Writer identity 146, 151
Writer's block 145
Writers' circle 152
Writing
    Group 152
    Standards 151
    Workshops 75, 142, 152

INFORMATION ABOUT THE AUTHORS

Soraya Abdulatief is currently registered as a PhD candidate at the Graduate School of Education at the University of Cape Town. She holds a Postgraduate Diploma in Education from the University of Cape Town and an MA in English Literature from the University of the Western Cape. She has lectured English Communication at a university of technology. Prior to her return to postgraduate studies, she was an online editor and technical writer. Her PhD research is on teaching critical literacy and academic literacy practices to higher education students. Other research interests include multimodalities with an emphasis on the visual, using technology in education and debates around race, gender, language and literacy. She can be contacted at sabdulatief@gmail.com.

Collium Banda is completing PhD studies in the Department of Systematic Theology and Ecclesiology at Stellenbosch University. He completed a Licentiate in Theology and BA Hons at the Theological College of Zimbabwe and an Honours BTh and MTh at the University of South Africa. He has held a church pastorate and military chaplaincy in Zimbabwe, and lectures at the Theological College of Zimbabwe in Systematic Theology and Theological Ethics. His research interests are Christian doctrines and the African public space, African traditional religions, African indigenous knowledge systems and religion in contexts of poverty. He can be contacted at collium@gmail.com.

Kasturi Behari-Leak is an academic and professional staff development lecturer at the Centre for Higher Education Development (CHED) at the University of Cape Town. She currently convenes the New Academic Practitioners' Programme, the Short Course on Teaching, and the Learning and Teaching in Higher Education modules of the PGDip/Master's coursework, all of which focus on the development of emerging, new and established academics. Her PhD study, which is part of the NRF Social Inclusion PhD project, is a social-realist analysis of the conditions that enable or constrain the exercise of agency among new academics. The study is focussed on examining the interplay between structures (national, institutional, departmental and disciplinary), institutional culture and lecturer agency within the framework of "Africanising the curriculum". Other areas of interest include critical pedagogies, social justice, and transformative staff development initiatives such as preparing and inducting the next generation of academics into higher education. She serves as an executive member of HELTASA and is a consultant for the professional development special interest group nationally. Kasturi can be contacted at kasturi.behari-leak@uct.ac.za.

Shakira Choonara is employed as a PhD research fellow at the Centre for Health Policy (CHP), South Africa (SA) and is involved in the multi-country project aimed at strengthening governance at the district (local) level of the health system in countries such as Kenya, Nigeria and South Africa. In addition, Shakira is pursuing Doctoral Studies (Public Health) at the University of the Witwatersrand (South Africa). She has extensive research experience in the field of malaria prevention and other health related issues. She has received numerous research awards and has participated in a number of prestigious leadership programmes, such as the Emerging Voices for Health Systems Research and the Ahmed Kathrada Youth Leadership Programme. Recently, Shakira was selected from 172 applications from around the world as a Future Leader at the European Union's Development Days 2015 (EDD15) in Brussels. Shakira can be contacted at shakira.choonara@wits.ac.za.

Sherran Clarence is an AW Mellon postdoctoral research fellow in the Centre for Higher Education Research, Teaching and Learning (CHERTL) at Rhodes University. Prior to this, she managed the UWC Writing Centre at the University of the Western Cape from 2009 to 2014. Sherran has worked in higher education as a tutor, mentor and academic developer since 2001, and her present research centres around enabling lecturers through their teaching, and students in their learning, to make meaning and build knowledge in their disciplines in ways that further students' ability to continue learning and growing in their fields beyond their studies. As a new PhD supervisor and long-time academic literacy practitioner, she has a particular interest in academic writing, both at under- and postgraduate level, as well as writing for publication, and building capacity for knowledge-making through writing. Sherran has published her research in international and South African journals and books, and writes two blogs about her higher education work: *Writing in the Academy* and *How to Write a PhD in a Hundred Steps (or More)*, both hosted on Wordpress.com. She can be contacted at sherranclarence@gmail.com.

Liezel Frick is an associate professor in the Centre for Higher and Adult Education at Stellenbosch University. Her research focusses on doctoral education and postgraduate supervision. In 2012, she received the Emerald Literati Network Award for Excellence together with Prof Eva Brodin (Lund University, Sweden) for the article, *Conceptualising and encouraging critical creativity in doctoral education*, published in the International Journal for Researcher Development. She was awarded the Best African Accomplished Educational Researcher Award for 2013–2014 by the African Development Institute (ADI) and the Association for the Development of Education in South Africa (ADEA) for her contribution to educational research in the African context. She currently holds a Y2 (Young Researcher) rating from the National Research Foundation. Liezel can be contacted at blf@sun.ac.za.

INFORMATION ABOUT THE AUTHORS

Daniela Gachago is a senior lecturer in the Educational Technology Unit at the Centre for Higher Education Development at the Cape Peninsula University of Technology. Her research interests lie in the potential of emerging technologies to improve teaching and learning in higher education, with a particular focus on using social media and digital storytelling for social change. She completed a Master's in Adult Education at the University of Botswana and is a PhD candidate at the UCT School of Education where she explores the role of emotions in transforming students' engagement across difference. Daniela can be contacted at gachagod@gmail.com.

Delia Layton is a Senior Lecturer at the University of Johannesburg's (UJ) English department where she teaches and co-ordinates a first-year academic literacy module. She completed her MA in Applied English Language Studies (AELS) at the University of Witwatersrand in 2008 and her PhD in Education at Rhodes University in 2012. She participated in the NUFFIC programme: Strengthening Doctoral Supervision, and is currently co-supervisor on an NRF funded doctoral research programme on Institutional Differentiation. Delia is an active research participant and member of UJ's Scholarship of Teaching and Learning (SOTL) project on Social Justice in pedagogy. Her work focusses on academic literacies, epistemological access, educational transformation, student access and academic success. Recent publications address the value of dialogue in developing cognitive academic language proficiency (CALP), relationships in tutorial programmes, and the role of the tutorial system in enabling epistemological access. Delia can be contacted at delial@uj.ac.za.

Guin Lourens manages the Centre for Rural Health at Stellenbosch University's Faculty of Medicine and Health Sciences. She completed her doctoral studies in 2015 in the field of Public Management with a focus on hospital revitalisation programmes. An avid member of the women's forum at Stellenbosch University, she also lectures in health service management and supervises students in the postgraduate programme of the Nursing Division, where she also completed her initial B.Cur degree. Lourens is the founder of the Rural Nursing Network South Africa (RuNuRSA) and has worked in community Psychiatry and mobile primary health care services, while completing post graduate qualifications in Health Services Management (UNISA), Education (NWU), Occupational Health (US) and Primary Health Care (UPD). She applies community service and interaction through knowledge partnerships and serves on a variety of community and health sector boards. Her research interests are quality and risk management in healthcare. Guin can be contacted on guin@sun.ac.za.

Heidi Lourens is a counselling psychologist and a lecturer at the University of Johannesburg where she teaches psychology. She obtained her doctoral degree in March 2015 from Stellenbosch University. Her research interests include matters related to disability and inclusion. She presented her research at various conferences, amongst others the Nordic Network of Disability Studies in Norway, The International Conference on higher Education and Disability in Austria and the 9th Biannual International Society of Critical Health Psychology Conference at Rhodes University. Heidi may be contacted at hlourens.psych@gmail.com.

Jacqueline Lück has taught English at high school and in higher education for the past 25 years. She completed her MA studies at Stellenbosch University and her PhD in higher education studies at Rhodes University. She currently lectures at the Nelson Mandela Metropolitan University in the Department of Applied Language Studies. She lectures academic literacies, discourse analysis, language, identity and ideology, language policy implementation and language acquisition to students ranging from first year to Honours. She is also a Tesol (Teaching English to Speakers of Other Languages) trainer. Her research interests are disciplinary knowledge and academic literacies, language, identity and ideology and social inclusion in education. Jacqueline can be contacted at Jacqui.Luck@nmmu.ac.za.

Langutani Masehela is an educational development practitioner in the Centre for Higher Education Teaching and Learning at the University of Venda, South Africa. Langutani holds a Master's degree in Applied Linguistics from the University of Johannesburg and a PhD in Higher Education Studies from Rhodes University. Her research interests are quality assurance in teaching and learning, and student academic support in the higher education sector. The focus of her PhD study was exploring the conditions that constrain or enable academics from implementing quality assurance policies. Her current portfolio requires her to design, develop and implement student support programmes such as mentoring, tutoring, academic development workshops, induct new staff members at the University of Venda, amongst other duties. Her current major responsibility is to set up the First Year Experience programme. Langutani can be contacted at mary.masehela@univen.ac.za.

Simangele Mayisela is a PhD candidate at the School of Education, Humanities, at the University of Cape Town (UCT). Her field of expertise is Psychology and Education. She has a keen interest in intergenerational trauma and violence, and how these impact learning and development. For her doctoral research project, she received the Next Generation Social Sciences in Africa Fellowship 2013, 2014 and 2015, NRF's Innovative Doctoral Research Scholarship from 2013 to 2015, and the

INFORMATION ABOUT THE AUTHORS

UCT's Crasnow Postgraduate Scholarship for International Travel. As a registered Psychologist with the HPCSA, she is a consultant in this field, and as her social responsibility project she serves on the Executive Board of the Centre for the Studies of Violence and Reconciliation. Her contact details are smangele.mayisela@uct.ac.za.

Christopher McMaster has been lead editor on all editions of the *Survive and Succeed* series. He completed a PhD in education based on a critical ethnography of developing inclusive culture in an Aotearoa New Zealand high school. He designed a thesis topic that incorporated two of his passions – community activism and inclusion – and builds on the experience of 15 years as a teacher and 25 years as a parent. He received a Master of Arts from the University of London, specialising in post-war United States foreign policy, before becoming a primary teacher in the UK. Returning to his native US, he specialised in special education, earning a postgraduate diploma from the University of Alaska Southeast, teaching in special education for three years. He lived in New Zealand for over eight years, where he taught at primary and secondary levels, and worked for the Ministry of Education as Special Education Adviser and Resource Teacher. Chris was most recently an assistant professor of education at Augsburg College, Minneapolis, USA. Christopher can be contacted at drchrismcmaster@gmail.com.

Zondiwe Mkhabela is a senior manager for the Bushbuckridge local municipality in Mpumalanga, South Africa. His research interest is in leadership learning in municipalities. He worked as a school teacher for 15 years and as a part-time lecturer for seven years prior to joining the municipality. He completed his Master's degree at the University of Johannesburg and his PhD at Stellenbosch University. Zondi may be contacted at mkhabelazondi@gmail.com.

Karien Mostert-Wentzel is a senior lecturer at the Department of Physiotherapy, University of Pretoria, South Africa. She coordinates the community-based education placements. These service-learning programmes offer care in less-resourced communities. In her PhD study she developed a kaleidoscope model for an undergraduate curriculum for community and public health physiotherapy in South Africa. As a fellow of the Sub-Saharan African Regional FAIMER Institute (SAFRI), she contributes to the promotion of health professions education, amongst others, through mentoring education innovation projects. She can be contacted at karien.mostert@gmail.com.

Puleng Motshoane is currently employed as a Teaching and Learning Consultant in the Centre for Academic Technologies (CAT) at the University of Johannesburg. She comes from a school teaching background and has an interest in the ways in which higher education meets the needs of a transformed South Africa. She is especially interested in the postgraduate sector and the extent to which we are building the next generation of researchers needed to ensure a stable economy. Her doctoral study focusses on how institutions support the supervision process with the aim of increasing doctoral outputs. She is also a member of the International Doctoral Education Research Network, as well as the first recipient of the Liz Harrison Scholarship. Puleng can be contacted at pulengm@uj.ac.za.

Ndileleni Paulinah Mudzielwana holds a PhD in Early Childhood from University of Pretoria, a PGDIP in Higher Education from Rhodes University, a Master's in Early Childhood Education from the Australian Catholic University in Melbourne, and a Bachelor's Degree and a BEd Honours from the University of Venda. She specialised in Early Childhood Education during her BEd Honours with additional modules from the University of South Africa. She holds a Further Diploma in School Readiness from the University of Johannesburg. She worked for 20 years as a primary school teacher, and for five years as a lecturer in the then Tshisimani and Makhado training colleges in Limpopo. She is currently working at the University of Venda as an Associate Professor and HOD in the Department of Early Childhood Education, where she specialises in literacy teaching. She is also the co-author of a Tshivenda Foundation Phase package of readers, learner's book and teacher's guide, as well as the author of various academic articles and papers. Ndileleni may be reached at ndileleni.mudzielwana@univen.ac.za.

Caterina Murphy is an experienced book developer, presenter and academic writer, and has partnered with Chris McMaster across the global *Surviving and Succeeding* series. She has worked in the education sector for 29 years, and held senior roles in tertiary education since 1999. Her Master of Education (Hons) from Massey University investigated the play patterns and behaviours of gifted young children and her PhD (Indigenous Studies) from Te Whare Wānanga o Awanuiārangi examined the cultural identity of families through the lens of cooking traditions. Her professional and research interests include early years education, teaching practice, mentoring, qualitative research, gifted education, anthropology, and oral history methodology. She actively mentors adolescents, undergraduates and postgraduates in Aotearoa New Zealand and freelances her academic leadership services through *AcademicExpressNZ*. Caterina can be contacted at academicexpressnz@xtra.co.nz.

Mariana Pietersen is a lecturer in the Department of Sociology at the University of Pretoria, South Africa. Her research focusses in the field of Medical Sociology, Sociology of Health, Social Epidemiology and Zoonosis. She specialises in Diabetes Mellitus, the Poverty of Health, and HIV and AIDS. She has 16 years practical experience in management within in a health and communication related environment and 20 years in the academic field. In her DPhil thesis, Mariana investigated the influence of population-based factors on self-care of patients with diabetes mellitus, specifically those questions that might provide possible answers to the underlying causes of diabetes, and the causes of hyperglycaemia and factors in society that contribute to the causes, thereby providing a knowledge base for interventions that might be the most successful in this regard. She can be contacted at mariana.pietersen@up.ac.za or pietersenmariana@gmail.com.

Catherine Robertson has always had a love of language, reading and writing which is why she completed her Master's in Linguistics at Stellenbosch University. She spent many happy years teaching English, Communication and Public Relations at schools, a teachers' training college and a TVET college, thereafter working at an executive level at a TVET college. Her main research focus is leadership in post-school vocational education institutions, which is the area in which she completed her PhD. As a research associate at Stellenbosch University, she hopes to continue with her research, writing, editing, reviewing and sharing her research focus at workshops. Catherine can be contacted at cathy@tcrobertson.co.za.

Emmanuel Sibomana taught Kinyarwanda, English and French at several high schools in Rwanda. He also taught the following courses at the University of the Witwatersrand (Wits) as a part-time lecturer: New Literacies for Teachers, Communication and Learning Skills and Basic Research Skills. He completed his MA and PhD study programmes in Applied English Language Studies (AELS) at the University of the Witwatersrand in 2009 and 2014 respectively. He is currently working as a lecturer in the Humanities and Language Education Department of the University of Rwanda's College of Education. His research interests are language education, language in education policy, language teacher education pedagogy and distance education. Emmanuel may be reached at siboemma14@yahoo.fr.

Hannelie Untiedt is currently working as a Senior Instructional Designer at the University of Pretoria in the Department for Education Innovation. Formerly she was a mathematics teacher. She holds a Master's degree and PhD, and the latter focussed on the use of computers in education. She is responsible for facilitating staff development workshops and guiding and supporting academic staff on the integration and use of technology into their teaching and learning plans. To further support academics, she presents student orientation sessions in the use of specific online functionalities for a particular programme. In her thesis she focussed on evaluating the use of the online environment (i.e. learning management system) in teaching and learning, and the specific (changing) needs of academics when they are expected to continuously master new (or updated) software in a time-restricted teaching environment, especially in medical education. She can be contacted at hannelie.untiedt@up.ac.za.

Andre van der Bijl is a senior lecturer at the Cape Peninsula University of Technology's Faculty of Education. He qualified as a business studies teacher at the University of Cape Town and obtained graduate qualifications at Stellenbosch University. His Master's thesis involved an investigation into the use of marketing principles in education and his doctoral work analysed teaching development strategies for new lecturers employed at TVET colleges. His special interests are classroom related management and policy issues, with a focus on the adaptation of teaching to vocational and higher education. He also served on a number of national working groups, primarily aimed at developing teaching competencies within vocational education. Andre may be contacted at vanderbijla@cput.ac.za.

Bella Vilakazi is a doctoral scholar at Rhodes University. She is employed at the University of South Africa (UNISA) as a Curriculum and Learning Development Specialist. Her work at UNISA involves supporting academics in curriculum and learning design, module development, teaching and assessment practices and how to teach effectively in Open Distance Learning (ODL). Her PhD study aims at analysing how formative feedback, a pedagogic practice, influences undergraduate students to gain epistemological access. This study is located within the wider field of Higher Education Studies. Formative feedback is also central during a doctoral journey that a scholar and her supervisor undertake. It involves comments given by the supervisor in writing or verbally on work that a scholar has submitted. Formative feedback creates a space for engagement between a scholar and her supervisor. Bella can be contacted at vilakbp@unisa.ac.za.

Liz Wolvaardt is a senior lecturer in the School of Health Systems and Public Health at the University of Pretoria. Her research interests with her postgraduate students focus on health system strengthening. Her personal research interests extend to strengthening public health in the undergraduate medical curriculum which was the focus of her doctoral studies. Liz has won awards for Education Innovation from the University of Pretoria for her work in the undergraduate medical curriculum. She is a Sub-Saharan African FAIMER regional institute (SAFRI) fellow and contributes to the strengthening of health professions education in Africa through her continued work in this programme. Liz is also a sub-editor for the African Journal of Health Professions Education (AJHPE) that aims to develop educational research scholarship in the region. She has successfully supervised eleven Master's students to completion and has published 16 articles to date. Liz can be contacted at liz.wolvaardt@up.ac.za.

www.ingramcontent.com/pod-product-compliance
Lightning Source LLC
Chambersburg PA
CBHW080322170426
43193CB00017B/2875